D1248541

REMEMBERING WORLD WAR I IN AMERICA

Studies in War, Society, and the Military

GENERAL EDITORS

Kara Dixon Vuic
Texas Christian University

Richard S. Fogarty
University at Albany, State University of New York

EDITORIAL BOARD

Peter Maslowski
University of Nebraska–Lincoln

David Graff
Kansas State University

Reina Pennington
Norwich University

Remembering World War I in America

KIMBERLY J. LAMAY LICURSI

University of Nebraska Press

LINCOLN & LONDON

© 2018 by the Board of Regents of the University of Nebraska

Portions of chapter 1 were previously published as "State Great War Histories: An Atom of Interest in an Ocean of Apathy," in *The Great War From Memory to History* (Waterloo: Wilfred Laurier University Press, 2015), 19–57.

All rights reserved
Manufactured in the United States of America

Library of Congress Cataloging-in-Publication Data

Names: Lamay Licursi, Kimberly J., author.
Title: Remembering World War I in America / Kimberly J. Lamay Licursi.
Description: Lincoln: University of Nebraska Press, 2018. | Series: Studies in war, society, and the military | Includes bibliographical references and index.
Identifiers: LCCN 2017030480 (print)
LCCN 2017030988 (ebook)
ISBN 9780803290853 (cloth: alk. paper)
ISBN 9781496205674 (epub)
ISBN 9781496205681 (mobi)
ISBN 9781496205698 (pdf)
Subjects: LCSH: World War, 1914–1918—Social aspects—United States. | Collective memory—United States. | Memory—Social aspects—United States. | World War, 1914–1918—Influence.
Classification: LCC D524.7.U6 (ebook)
LCC D524.7.U6 L36 2018 (print)
DDC 940.3/10973—dc23
LC record available at https://lccn.loc.gov/2017030480

Set in New Baskerville ITC Pro by E. Cuddy.

For Steve and Willa

CONTENTS

List of Illustrations ix

Acknowledgments xi

Introduction xiii

1. State War Histories: An Atom of Interest in an
   Ocean of Apathy 1

2. War Memoirs: They Pour from Presses Daily 43

3. War Stories: Fiction Cannot Ignore the Greatest
   Adventure in a Man's Life 93

4. War Films: Shootin' and Kissin' 147

   Conclusion 191

   Appendix 1: Selected Bibliography of
   World War I Personal Narratives. 195

   Appendix 2: Selected Bibliography of
   World War I Novels. 211

   Notes 215

   Bibliography 241

   Index 259

ILLUSTRATIONS

FIGURES

1. Virginia War History Committee poster. 20
2. Cover of *War Stories*, February 1928 135
3. Cover of *Battle Stories*, December 1930 137
4. Cover of *Sky Aces*, February 1941 140

TABLES

1. Best-selling books of fiction about war 96
2. Books by Sinclair Lewis and Ernest Hemingway in
   three public libraries in 1933 117
3. War-related pulp-fiction magazines 138
4. War-related movies and studio revenues 150

ACKNOWLEDGMENTS

The genesis of this book was a challenging research semi-
nar taught by Carl Bon Tempo and a readings class facilitated by Dan White at the University at Albany, New York.
Both gentlemen deepened my interest in a war that, while
so pivotal to the shape of the world today, is poorly understood by most Americans. Richard Hamm, Kendra Smith
Howard, and Rick Fogarty provided continual encouragement and instilled in me the confidence that I could craft
something worthy of publication. Richard and Kendra challenged me to bolster my arguments in a larger context and
readily suggested innumerable ways to make this manuscript stronger. Rick tirelessly read through draft after draft,
made my words much more eloquent and sharpened the
content in countless ways. My debt to him is substantial.

The New York State Archive was the starting point for my
research and their large collection of World War I materials fueled this work. The State of New York, like many
others, has a sizable assortment of documents that were
collected as part of an effort to publish a memorial book
for soldiers of the Great War. That book never came to fruition and the haste with which fellow New Yorkers seemed
to forget those who fought was the provocation for further study on memory and World War I. Staff at the New
York State Archive provided invaluable assistance as did
the knowledgeable and helpful people at the Kansas State
Historical Society, the Library of Virginia, Yale University

Library, the Library of Congress, the library of New York University at Albany, and the office of the city historian of Rochester, New York.

I am grateful for the time and talent of Steven Trout. His review of this manuscript and insightful commentary significantly improved the end result. Steve, and Bridget Barry, Ann Baker, and Emily Wendell at the University of Nebraska Press, were tremendously helpful as I navigated the unfamiliar territory of revisions and publishing.

Family and friends have also been instrumental in the completion of this work. My close friend Annie Gartelman provided much needed copy editing and moral support. My family supported what could have been folly in leaving a successful career to return to school to follow my passion for history. Moreover, they were helpful in countless ways during the six years I engaged in research for this book. My husband, Steven, put up with my incessant fascination with the Great War without complaint and has been my biggest champion in life, and in the writing of this book. My daughter, Willa, inspires me to continue chasing my dreams so that she might follow my example. May she never stop striving for what makes her happy.

At the close of World War I in November 1918 the United States was poised to become a player in the new world order. The country had raised an army of over four million men and sent two million across the Atlantic as the American Expeditionary Force (AEF) under Gen. John J. Pershing. It was an infusion of fresh manpower critical to boosting French and British morale, weakening German resolve, and winning the war. Americans marched into a demoralized and desperate French countryside and marched out heroes. Pershing reputedly claimed that "the deadliest weapon in the world is a Marine and his rifle." Hyperbole aside, American doughboys, through sheer numbers, had played a pivotal role in turning the tide of war, but they had gone through hell to do so. One of their more daunting trials by fire had been the Meuse-Argonne Offensive, to this day America's largest military battle. One million soldiers fought for forty-seven days to defeat a German stronghold in the Argonne forest and over 26,000 men lost their lives in the process. It was not the Americans' only test, but it was their bloodiest.[1] Overall, the war claimed more than 116,000 combat fatalities and more than 200,000 wounded, not counting the 43,000 who died from the 1918 influenza pandemic that was exacerbated by the war.

The cost was steep, but the AEF not only established a new military pecking order, they unleashed a juggernaut of American culture through the army jazz bands that traveled to France and the Hollywood films that would follow. James Reese Europe's 369th Regiment Harlem Hellfighters band and other African American regimental bands made quite an impression abroad, including recording on the French Pathé label before coming back to the United States. Hollywood stepped up to the plate as the film industry in France and Germany struggled to regain its footing after the war. Charlie Chaplin, Douglas Fairbanks, and Lillian Gish became international celebrities, and they spread the gospel of the American way of life with each film that crossed the ocean. America truly came of age during and after World War I, yet many Americans think of it as merely the numerical precursor to World War II—the "good" war—the one that was worth fighting.[2] Their only consciousness of the earlier global conflict is a hazy vision of parades, doughboys, and trenches. Some may also remember the war as a time of copious propaganda, epitomized by the thousands of posters crafted to encourage unified support for the war effort. James Montgomery Flagg's iconic poster of Uncle Sam pointedly encouraging recruits, or Howard Chandler Christy's ethereal girls in gauzy dresses and sailor uniforms, exhorted Americans to enlist, buy more war bonds, or volunteer with the Red Cross. But Americans' common perceptions of the war end there.[3] Notable leaders and battles and a general understanding of why war was waged come fairly easily to mind for World War II and the Civil War, but not so for World War I.

As this study demonstrates, if cultural production like books and movies are any indicator of public sentiment, Americans simply forgot the war after the first few parades welcoming doughboys home. Specifically, in this work I identify the documents, books, and films produced by the interwar generation and analyze what they suggest about how Americans came to terms with the war. Did they forge a consensus or myth about the war that most could agree with, and why does the war have such a light footprint on American memory? The evidence suggests a two-fold response. First, American memory of the war was a casualty of competing perspectives among the populace. Public discourse about the war never congealed into a consensus view, which would have helped create a sustaining and coherent memory. Instead, memory of the war concentrated around two poles of thought, one that patriotically supported participation in the war and another that questioned the purpose of any war and lamented the "lost generation" that emerged from the conflict. Second, there are few cultural touchstones of the war because a pervasive apathy about anything war-related arose in 1918 and was slow to abate.

Contemporary disregard for World War I seems to build upon the indifference that dominated attitudes about the war in the 1920s and 1930s. Most of the war generation seemed content to let the war fall into obscurity shortly after the armistice. Because of this there are few iconic people, places, or events memorialized in popular books or on film that encouraged the development of a collective memory of the war. No consistent images or messages about the war arose that resonated with a significant segment of the American population. There was no World War I equivalent to the flag raising at Iwo Jima or the bright imagery of Rosie the Riveter, and no military leaders who gained lasting fame. Collective memory of a past event fades like any private memory if it is not fostered over time by acts of remembrance, and the cultural production of the interwar generation failed to produce the touchstones that might have spurred remembrance.

The reluctance to remember war in any way is understandable, but American disinterest in World War I, especially over the two decades that memory had time to take root before World War II, defies logic in two ways. First, it ignores the commonly held belief today that society should recognize and lionize soldiers for their sacrifices. Warriors from time immemorial have been lauded and condemned, studied and admired, but rarely ignored. The majority of soldiers who served in France did so because they were compelled by their government, not by choice. Men left their jobs to cross the ocean and face death from machine guns and artillery shrapnel. They witnessed death and destruction on an unimaginable scale. Moreover, those who were lucky enough to return home often found that their jobs, or their girls, had been taken by others. Tens of thousands of soldiers came back to a teetotaling nation that offered little promise of reward for their service. Many others, of course, remained interred in French soil. One might expect that the tremendous loss of life and the innocence with which so many entered into this first industrialized war was worth remembering. Moreover, forgetting war means forgetting its social and cultural implications, disregarding its hard-earned lessons, thereby risking a repetition of historical mistakes. The conventional wisdom that past wars are an admonition against future war would seem to suggest that the Great War should have served some didactic purpose for Americans. Still, nothing in American culture generated or sustained a vibrant or lucid public memory in the war's immediate aftermath, or in the years that followed before World War II took a primary place in Americans' lives and consciousness. It is surprising that the cultural footprint of World War I is so light, given all the reasons Americans had to remember.

What Is Collective Memory?

Many historians have grappled with the concept of "collective memory." Two of the most prominent war historians to tackle this issue are Jay Winter and Samuel Hynes. Winter defines collective memory as "the process through which different collectives, from groups of two to groups in their thousands, engage in acts of remembrance together."[4] Hynes argues that collective memory of war might be more appropriately called collective *vicarious* memory, or a shared myth. It is vicarious because most people have no personal memories of the war. The collective memory, or myth, of the war is the "simplified, dramatized story that has evolved in our society to contain the meanings of the war that we can tolerate."[5] The present study defines collective memory in a way that incorporates both Hynes's and Winter's interpretations. Collective memory of World War I is simply the public's common perception of the war and the extent to which that memory is expressed in acts of remembrance like the production of cultural artifacts related to the war.

The most common response to the argument that Americans lack a collective memory of World War I is that they escaped the full impact of the war. The United States fought for a relatively short period of time in a land far removed from the everyday lives of most Americans. But generalizing the American experience in this manner is a disservice to those for whom the war was neither foreign nor benign. There were hundreds of thousands who fell into this category and many millions more who would have commiserated with their sacrifice. Perhaps Americans are heedless of World War I because it deviates from the myths that have sprung up around other more agreeably remembered wars. The Revolutionary War, Civil War, and World War II support the paradigm of "American exceptionalism." They bolster the idea that Americans stand apart, either as bold patriots who fought for a semblance of equality among men, as noble warriors who fought to avert the breakup of an unprecedented national experiment, or as the forces of democratic good against Fascist and Nazi evil. World War I can make no claim to such pretensions, and its purpose was challenged almost immediately after it ended. An antiwar backlash arose as the revelry of the parades faded and the vast majority of soldiers came home unheralded, unsure of what they had fought for, and uncertain of their future in an economy that was reeling from a postwar economic slump. Criticism of the war grew in the 1920s and 1930s, when the banking and munitions industries came under increasing scrutiny for the role they might have played in pushing the country toward war. This was not a war that would fit easily into the American narrative.

There is little modern scholarship that specifically addresses American collective memory of World War I. While Winter, Hynes, and other prominent historians of the war have analyzed the larger European collective memory, or myth, of World War I, they have usually ignored the American experience. As a token reference, some may invoke Ernest Hemingway's contributions to literary memory, but rarely in the context of American perceptions of the war. The preeminent scholar of memory and the war, Paul Fussell, suggested that early nineteenth-century Americans were literary naïfs and devoid of the skill required to capture the public's imagination and contribute works of enduring value about the war.[6] Hynes posits that American writers lacked the necessary experiences from which to construct a valuable soldier's story. He believes the short tenure of American soldiers in the trenches, and their relatively limited experience in battle, provided little fodder for great literature.[7] Even the great writers of the time, like Hemingway and John Dos Passos, had only a fleeting impression, if any, of the real war. As my analysis will point out, however, many soldiers did experience much more of the war than Hemingway and Dos Passos did, and while their service may have been much briefer compared with French and British soldiers who were at war for years, their experiences of war were often no less intense or traumatic and their literary skills were no less refined.

One of the most recent books on American war memory, Steven Trout's *On the Battlefield of Memory: The First World War and American Remembrance*, provides a literary historian's analysis of the competing visions of war that emerged from some of the leading writers in the 1920s and 1930s. Trout also explores the numerous acts of commemoration manifested in monuments, public memorials, and commemorative products as evidence that Americans did not forget the war. However, many of the resulting monuments, in the United States and abroad, were the product of government and American Legion efforts to memorialize a victorious army and shape public opinion about the war and do not necessarily indicate that the prevailing public mood was one of remembrance. The legion, which represented no more than 20 percent of veterans in the 1920s, was promoted by the government as a bastion against left-wing radicalism, and the goals of the legion's leaders were not necessarily the views of the rank-and-file membership.[8]

Another recent analysis of memory, Lisa Budreau's *Bodies of War*, calls collective remembrance in America "a politically motivated exercise."[9] Her book primarily focuses on the repatriation of soldiers' remains, the American Battlefield Monuments Commission and its work to erect memorials abroad, and the government-sponsored pilgrimages for relatives to visit soldiers' graves in France. She argues that government attempted to shape remembrance in America to suit exigent political imperatives, including crafting a memory of war that might unify a nation fractured by ideological, racial, and cultural divides. This study contrasts with Budreau's in that it examines the memory that evolved, or failed to evolve, organically from the efforts of civilians to synthesize information from cultural production outside the realm of politics and the state.

The cultural legacy of the interwar years suggests that Americans hastened to put experiences and memories of the war behind them, not looking back to the war for a sense of identity or place as they forged into the tumultuous twenties. An attitude of purposeful indifference prevailed after the war and substantially hindered the emergence of war documentation, including soldiers' stories—the reflections of war that seep into the collective conscious- ness and become ingrained in popular culture. Those stories that did emerge often failed to portray the Ameri- can war experience or presented conflicting images that hindered the coalescence of a larger narrative. This book explores how war stories were disseminated through four different vectors in the interwar years—war histories, sol- dier memoirs, war fiction, and war films—and how the public received those stories.

The first chapter of this study explores a postwar effort to publish official state war histories that might have shaped public memory about the war. State and local governments went to great lengths collecting information on veterans and volunteers in an attempt to recognize the sacrifices of each. Approximately thirty-five states began efforts to publish comprehensive war histories memorializing the dead and acknowledging the contributions of the living, but few finished the task.[10] The systems created to procure information for these histories foundered when it became apparent that the public preferred to forget the war. Vet- erans either joined citizens in trying to put the war behind them or were likely silenced by the lack of interest shown by those whose lives they fought to protect. Local officials achieved greater success producing less ambitious books, but often faced the same obstacles that state officials had faced. War histories might have played an important role in leading postwar commemoration, and later successive generations might have used them to study local history, military history, or explore their family trees. Rather than demonstrating a nation's gratitude, never-completed war history projects indicate the pervasive apathy that characterized American attitudes toward the war.

Apathy was also evident in the market for war stories. Many soldiers may have been less than cooperative in state efforts to record their stories, but they were fairly prolific in creating their own war histories. American veterans published approximately five hundred personal narratives between 1914 and 1941. Chapter 2 reviews notable memoirists, including Hervey Allen, John Thomason, Alvin York, and Eddie Rickenbacker. These veterans, who gained acclaim in their day, provided firsthand accounts of some of the most iconic battles involving American soldiers: the Battle of Belleau Wood, the Aisne-Marne Offensive, the Meuse-Argonne Offensive, and the war in the air. Veterans vividly described the war in these and many other personal narratives, but they are largely unknown today. After 1918, manuscripts about the war were a tough sell because many publishers believed the public was tired of war. To some extent they seemed to be justified in that claim since most memoirs published sold pitifully few copies.

Fiction writers produced books with greater commercial appeal but their work generally presented the war from one of two perspectives. It was either a war of necessity that could bring out the best in a man, or, alternately, it was a shameful affair that resulted in the senseless slaughter of American youth. This dichotomous message, the former offered mostly by an older generation of writers, and the latter offered by a younger, disaffected generation of writers, hampered the formation of a coherent collective memory of the war. Chapter 3 examines these two strains of thought as well as another form of fiction writing about the war found in pulp magazines. Novels had a relatively limited audience, but millions of young men devoured "the pulps"—cheap magazines that told vivid tales of adventure in a number of formats—every month.

Literary critics derided the pulps at the time, and many later historians classified them as ephemeral pop culture, so their usefulness in exploring the popular memory of the war has been neglected. In this study I use novels to present the bifurcated opinion about the war and pulp fiction to counter the myth that most of the postwar generation was disaffected by the conflict.

Chapter 4 explores the war's depiction in films, which could be much more formulaic than novels. War films were hampered by their need to appeal to a large segment of the audience that wanted, as one viewer put it, "shootin' and kissin'," something for which a military setting provided plenty of opportunity.[11] In their quest for commercial success Hollywood studios offered more show than substance, which made them flawed vehicles for remembrance. Films, however, had more potential to affect the consciousness of Americans than all the hundreds of war books combined. Film audiences numbered in the millions every week, and, after a brief hiatus shortly after the war, there were many popular war films produced during both the silent and sound film eras. However, as was true of war fiction, many films focused primarily on a European war, told conflicting stories, and incorporated additional plot lines that made them more palatable as entertainment but diluted their war-focused content. This was just fine with American audiences who, when they thought about the war at all, one contemporary historian noted, "still felt obliged to pretend to [themselves] that the war had been a fine experience."[12]

All four vectors of memory—war histories, memoirs, fiction, and film—had the potential to craft a public memory of the war, yet all four failed in different ways. Most war histories never materialized, American war memoirs did not capture the public's attention, and war novels and films presented a fictional war that either bore little resemblance to the doughboys' experience or offered discordant views about what the war meant. Novels and films also tended to adopt an escapist mentality that soft-pedaled the war as a central theme by conflating the war with romance, adventure, and heroism. In the end, Americans emerged from the interwar years with narrow pockets of public memory about the war that never came together in a dominant myth.

World War II was also an important factor in curtailing memory and further removing World War I from public consciousness. Not only was the war bigger, fought by a seemingly more unified populace, and thought to be more just, but it was fought by the very generation of young men who were a prime audience for books and films about World War I. In the 1920s and 1930s, young men and boys consumed war novels, war pulp fiction, and war movies to experience vicariously the drama and adventure of war. It was a war that happened before they were born, or before they were old enough to understand it, and it was a topic that many fathers and grandfathers may have avoided discussing with their sons and grandsons. Movies and books filled the void left by the silence of the men who fought and ultimately prepared the next generation for war. As the largest audience for war books and films, boys and young men would have been most effective in carrying the memory of the war forward if a second war had not intervened. Instead of telling their offspring about the Marines at Belleau Wood or the victory at Saint-Mihiel, the boys who learned of the Great War through books, films, and magazines would share their own personal stories of Normandy or Okinawa. Their personal experiences with war would displace the fictional version of war that they grew up reading and watching. The lived experience blotted out the imagined experience, and World War I has been marginalized by the "good war" ever since.

REMEMBERING WORLD WAR I IN AMERICA

State War Histories

An Atom of Interest in an Ocean of Apathy

When Frank Buckles died in 2011 he was the last American veteran of World War I, and his death was marked by a few fleeting stories that prompted very little reflection about the war's meaning in the United States. His family and other supporters were denied their request that Buckles be allowed to lie in the Rotunda of the Capitol so that his passing might serve as an occasion for remembering and honoring all American veterans of World War I. Buckles's family was instead allowed to use the amphitheater at Arlington Cemetery for a service attended by two hundred people. This stands in stark contrast to the last French and Canadian veterans of World War I, who were offered state funerals, and to the thousands who attended a ceremony for the last British veteran in 2009. Americans greeted Buckles's death in a manner that was not surprising, given their general disinterest in World War I in favor of the Civil War and World War II, which are thought of as more poignant and more justified, respectively. News of the death of the last Confederate widow in 2004 merited about as many lines in the *New York Times* as that of the last American soldier from the world's first great war. The American collective disregard for the war is ironic, given the tremendous postwar efforts exerted by some to create war histories ensuring that it never be forgotten.

The fervor that swept America during World War I focused not only on winning the war but on memorializing the people who would eventually secure victory. American soldiers had not yet reached the shores of France, and government agencies and citizens had formed war history organizations to highlight their sacrifice for the cause. Each state would have their own story to tell about their contributions to the war effort. Many states planned to publish ambitious multivolume tributes, the sort of gilt-decorated, leather-bound volumes that preserve the most sacred narratives of history. By 1919 thirty-five states had made systematic efforts to collect and preserve historical data about the war, either by delegating the task to a state historian, war history committee, war records commission, or historical agency.[1] These organizations solicited information from soldiers, war agencies, churches, schools, government agencies, and a host of other sources. States collaborated under the auspices of the National Board for Historic Service (NBHS), an organization formed in 1917 as an outlet for historians who wanted to offer public service during the war, much like the public service that was offered by scientists, engineers, or munitions workers.[2] Historians hoped to create vast archives of information that would assist future historians in a way unprecedented in previous wars.

State governments worked in collaboration with historians to preserve war-related information because it was in their best interest to remind people of the nation's collective effort in support of the cause in order to preserve a united front during and after the war. Citizens pulled together by war were less likely to fall prey to leftist or radical thoughts about government. The war propaganda machine did not shut down after the armistice; it was functioning well into 1920, packaging the war as a patriotic endeavor and honorable fight for democracy. Therefore state agencies, in one form or another, were often integral to war data-collection efforts. The NBHS dissolved at the close of the war and was succeeded by the National Association of State War History Organizations (NASWHO), which would carry out the mission of encouraging the collection and preservation of war-related records. A core group of fifteen or sixteen states, including New York and Virginia, collaborated to discuss issues related to their respective projects for many years after the war, but even the most concerted efforts often met with failure.

Ultimately only seven states (Illinois, Indiana, Iowa, Maryland, Massachusetts, Minnesota, and New Mexico) and the territory of Hawaii published a war history before 1940.[3] The relatively paltry number of states publishing histories would not have been a surprise to state or national coordinators at the time. Leaders noted both "indifference of men" and "indifference to the history of the war" were obstacles nationwide.[4] Lack of funding was another stumbling block that many state organizations found insurmountable. State legislatures were not only miserly in their appropriations for war histories, they were wary of creating a precedent for publishing war histories that might continue after future wars.[5] These problems only worsened with time. Enthusiasm for memorializing the war was strongest in the weeks and months after the war and then waned considerably thereafter. A city clerk reflecting on his experience putting together a history for Buffalo, New York, noted, "You ask me what I would do if I had the job to do over again, and I am frank to tell you that I would enlist in the Army and let somebody else write the history."[6] Historians had no way of knowing that the war would become a taboo conversation topic in the years and even months after the armistice—much less a subject for triumphant commemorative writing.

There was little precedent for the creation of "war histories" as envisioned by many states. There was no organized effort during or after the Civil War to create similar histories by states, but crafting honor rolls of the dead was a fairly widespread activity at the local level. Additionally, the quartermaster general of the Union army produced an eight-volume *Roll of Honor* listing the names of Union dead that was completed six years after the end of the war.[7]

In fact, organizers during World War I noted that the lack of accurate state-by-state rosters of soldiers who fought in the Civil War provided motivation for collection efforts. One historian noted that a complete list of the soldiers from New York who fought in the Civil War had not been developed until 1920 and cost $500,000 to compile.[8]

World War I did, however, create a precedent for data collection during World War II. Some historians noted that the paucity of information preserved from World War I was the impetus for reinvigorated efforts in some states during World War II. One estimate indicated that by 1945 forty states had begun collecting information and records related to the war.[9] The focus was shifted from the collection of personal war service records to a larger number of sources, and an emphasis was placed on quality over quantity. During World War I, some state agencies had preserved every item offered with the thought that it might someday serve valuable to historians. Document and artifact collection during and after World War II was much more circumspect.[10] After all, the number of participating individuals and agencies had grown exponentially. Ultimately, there were no fewer than eight state histories or honor rolls published as well as many local and county works. It is a level of publication comparable to that produced after World War I. Of course, the lesson of the World War I history project lies less in the number of volumes produced than in the insight gleaned through the process of collecting individual war service records. With more than three times as many soldiers deployed during World War II, it is not surprising that efforts after the war were not focused on collecting individual records, especially given the logistical nightmare faced by historians after World War I, with a much smaller cohort.

Many states have extant archives of records documenting the collection process undertaken to produce their respective war histories. These archives provide a better understanding of the lack of interest on the part of soldiers and communities that was continually cited by project coordinators. In this study I look specifically at the records in New York, Kansas, and Virginia. These states were chosen because they represent a diverse geographic area and disparate American communities. The study includes rural and urban, north and south, conservative and liberal, and black and white parts of the country. New York is a particularly compelling state for study because officials there were in front of the organizing efforts for other states and as such had a strong incentive to succeed in publishing a war history and lead by example. New York also provided more than 10 percent of the nation's soldiers during World War I.[11] Virginia was active in the collection of war materials as well, had one of the most ambitious questionnaires, and published seven volumes of source material for use by later historians. Kansas represents the Midwest, a portion of the country with conservative values and a strong academic reputation for preserving and researching its history. All three states were better poised than most to complete their war histories, which makes their failure to do so that much more instructive.

The experiences in New York, Virginia, and Kansas establish a pattern of behavior that demonstrates a pervasive apathy, if not disdain, for war remembrance in postwar America. Organizations in these states focused most of their time, as did other states, attempting to collect individual war service records, and not without good cause. The desire for individual service records was born as much by necessity as it was from historical curiosity, since no accurate roster of the soldiers from each state was available until years after the war. Branches of the armed services kept records on soldiers, but did not arrange them according to political boundaries and had never published the information. One could search the federal records by person, but could not generate a list of individuals native to a particular state. The adjutant general of the army had attempted to produce a central roster of soldiers in the 1920s, but NASWHO members discredited it as largely inaccurate.[12] The testimony of soldiers was the only reliable way to compile accurate lists of state residents in uniform during the war and where they fought. Each state would use questionnaires directed at veterans to acquire information on various topics, including their dates and places of service, their training and combat experience, and their reactions to the war and military life. Following is an analysis of how three states attempted to document those who served.

New York

James Sullivan, a major propaganda operative during World War I, spearheaded the documentation of New York's part in the war. Sullivan was a Harvard-educated principal of a boys' school in Brooklyn when New York State "drafted [him] for the State service" in 1916 by appointing him state historian.[13] He began collecting information on the Empire State's role in the war shortly after the declaration of war against Germany in 1917. In April 1919 the state legislature directed him to create a publication highlighting the state's contribution to the war effort. By 1919 Sullivan had become president of the NASWHO and was also deeply involved in other war efforts, including his service as the home director of the YMCA, a lecturer for the National Security League (NSL) and Committee on Public Information (CPI), and an educational commissioner for the American Expeditionary Forces in Europe.[14]

Sullivan seemed to relish his role as president of the NASWHO, and he carefully cultivated the creation of a New York State war history as a model for others to follow. He had a herculean task ahead of him. Five hundred thousand New Yorkers from every corner of the state served during World War I, and more of them would die than from any other state.[15] For seven years Sullivan challenged, shamed, and cajoled citizens and historians to fulfill their patriotic duty and document the men who fought to preserve democracy abroad. Although the story of New York in the war never made it to print, the failure was certainly not due to Sullivan's lack of resolve. The effort failed for the very simple reason that many veterans and their families refused to share information about their war service with local historians.

When the legislature supported the plan to capture New York's war history, they had also authorized the appointment of 1,500 local historians to serve as Sullivan's field staff to collect soldier data.[16] By 1921 Sullivan reported that 1,027 local historians had been appointed and that nearly 75 percent of the war histories from these local historians had been received.[17] His appraisal of the situation was generous at best. He may have been trying to drum up enthusiasm for the project or bolster his reputation among NASWHO members, because records indicate that in reality Sullivan was having trouble finding local historians, and many of those who were appointed never sent in the required information. Local historians expressed unequivocal disappointment in their inability to extract information from soldiers and war service organizations. The questionnaire provided to soldiers was not standard, but communities in New York typically asked for basic information, including address, date of enlistment, regiment, and rank. Some were much more detailed, asking for information about battles fought, honors and awards received, and copies of letters sent home.[18] Local historians faced an uphill battle to secure any of it.

In Sinclairville, the historian reported finding, "A very strange condition among the soldier boys, their relatives and friends. None of them, or perhaps not more than one in ten seem to care to give me . . . the details [of their service]."[19] Numerous historians sent letters apologizing to Sullivan about paltry returns and long delays. In Fairfield, just five out of fifty soldiers supplied the requested information.[20] In Hudson Falls, local officials reported that the "men were too careless to participate," and submitted the stories of only twenty out of three hundred soldiers.[21] Another official bemoaned the lack of soldier participation and regretted that there was "[regarding the collection of information] no teeth in the law, and no penalty to enforce the same."[22] The necessity for "teeth," or a penalty to encourage participation in the war history effort, spoke volumes about postwar attitudes. This apathy, and even outright opposition, would sideline war histories in New York and many other states.

Sullivan told one distraught historian that there was no generalization to be made about the situation. "In some cases the men and women have entered into the spirit of the matter with vim and energy. . . . In others they have been what we might popularly term 'the limit.' What creates this state of mind is difficult to say."[23]

Letter after letter to Sullivan indicates soldier and community apathy toward the project. One historian told Sullivan that Civil War veterans were proud of their service and would share their stories freely. When he sought out the stories of Great War veterans, he claimed that "never have I worked with greater zeal or spent more time and effort than on the subject in question [soldier questionnaires] and never have I met with as little response and manifest interest on the part of those who ought to have been interested."[24]

Plattsburgh City historian George Bixby decried the meager responses he had gotten from soldiers and city war agencies and published a statement in the local paper urging "all persons and families interested in having proper credit given to the city, its martyrs, its ex-service men . . . to do their part in furnishing information."[25] Bixby elevated those who died in the war to the status of martyrs to encourage participation, but his request met with little response.[26] Historians mailed questionnaires once, twice, even three times, with little effect. Personal visits soliciting information were often met with a stern refusal. One historian noted that soldiers rebuffed even basic inquiries about the unit in which they enlisted. Veterans told the Saratoga Springs historian that "they got little recognition for their sacrifice and suffering and felt that it was useless for me to try [and] give them any now."[27]

Despite exerting considerable effort over eight years, New York State officials never published a history of the state's role in the war. The published history of the participation of New York State in World War I is represented only by works at the local and county level. At least ten counties published histories or rosters (including Albany, Chautauqua, Erie, Franklin, Jefferson, Madison, Monroe, Oneida, Otsego, and Yates), and many localities published works that ranged in scope from brief pamphlets to multivolume publications. There seems to be little geographic correlation for those upstate counties that completed the project and little distinction between urban and rural areas.

Why were some communities able to successfully complete the task, while others reported overwhelming difficulties? Sullivan asserted that smaller communities and those employing highly motivated and patriotic individuals were more likely to engender cooperation and compile comprehensive reports. However, as the following examples demonstrate, determination and patriotism were not necessarily the keys to garnering support from returning soldiers and recording a community's history. Persistence was important, as historians might have better luck if they repeatedly contacted a soldier. However, this too is indicative of the general mood of the soldiers. If soldiers had to be compelled through repeated visits or letters to share their stories, they were clearly troubled by their experience and, by extension, the government and community that sent them to France.

Many of the war histories that came to fruition were direct products of the extension of the state's war propaganda infrastructure into the postwar period. County Defense Committees were established during the war in all sixty-two New York State counties. After the armistice, these committees were authorized to continue work until May 1920 and were encouraged to prepare honor rolls of those from the county who served and died.[28] In Oneida County, the Defense Committee published a notice requesting the names of all servicemen and women from the war for the purposes of preparing the roster for the honor roll, urging residents to "Do it as a Duty." They made their final appeal to citizens in April 1919, in all newspapers of the county, including those in Italian and Polish languages, before publishing the honor roll in August 1919. Through rosters from the National Guard, recruiting stations, and draft boards, the Defense Committee estimated 8,100 people had served in various home front and military capacities. When the roll was published, the committee had received response cards from only 364 individuals. The chairman of the committee suggested the poor response rate "must bring unpleasant reflections and regrets to the minds of those who failed to render that co-operation so solicitously sought."[29] Although Oneida County published a war history, it consisted of little more than a list cobbled together from different war agencies, and it did so without significant community support.

Emmett Harrison, the compiler and publisher of *Yates County in the World War 1917–1918*, appeared to have succeeded where others had failed. A reviewer lauded Harrison for the amount of information, including photographs, he was able to extract from some soldiers. However, while Harrison was successful at compiling full reports on select soldiers, he is forthright in his admission that his task was not met with universal support. The reviewer absolved Harrison of responsibility by stating, "That there were some [soldiers] that he could not get is evidently no fault of his own, but of a silly spirit prevalent with some men who think they acquire a sort of big boy credit by replying, 'I want to forget the war.'"[30] It is difficult to know exactly what the reviewer means to convey by this comment, but it is clear that he has disdain for those soldiers who came back from the war lacking the proper civic spiritedness that would impel them to cooperate with the state and its agents. According to Harrison, the "really hardest part of the work was the securing of the records of the service man." Harrison blamed it on the fact that men became "'tired,' 'disgusted,' 'had enough of it,' etc. . . . Some of them 'turned me down cold,' refusing to give me any information and it was impossible to secure it."[31] Veterans could indeed have been "tired" of requests for information about their service, which, depending on their location, could have come from any number of sources, including the adjutant general, local or state historians, civic organizations, or even for-profit publishing enterprises. Their "disgust" and pointed refusal to cooperate, though, seems to suggest a visceral reaction that goes beyond simple annoyance.

The difficulty in securing information appears to have

been overcome in Erie and Monroe Counties as both compiled what are, without a doubt, the two largest war histories produced in New York. In 1920, Erie County and the City of Buffalo, through the "Committee of One Hundred," produced a 733-page tome, reportedly at a cost of $40,000, outlining the illustrious work of the county during the war. The first 450 pages are dedicated to the years leading up to war, civilian efforts on the home front, and histories of the units containing many Buffalo and Erie County soldiers. Again, however, the publication suggests difficulties in obtaining the limited information available. The roster lists only soldiers' names, occasionally with rank and unit affiliations. There are no photographs, except for those of local elected officials and dignitaries, and little distinction is made to recognize those who died in service. The book is basically a compilation of documents produced by wartime propaganda agents with the addition of an incomplete roster of soldiers at the end.[32] To the extent that information is available on select soldiers, much of it was procured through the long arm of the state. City policemen brought a card to the home of each veteran soliciting data. Many, however, disregarded this not-so-subtle attempt to bully veterans into compliance. A civic organizer in Buffalo suggested that the effort would have yielded more responses if the police had also been assigned the task of collecting the cards, and he lamented that, "we thought there would be enough pride in the house to have the cards sent in."[33]

Less threatening inducements than a knock from the friendly local police officer were used elsewhere. For example, the city historian in Rochester, New York, became an agent for the adjutant general in the distribution of the state's World War I service medal, allowing him to hold the medal as ransom for the prize of a completed questionnaire.[34] In other states the questionnaire was secured with the administration of a bonus of some sort. The secretary of the Maryland War Records Commission estimated that the return rate for questionnaires absent a lure of some sort was substantially less than 50 percent.[35] Many war histories that did come to fruition simply used existing rosters produced by draft boards, recruitment offices, civic organizations, and state adjutant generals. These somewhat bureaucratic memorial volumes often give disproportionate recognition to local elected officials and others on the home front rather than combat veterans.

Monroe County historians proved exceptional, however, in their ability to produce a memorial volume that exceeded the bar of mere "government work" in a monumental effort chronicling native sons and daughters. In three volumes totaling an overwhelming 3,300 pages, the City of Rochester and Monroe County crafted an extremely detailed account of citizens' and soldiers' contributions to the war effort. The first volume of the *World War Service Record of Rochester and Monroe County New York* memorialized those who died and includes photographs of the war dead.[36] The second volume is a thorough accounting of more than twenty-three thousand men and women who served during the war. Each individual is identified by name, address, place of birth, the date he or she entered service, places of service (including training camps), and discharge date. Of those included, just over three thousand were civilians on the home front. Rochester city historian Edward Foreman estimated that as many as twenty-four thousand men had served during the war, which would suggest that the book documented more than 80 percent of those who served.[37]

While Rochester provides a success story, the city still faced some of the same problems found in other communities. Initial resistance to data collection efforts was tackled through the use of teams of volunteers to blanket the streets and counteract apathetic soldiers. The Red Triangle Club, an outgrowth of the YMCA during the war,

fanned out across the county in seven teams, each com-
posed of a captain and four other members. The club was
made up of primarily young women who would use all the
resources at their disposal to secure information on the
county's war heroes.[38] The efforts of the "Red Triangle
girls" were supplemented by myriad other organizations.[39]
Other tactics included outreach to men's Bible classes,
large factories, and American Legion Post meetings. The
East Rochester Legion Post offered a five-dollar prize to
any high school student who could collect the most information from veterans. Leads were also secured by hiring
two workers in Albany to scour the records of the adjutant
general's office. Most notably, the county even hired ex-
servicemen to assist with the collection of data.[40] Basically
no rock was left unturned under Foreman's leadership.
He attacked the project with unparalleled zeal, including
writing to other local and statewide war history organizers, keeping up regular communication with James Sullivan, and devotedly collecting published memorial volumes
from around the country.

Yet, even Foreman had to admit the difficulties he faced,
noting that the commander of a local American Legion Post
tried to acquire records after a local historian could not
be found "who was grateful enough to compile the data."[41]
The ex-servicemen who were hired to solicit information
told organizers that veterans engaged in both open and
covert opposition to their entreaties because "they think
the country has been ungrateful to them for not supply-
ing them with jobs or with a bonus."[42]

However, it seems that an organized, well-financed cadre
of individuals willing to use creative means to track down
soldiers definitely helped overcome the apathy evident
in other communities. There are, however, a few other
factors that may have contributed to Monroe County's
success. First, the county claimed that 11,064 of 20,211

soldiers volunteered for service, the remainder having been drafted, indicating a 55 percent enlistment rate, almost double the national average of 28 percent.[43] The City of Rochester was also one of many communities that bestowed on each soldier an honor medal, hung from a ribbon of blue, white, and gold, with the inscription "For Democracy, Liberty & Justice." It appears that they also gave similar medals for "Mothers of Defenders of Liberty."[44] These efforts attest to stronger community support for the war and created an environment of gratitude that may have made soldiers more amenable to participation. Monroe County's effort and the resulting volumes were unique among New York's communities. Their ability to publish a comprehensive war history was not based primarily on enthusiastic and voluntary participation by veterans, but a determined community effort to recognize war service.

Monroe County historians also made significant efforts to be ethnically inclusive, as did many other communities. Monroe County's history captured the wartime activities of Italians, Poles, Canadians, French, Lithuanians, Ukrainians, Armenians, and Greeks, many of whom were not naturalized citizens. Rochester officials sought the assistance of the Italian Consular Office to secure the names of those who were called back as reservists in the Italian army. In Oneida County, Polish and Italian veterans were encouraged to participate in the war history through advertising in newspapers published in their native tongue. The "Americanization" campaign to transform immigrants into loyal citizens that was in full swing during the war clearly spilled over into postwar attempts to package the war story. There is, however, much less evidence of outreach to African American communities. Within all the New York publications I reviewed, African American soldiers are only readily evident in two local histories, and in one of these, they are represented by a separate list for African Americans.

African Americans represented only 1.9 percent of New York's population in 1920, so it is possible that black veterans are integrated into the lists of white soldiers, or simply chose not to participate. But there is some evidence that racist sentiment hindered data collection efforts. James Sullivan expressed concern about difficulties that had "arisen from the failure to distinguish between colored and white soldiers."[45] The questionnaire developed by the state historian's office failed to include a line identifying race; however, race could easily have been determined based on a soldier's unit, as servicemen were strictly segregated. The paucity of black representation in the histories that were produced in New York, and the fact that this minor paperwork issue caused consternation, attests to a level of racism that probably worked to suppress or exclude black participation. As demonstrated later in this chapter, Virginia officials, working in an environment permeated by official segregation and overt assertions of white racial superiority, were much more active in courting African American participation in war histories. If war histories were to bind up the wounds of the country and encourage unification in the face of bolshevism during the Red Scare, the large black population in Virginia necessitated outreach to African Americans much more compellingly than in the North.

Ironically, the most celebrated African American unit during the war was from New York, the 369th Infantry, which was partially raised in Harlem. French and German soldiers nicknamed them the Hellfighters because of their determination in battle.[46] The French bestowed the first Croix de Guerre to an American to Henry Johnson, a Hellfighter from Albany, New York.[47] Johnson received his Distinguished Service Cross posthumously in 2002, and the Medal of Honor in 2015, following an effort to redress what many had called a racist snub on the part of American military officials.[48] Johnson lived just blocks from where James Sullivan would orchestrate his war history at the state capital.[49]

Ultimately, the purposeful exclusion of black soldiers, if it happened, is mostly moot, as so few soldiers are represented in the limited war histories that were published. African Americans joined white New York veterans who were missing from the public record, many of the latter, at least, of their own accord. As the record in Virginia demonstrates, however, it is just as likely that black soldiers refused to participate as it is that they were excluded. The indifference and outright opposition expressed by soldiers in New York was evident in Virginia as well, and the sizable population of black soldiers there were no exception to this rule.

Virginia

Gov. Westmoreland Davis created the Virginia War History Commission (VWHC) in 1919. The commission was made up of sixteen community leaders and chaired by Arthur Kyle Davis, the president of Southern Female College in Petersburg, Virginia. The commission oversaw local branches set up in Virginia's one hundred counties and twenty-one cities.[50] Davis's 121 commissioners would serve the same role as Sullivan's locally appointed historians. In terms of organization alone, it would appear that Davis faced a less formidable task, but where Sullivan at least had a fairly stable army of local historians, Davis was stuck with a continually changing list of commission "volunteers," who offered numerous reasons why they could not complete their appointed tasks. Davis combated this recalcitrance with between one and six field workers who canvassed the state to keep commission volunteers on target.[51]

Davis asked his field workers to collect individual service records along with several other categories of information, including:

1. Virginians of distinguished service
2. Prewar conditions and activities
3. Virginia churches in war time
4. Virginia schools and colleges in the war
5. Draft law and Virginia organizations
6. Economic and social conditions
7. The Red Cross in Virginia
8. War work and relief organizations
9. War letters, diaries, and incidents
10. Postwar conditions and activities

However, as in New York, the commission stressed the importance of collecting individual service records, telling county commissions that the collection of service records was the "gravamen of the history. The history will fail of its purpose unless we have a fairly accurate roster of all Virginia troops with something more than a mere list of names."[52] They had no idea how prescient that claim would be. The success of each county commission was rated, largely, on the number of records collected. So, while the county commission exhibited limited success collecting reports on other topics, their efficacy would be rated according to the number of soldiers' records collected, which was more often than not meager.[53] The four-page questionnaire sent to veterans was more comprehensive than that in New York, including basic information about a soldier and his service as well as queries about attitudes toward military service, the effect of experiences at training camps and overseas, the effect on religious beliefs, and any changes in the soldier's overall state of mind after the war.

Davis asked county and local commissions to appoint chairmen who would coordinate data collection efforts.

Many of those appointed seem to have been obliged to participate rather than having volunteered, and the roster of commissioners was continually updated with resignations and replacements. By the end of 1923, forty-six of one hundred counties were either no longer responding to letters from the VWHC, had no chairman in place, or had submitted no reports.[54] Without the constant prodding of War History Commission field agents, it is unlikely that most county organizations would have been appointed at all, a situation analogous to the appointment of local historians in New York State. In Richmond, the field agent found that none of the named members of the county committee had agreed to serve, and "most had positively refused the use of their names."[55]

Field workers who submitted regular progress updates to Davis often bemoaned the lack of interest in the topic. One reported, "I am already beginning to feel like an atom of interest in an ocean of apathy as regards war history."[56] The effort suffered from two fundamental problems: an inability to keep commission members active in the counties; and, in those counties where commissioners made some attempt to complete their task, an inability to get soldiers to share their war histories. Virginia's war history foundered on a double-barreled problem of community and veteran indifference.

An American Legion officer wrote Arthur Kyle Davis that he believed Virginians were apathetic about a war history because they did not care about soldiers and that their efforts on the battlefield were not appreciated. The legion official noted that he would not lobby the legislature for funding for a war history because, "If what the young men of the state did constitutes meritorious and patriotic service, you may depend that a history will be made of the same, for outstanding appreciative work will always become known." He believed that "the record of

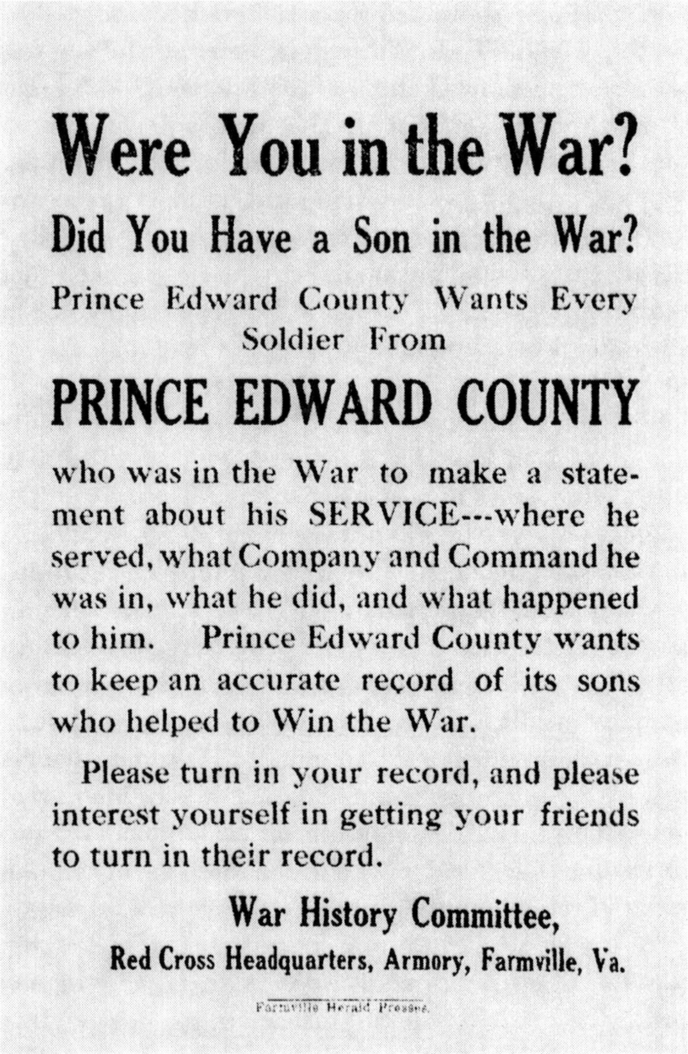

Were You in the War?

Did You Have a Son in the War?

Prince Edward County Wants Every Soldier From

PRINCE EDWARD COUNTY

who was in the War to make a statement about his SERVICE---where he served, what Company and Command he was in, what he did, and what happened to him.   Prince Edward County wants to keep an accurate reçord of its sons who helped to Win the War.

Please turn in your record, and please interest yourself in getting your friends to turn in their record.

War History Committee,
Red Cross Headquarters, Armory, Farmville, Va.

Farmville Herald Presses.

FIG. 1. Virginia War History Committee poster soliciting soldier data. Virginia War History Commission, Series 11, Office Files, 1917–27, Library of Virginia.

service and sacrifice of those who bore the brunt of this war, is not history if we have to beg for money to compile it in book form; no more than the compliments in a eulogy delivered by a paid agent." In effect, he argued, if society does not provide the momentum for such a memorial to be completed, "what some of us think is history is only unimportant events to the majority."[57]

In Lexington, a field worker encountered a chaplain who served in the war who "offered the most bitter opposition to the military questionnaire I have yet encountered and that is saying a great deal for I met it everywhere."[58] The commissioner for Cumberland County was ashamed that she was unable to secure individual records from men in her community after personal visits to soldiers' homes, reporting that they were "'disgusted with the whole affair,' 'wish they could forget it all.' . . . The people too seem very tired of the thoughts of the war and all that has followed."[59] In Richmond, county organizers had the police bring veterans surveys with the admonition that they would be back to collect the completed forms. This strong-arm tactic may or may not have produced significant results. Of the six or seven thousand soldiers recruited from Richmond, at least 2,500 were recipients of hand-delivered questionnaires, and 2,814 are extant in the archive.[60] In Shenandoah County, high school students solicited responses as part of a competition for prizes. This strategy may have garnered some success, as the county submitted records for 66 percent of its soldiers.[61]

Most field reports contain some reference to the attitude of ex-soldiers and citizens, which generally ranges from general apathy to harsh opposition. The response suggests a far-reaching repulsion to the war and its aftermath. Approximately one in seven of the extant questionnaires in the archive at the Library of Virginia indicates a negative opinion of the war. Soldiers mentioned the senselessness of war, disgust over the way government handled disabled soldiers, and criticism for the way enlisted men were treated. One veteran disclosed that war "is a horrible useless waste of our young men," another offered that a new law was in order, one that ensured that "a few of the flat-top-desk-officers of the last war, and as many of the war profiteers as the army can accommodate, be induced into the service to help fight the next war."[62] Veterans recognized the inequities of the system that sent them to fight, and resentment for those who stayed home festered just under the surface for many.

African American veterans expressed the same cynicism. Some even expressed a fear that signing government papers of any type would only result in their obligation to serve in a future war. Some black veterans held out for a cash payment in return for submitting their records.[63] Others took the opportunity to snub the government because of any complaint they had with the bureaucracy during the war. A field officer reported, "Everybody who had a grievance against the Red Cross, Liberty Bond or any war organization has told it to me and then positively refused to cooperate with the History Commission."[64] Many scholars, including Jennifer Keene, have explored the state of mind and written of the grudge that returning soldiers had against a government that sent them to fight for unclear purposes and welcomed them home to a dry country suffering from both high prices and high unemployment. One soldier put it very succinctly, "We fought for democracy and you gave us Spanish Influenza and prohibition."[65] Black soldiers, particularly in the South, cited the added injury of Jim Crow. One black veteran had been turned away at Red Cross headquarters because of his color and "still nursed his wrath all through the war and promised to not assist [with] anything."[66] After the war, black soldiers faced ridicule and hostility in many Southern towns, black officers were prohibited from staying in the army, and most veterans were barred entry in the newly formed American Legion. A black newspaper reported, "For valor displayed in the recent war, it seems that the Negro's particular decoration is to be the 'double-cross.'"[67]

The poor state of race relations in postwar Virginia made the daunting task faced by such a small number of VWHC field workers even worse. Of the three states analyzed, only Virginia had a substantial African American population, and field workers had to overcome significant barriers to gain black participation. Although white Virginians often saw their state as being particularly benevolent toward African Americans, black citizens saw the situation quite differently. The paternalistic attitudes of whites were aimed primarily at controlling blacks. After experiencing unprecedented freedoms in France, many black veterans would chafe considerably upon returning to the oppression of the segregated South. Where "benevolent" whites were unable to maintain control, the rising postwar ranks of the Ku Klux Klan stepped in.[68]

African American veterans may have faced greater tension as they returned as victorious soldiers back to a segregated South, but officials courted them for their war stories as vigorously as they did white soldiers. There was no lack of black Virginians in the war—fully 25 percent of the forces sent from the state (which represented 30 percent of the entire state population) were African American.[69] Early in the war, county history committees were charged with gathering the records of both white and black soldiers, but it soon became evident that almost no information was coming in from African American soldiers or war-related organizations. By February of 1920 a plan was in place to appoint a Board of Negro Collaborators to assist in compiling this information. A white section chairman, Julia Sully, coordinated the new plan and argued condescendingly that "it will have a good effect on some of our critics to the North when they find that we have treated the negroes not only with justice in allowing them to have a separate and distinct representation, but with generosity in making it interesting and sympathetic."[70] As it turned out, only one white chairman "attempted to do anything for the Negroes."[71] An advisor told Sully that the only way to get information from the African American community was through personal contact or through the churches.[72] However, even after the appointment of black collaborators, African Americans were less than forthcoming with information. Interestingly, but perhaps predictably, members of the War History Commission found that either the Board of Collaborators was negligent in pursuing the information or that African Americans were not fulfilling their patriotic duty.[73]

Ora Brown Stokes, a black field agent, seemed to take great pride in getting black soldiers the recognition they deserved. In one of her monthly reports she noted that there were several prominent black Virginians in the war, including Tym Brymn, one of the most well-known Jazz band leaders in the army; Capt. J. Wormly Jones, who led a notorious and heroic charge at the Argonne; Lt. Park Tancil, a dentist who was awarded the Croix de Guerre for providing medical attention to the wounded while under enemy fire; and Lt. Urban F. Bass, a black physician who died at an aid station on the battlefield after he was hit by a shell that severed both of his legs. Stokes put forward Bass, Brymn, Jones, and Tancil as symbolic of the determination and dedication of their entire race, but ironically none of these men are represented in the extant files of the vwhc.[74]

Because of the treatment many received from white Americans during their time in uniform and after, black veterans had little reason to participate in war histories. War veteran George Schuyler, a prominent black journalist and novelist of the 1920s and 1930s, described the particularly demoralizing experience of being called a "nigger" by a recently arrived Greek immigrant who refused to shine his leather puttees. On another occasion a bartender reluctantly served Schuyler and his fellow soldiers but made the point of smashing glasses after each black patron finished his drink.[75] Black soldiers abroad found no more encouragement, as they were largely relegated to roles other than combat, including labor battalions, stevedore regiments, and grave diggers.[76] Even as Arthur Kyle Davis was soliciting information from Virginia's heroes after they returned from war, black soldiers faced violence and intimidation. Black sailors in Norfolk, Virginia, became part of the wave of racially motivated violence that engulfed the country in the Red Summer of 1919 when they intervened as a police officer attempted to arrest a black soldier. Two men died and two police officers were wounded on a day that the City of Norfolk had scheduled a parade to celebrate the return of black troops from France.[77]

Virginia fielded thirteen black officers during the war, four of whom completed war history questionnaires.[78] Two of these soldiers had been students at the Hampton Institute and indicated that they filled their questionnaires out at the institute, perhaps at the urging of Hampton officials who had struggled during the war to prove that African Americans were loyal to the country.[79] One of those officers, 1st Lt. Edward Dabney, exudes pride in his service when answering the question, "What was your attitude toward military service in general and toward your call in particular?" He responded, "Being an officer answers that in full." He also noted the welcoming environment in France, "the hospitality given by the French [is] better than that of Americans."[80] The hospitality that black soldiers received when they returned home would have quickly brought these officers back to the reality of life in the Southern states. The governor of Virginia declared October 12, 1919, as War Memorial Day and urged the collection of soldiers' records so that their names might be placed in the "Virginia Valhalla." Of course, October 12 was also the anniversary of the death of Robert E. Lee, and War Memorial Day was a consecration of the men who fought for the Confederacy.[81] It is unlikely that black Virginians would have appreciated the coincidence.

Black and white officers were more likely to complete questionnaires because they had a larger stake in the war as professionals and had more to brag about. A sample of five hundred of the Virginia surveys found that the distribution "skewed heavily in favor of those higher in rank, better educated, more literate, and more eager for one reason or another to record their experiences."[82]

African Americans were much less likely to be officers, literate, or educated, but might have been eager to record their war experiences because it would give them a sense of standing in the community. Many black leaders believed that African American soldiers would grant a new legitimacy to black citizenship in the South. In fact, more than 2,500 black soldiers submitted questionnaires, a response rate that is lower than white soldiers, but the minor difference can probably be attributed to a dramatically lower number of black officers and marginal black literacy rates.[83] About half of African American respondents indicated an obligation to the nation, with one noting, "it was my duty to defend the standards of *My* country wher[e] my Freedom is sought." Another said that he felt obligated to the country and that he should "do all in my power to save its honor."[84] Of course, it is unlikely that a black man would be overtly critical of the government, or his wartime experience, in a document submitted to the State of Virginia. For many black soldiers the point of completing the questionnaire would have been justifying their value to the country, not inciting more discrimination and racism.

Recent scholarship by Edward A. Gutiérrez focuses on the military experience revealed by soldier questionnaires. He combed through fifteen thousand questionnaires in the Virginia State Archives to better quantify what he believes is a poorly documented American experience through all phases of the war. Gutiérrez argues that the extant questionnaires suggest that doughboys fought because they heeded their obligation as Americans. They were "duty- and honor-bound" to take up their rifles.[85] Gutiérrez states that he relied more heavily on the responses of enlisted men than officers, but he was still dealing with a self-selecting pool of respondents who likely had a more positive experience at war. It may be an overreach to suggest that extant questionnaires provide a definitive view on veterans' attitudes.

Maj. Hierome Opie of Staunton, Virginia, is a perfect example of someone who was likely to fill out a questionnaire. Opie was thirty-seven years old when he went to war, a veteran with sixteen years of service in the National Guard. He was the founder and editor of the local paper, the *Staunton Leader*, was married with a young daughter; and was a member of both the Masons and the Knights of Pythias. Major Opie served with distinction in the war and was awarded the Distinguished Service Cross and received the Croix de Guerre from no less a legend than Marshall Foch for his bravery in battle near Samogneux, France, in October 1918.[86] Opie dutifully filled out his War History Commission Military Service Record and encouraged others to do the same by agreeing to grant the vwhc a column per week in his newspaper for a period of one year in order to publicize efforts to preserve military records. He told Arthur Davis that this was the least he could do to help, considering that most Virginians have "forgotten that we had a war."[87] However, Opie's questionnaire hints

at the frustration also felt by others who were less cooperative with the vwhc; he states there that his mental health
was affected during the war by "inexcusable incompetence
in so many quarters."[88]

Ultimately, however, most black and white soldiers joined
in an unwitting solidarity that circumvented the original
plans of the vwhc. The State of Virginia was unable to
produce the four-volume war history that had been envisioned. As late as 1923 Arthur Kyle Davis told John Pollard,
the president of William and Mary College, that only six
cities and twelve counties had provided war information
that could be considered adequate. Davis asked Pollard
to consider a plan under which the colleges in Virginia
would send students throughout the state during the summer to collect the information.[89] No such plan appears to
have been implemented. Less than half of Virginia's communities submitted a narrative war history, and far fewer
would publish anything independently. There are only
eight extant independently published community histories in the Library of Virginia. Of these, only one is not
merely a reprint of the brief history (typically less than
thirty pages) that was submitted to the War History Commission. Seven of the eight histories provide a few narrative paragraphs about a varying number of the original
fifteen topics suggested by Davis. None include a roster
of soldiers, a roster of those awarded medals or honors,
and only one contains a roster of those who were killed
or wounded in action. None contain photographs.[90] One
of the seven, from the City of Norfolk, was not even completed by community members, but compiled by Davis to
serve as a model for other communities.

Veterans appear to have played a role in compiling only
a few of the community histories published by Davis, the
most notable being that of Rockbridge County. A field
agent with the War History Commission reported in 1921

that Capt. Greenlee Letcher had helped her convince an army chaplain that he should participate in the war history project and within a short time had taken charge of collecting soldier records.[91] He had pulled together his own National Guard battery of 160 men, christened the "Rockbridge Battery," and joined them in service at the age of fifty. The battery went abroad and secured training in time to join Pershing's push between Verdun and Metz in early November 1918. They marched to within one mile of the fighting before the armistice was signed. Captain Letcher kept in contact with many of the men of his unit after the war and was uniquely placed to encourage participation in the effort to collect individual war histories from his soldiers.[92] It would seem to be difficult to find anyone better primed for success, but it did not take long for Captain Letcher to recognize the complete futility of his task. He reported to the commission that he could "do nothing about securing them [the records]." Rockbridge is represented by twenty-two military records from a community that supplied at least 750 men for the war effort.[93] Captain Letcher's experience was the norm, and this left Davis coming up short in the quest to document Virginia's soldiers.

As time passed, the prospect of publishing a comprehensive history faded, and Davis focused his energies on publishing volumes of source materials that could be used by future historians. The War History Commission ultimately produced seven volumes of material compiled by the commission, all edited by Davis. The first, published in 1923, is a roster of Virginians who were recognized for wartime heroism by either the American government or one of her allies. Source book volumes two, three, and four provide documentation on Virginia's war agencies; clippings from state newspapers; and copies of war letters, diary entries, and soldiers' letters. Volumes five, six, and seven include information on Virginia military organizations and Virginia communities in war.

Davis's best effort to publish something, anything, to memorialize Virginia's contributions to the war is admirable, but he published a small fraction of what he had hoped to collect. After a protracted battle of many years, the VWHC had collected information on approximately 15 percent of its veterans. For a variety of reasons Virginia citizens and veterans were uninterested in packaging a patriotic war story for future generations. Their failure to acknowledge the sacrifices of those who waged war on their behalf would have long-term implications for the collective memory of World War I.[94]

Kansas

The war history campaign in Kansas was not led by as compelling a force as either Sullivan in New York or Davis in Virginia, and its scope would not be nearly as comprehensive. The effort to collect war information in Kansas was also much less formal than that in Virginia and New York, and a simpler approach did not garner better results. The Kansas Historical Society, based in Topeka, initiated the effort to collect the records of select Kansas servicemen and pursued the cause without a formal staff, local historians, or committees. Historical society staff placed ads in local newspapers and worked directly with numerous community and war organizations, including the Grange, American Legion auxiliary organizations, the National Military Sisterhood, and Gold Star Mothers. Their efforts focused on two divisions in which many Kansans landed: the Eighty-Ninth and the Thirty-Fifth. The Eighty-Ninth contained the 353rd "All Kansas Regiment" and was based at Camp Funston in Fort Riley, Kansas. The Thirty-Fifth Division had the most Kansans, close to ten thousand, and was made up of a combination of Kansas and Missouri National Guard units.[95]

William Connelly, the secretary for the Kansas Historical Society, sought information on Kansas veterans by appealing directly to family members in newspaper ads suggesting, "Friends and relatives of these soldiers are certainly proud of their record overseas. They would always regret it if there should be any failure on the part of any one to do all possible to make this record complete. As you love your soldier husband, soon [*sic*] or sweetheart, send his letters, his photograph."[96] Once the War Society of the Eighty-Ninth Division published a history of their own in 1920, Connelly focused only on the Thirty-Fifth, arbitrarily disregarding the service of Kansans in many other divisions.[97] Early efforts were guided by the desire to have an archive of information for future reference but with only vague notions of publishing the material at some point.[98] Unlike the efforts in New York and Virginia, the Historical Society did not solicit information from wartime organizations, schools, or government agencies; they were completely focused on publishing a complete list of Kansas soldiers with relevant biographical information.[99]

The society appears to have been working without any official direction from either the governor or the legislature, the latter having failed to appropriate any funds for the collection of materials.[100] Instead, it was an effort directed by the Historical Society that involved different partners at different times. One of the first partners was the National Military Sisterhood of America, conceived in 1917 by the wife of a general in the Kansas National Guard to help the families of soldiers. Chapters sprung up around the state as well as in Missouri, Oklahoma, Iowa, and Colorado during and after the war.[101] The Military Sisterhood sought basic information for Kansas soldiers, including the nationality of the soldier and his parents, when and where he served, and copies of wartime letters and photographs.[102] It is difficult to estimate how successful the Military Sisterhood was in this endeavor, but only a few surveys survive at the Kansas Historical Society. American Legion Auxiliary groups, the Gold Star Mothers, and Grange posts also assisted the Historical Society at various times. All circulated questionnaires to members and submitted some of the completed forms that the Historical Society retains in its archives. The many groups involved in collecting information resulted in a hodge-podge of forms in the archive with varying types and amounts of information.

The Gold Star Mothers limited membership to the surviving mother, daughter, wife, or sister of a soldier who died while in service, and, as such, they focused largely on the desire to memorialize the dead. At the first meeting of the Gold Star Mothers in 1921, members pledged to "collect and preserve the history and keep fresh the memory of the men and women who gave their lives at home or abroad."[103] By 1922 they were imploring American Legion Auxiliary chapters to collect this information by the end of the year. In 1923 they were still actively engaged in an endeavor to create a book memorializing "the 3,000 Kansas boys who gave their lives for America." The adjutant general in Kansas had published a list of Kansas soldiers who died during the war and their next of kin, but Connelly derided it as being "inaccurate and really of very little value."[104] The Gold Star Mothers planned a five-hundred-page document with five biographies to a page and approximately eighty-five words allotted to each soldier.[105] However, the project remained unfinished as of 1927 when a renewed call was made to complete the book by 1928. Ultimately, the ambitious idea faltered and nothing was published.[106]

As in New York, some Kansas veterans were memorialized in numerous county histories compiled by local organizations. Since there was not a war records commission or local historian at work in Kansas, these histories were generally commercially printed. At least eight such books were produced between 1919 and 1921. Six of these books were significant publications including relatively substantive lists of those who served. Of the six, Marion County holds the distinction of presenting the highest proportion of soldiers in the pages of their memorial book—close to 100 percent. Only 27 records were listed as "unobtainable," and their collection of 801 soldier vignettes, including almost 700 photographs, backed up that claim.[107] The Red Cross Home Service carefully compiled soldiers' war histories and printed a complete roster on the front page of the local paper, indicating which soldiers had not yet submitted information and asking anyone in the community to submit a questionnaire (included in the paper) with the required information. This meant that it was not necessary for veterans, or even family members, to participate for a complete accounting.[108] The organizers indicated that the collection of information was a "long and arduous task" that took, at the very least, nine months of dedicated effort. As in Monroe County, New York, public demonstrations of gratitude, or perhaps peer pressure, encouraged more participation. However, the results in Marion County were not typical for the rest of Kansas.

Shawnee County produced the largest of the six local publications (416 pages) that included thousands of photographs and probably accounted for over 60 percent of the county's soldiers.[109] Crawford County produced the second-largest publication (359 pages) and appears to have included information on about half of the men in the marines, army, and navy that the adjutant general reported as having enlisted from the county.[110] Two veterans, Woodson Ross and John H. Blair, compiled the book, and as in the case of a soldier-produced history in Virginia, Ross and Blair were both college-educated officers who never saw action on the battlefields of Europe. Neither were averse to tooting their own horn, either, as both have half-page photographs prominently placed in the book. In fact, Ross was not even from Kansas, let alone Crawford County, he was a native of Arkansas who was living in Missouri. Their venture may have been motivated more by the head than the heart. The Crawford County history was sold at the steep price of $12.50 per copy. Generously, payment plans were provided. Newspaper reports indicate that the complete run likely sold out.[111]

The Crawford County history also hints that midwestern pride may have contributed to the desire to create war memorial volumes and the relative success enjoyed by several counties. The editors take great pains to make readers aware that in the Midwest states between 70 and 80 percent of those entering the service passed both physical examinations, the highest proportion in the country. Virginians passed at a rate between 60 and 64 percent, and New Yorkers between 50 and 59 percent. Rural, white, native-born men were more likely to pass the examination than urban, black, or immigrant men, which helps to explain the high rate of Kansans accepted into the service.[112] However, advertisements promoting the publication of the Crawford County honor roll were published between March 26 and May 2, 1919, and the bulk of the county's men did not return home from the war until May 8, 1919.[113] Family and friends of soldiers probably provided any information secured by the honor roll organizers. Advertisements specifically targeted family members, chiding them by asking "What would one of our sons say should he find that his picture was omitted because of sheer negligence on the part of the stay-at-homes? . . . It is the duty of every Mother, Wife, Sister, or Sweetheart to keep an accurate record of the patriotic service HER Boy rendered."[114] Another told readers of the daily paper, "He Wants His Picture in Crawford County's Honor Roll."[115] If that subtle persuasion was not enough to convince residents, the ad cautions that dishonorably discharged soldiers will not be represented in the book, "If your boy's picture does not appear in the Honor Roll his friends may think that he was dishonorably discharged."[116] Family and friends were shamed into compliance.

Labette County patriots produced *Our Heroes in Our Defense*, with approximately 210 brief biographies and photographs of native men who served during the war. A few were community leaders who "served" on the home front, the remainder were soldiers, mostly officers, with eight black soldiers segregated on the last page. The book was beautifully illustrated and includes lengthy narratives of many of the home front activities in support of the war and descriptions of the major units with which Labette County soldiers served. However, the book is a far less compelling tribute when you consider that 85 percent of the fourteen hundred men who served are not included within its pages.[117]

Officials who compiled the history of the Horton community in the war acknowledged that their book excluded many names by inserting blank lines at the end of the alphabetical roster, at each letter, so that those who were missing might insert their own names in the history book at a later date. It's clear that veterans and their families in Horton were less than exuberant about the war history or community celebrations in their honor. Horton officials threw a splashy "Soldiers and Sailors" reunion parade and reception in the fall of 1919 for returning soldiers, but the local paper noted that "Enough food was prepared for 500 or more soldiers, but not over 200 at the most availed themselves of the grub . . . The soldiers who didn't attend the show, or who didn't put on the uniform, missed something."[118] The previous July a short story in the local paper told citizens not to worry about the "soldier problem," that the young men would gradually come around and were "only asking for the privilege of forgetting their disagreeable experience in France."[119] Interestingly, the Horton history provides recognition to Native American soldiers from local reservations, including members of the Kickapoo and Pottawatomie tribes. Privates Lyman Tapsee and Charlie Spear both died in France, one was gassed near Verdun and the other succumbed to wounds sustained during the Meuse-Argonne Offensive. They were lauded for being "pure Americans" who had made "the supreme sacrifice on the battlefield in France."[120] Native Americans were more likely to die abroad, as they were often given dangerous scouting assignments.[121]

Russell County, which produced the last of the six significant publications, memorialized just over 50 percent of their soldiers. The author, John Wilson, was not shy about pinning the blame for the poor showing on veterans. His preface begins with an admission that he would never have begun the process of compiling a history if he had known his spirit would be broken by the difficulties he would face. Wilson wonders, "Is it possible that any do not now wish the fact recorded that they fought against Germany in 1917 and 1918?" The answer was a resounding yes from many who "openly refused to submit a brief record of honorable service rendered." Wilson used blank spaces at the end of one page to note, "This is where the others ought to be, Were you one?"[122]

The Russell County and Marion County publications took the extraordinary step of publishing the names, and sometimes photographs, of those who did not serve. Russell County included noncombatants in a section titled, "They Didn't Go." Those named included men who claimed exemption as aliens and those who refused to serve on religious grounds.[123] Marion County had a section for "Alleged Non-Combatants or Conscientious Objectors," and to ensure that the requisite shame was heaped upon these poor souls, each entry included the name of the soldier, his hometown, parents' names, and date of birth.[124] Russian and German Mennonite families had settled in Marion and Russell counties in the 1870s, and, at least in Marion County, they seem to have been the bulk of those listed as either noncombatants or conscientious objectors.[125] Most listed were from two predominantly Mennonite towns, and the same surnames, like Duerksen, Klassen, and Knaak, appear repeatedly.[126] Only 23 of 323 Mennonite men who were drafted in Kansas joined the army in a combat role.[127] Some Kansans expressed considerable enmity against pacifist Mennonites during the war. Nightriders heaped insult and injury on Mennonites because of their perceived support for Germany and their religious views on war. Vigilantes shaved Mennonites' heads, tarred and feathered them, and burned their property in what many believed to be a demonstration of loyalty and patriotism.[128]

In the end, large numbers of Kansas veterans were not represented in the pages of these memorials, and the pleading calls for information and stinging rebukes against those who failed to participate are reminiscent of experiences in the other states. John Wilson's pointed comments in the Russell County book are the most compelling evidence of widespread apathy, and they deserve a great deal of weight. Memorial war histories were not the appropriate venue for airing a community's dirty laundry. The problems in Russell County must have been considerable if Wilson took the extraordinary step of venting his frustrations in the preface to his book. It is unlikely that these issues were unique to Russell County, and the general failure of the Kansas Historical Society and its partners to produce a war history bears this out. Extant questionnaires in the archives represent only approximately 5 percent of the Kansans who went to war, a meager showing at best.

In each state the officials in New York, Virginia, and Kansas took a different approach to the creation of war histories, whether it was the appointment of 1,200 local historians, the creation of 120 local commissions, or the use of a solitary agency. However, all failed to meet either of their goals: the collection of individual war service records or the publication of narrative war histories. They were unable to produce war histories because many soldiers and citizens wanted to forget the war, not write paeans to it. When soldiers did not respond to entreaties for information, some of the more diligent war history organizers sent in the police, young women, high school students, or fellow veterans to grease the wheels. When this too failed, as it often did, organizers gave up, published a compilation of reports about the war, or used draft and enlistment rosters to produce lists of those who served that would subtly encourage the next generation to bear arms when the world imploded once again. The resulting books and "honor rolls" of those who served suggest a unity of purpose that belies the reality. The fracture in attitudes about the war is evident in that some veterans effectively thwarted the efforts of many to package this war as a patriotic victory. The failure of these histories suggests more than just apathy. Simple carelessness does not explain the numerous references in the record to veterans who were "disgusted," "turned [organizers] down cold," offered "bitter opposition," or "positively refused [to participate]." The record is replete with responses that were emotionally charged, not apathetic.

Soldiers who adamantly rejected participating in the creation of war histories in the late 1910s and early 1920s were the first manifestation of what would be called the "lost generation" school of thought that was most evident in the late 1920s. Many men may have had traumatic experiences and, like soldiers of many wars, were less than eager to rehash memories of the trials they endured. One veteran wrote to a war history organizer that he and his fellow soldiers "can never see ourselves the heroes our relatives and friends would make us." He felt that generous praise was acceptable when demonstrated in "news stories" during the fighting, but praise in a "public document of the war" was in poor taste.[129] Still others were justifiably demoralized by their stark economic prospects in 1919, especially in contrast to those who had profited from the war, and sought any way to demonstrate their anger. Some veterans, too, had probably been bothered by numerous agencies seeking information and were annoyed by repeated inquiries. And, finally, there were veterans who felt that they had done nothing worth noting—they had never made it out of the states, or made it to France only to engage in the more mundane tasks of war.

Of course, a good number of veterans did participate, or their families did, and those veterans were likely less cynical in their beliefs about the war. These were the men who would, over time, focus more on the camaraderie of those who served, the shared experience in French estaminets, and, what would become for some, the adventure of a lifetime. These soldiers rarely required a second solicitation from war history organizers. They parted with their only photo in dress uniform because they took pride in their service or maybe to bask, if only fleetingly, in the glow accorded returning heroes. Many American soldiers would have fallen into this category, yet, even if a majority of soldiers had been willing to share information, compiling war histories would have faced challenges in other ways. Displacement after the war left a significant number of veterans far from their original place of enlistment, presenting an insurmountable obstacle for community war history organizers in an era well before the Internet would make it difficult for anyone to truly be unreachable. One historian estimated that up to a third of veterans could not be found at the address they provided upon entering military service.[130] Additionally, even with eager participants, many communities simply did not demonstrate a great desire to produce war histories. There was a constantly revolving door of local organizers in both New York and Virginia. Moreover, legislators and government officials who no longer had to sell the war felt quite comfortable ignoring requests for operating budgets and publishing costs. Veteran participation was a key part of the battle, but other factors played a substantial role as well.

The bold plan for comprehensive state war histories primarily resulted in three different outcomes—none of which reflected the original spirit of the project. First, some communities never put much effort into compiling information (or, as one organizer put it, had no one "who was grateful enough to compile the data").[131] These projects never really got off the ground, so it is not surprising that they failed to produce a memorial book. The second outcome, also failure, resulted from active war history organizations that were unable to get sufficient participation in the process. There was either trouble getting information from those who were averse to a government-sponsored attempt to package the war or simply wanted to forget it. There may also have been problems reaching highly mobile veterans or getting traumatized veterans to tell their stories. The third outcome was limited success. If success was publishing a memorial volume of any sort, then many communities would reach this bar. This included privately printed rosters of a few pages with only partial information gleaned from the files of war agencies. Very few communities, however, claimed success in compiling comprehensive lists of those who served and how they served. The work in Monroe County was truly an anomaly. An incredibly dedicated organizer used every opportunity available to track down information on veterans, working with numerous agencies that all had a vested interest in recognizing the service that veterans provided their country. A well-funded cadre of individuals and groups was able to overcome apathy, fear, and disgust to publish what many communities had first envisioned. It is ironic that the true legacy of war history projects in the United States is actually the fact that so few were successful. Instead of presenting an image of a country unified behind the war effort and grateful to its returning soldiers, this lack of success demonstrates a significant undercurrent of dissatisfaction with the war.

War histories and their supporting archives of information might have served as a reminder of World War I and its enduring significance for Americans. The professional historians who supported the NBHS and NASHWO believed that these archives were essential for future scholarship. Historians may have slipped the moorings of objectivity during the war, but their basic impulse to preserve testimony of the war was still sound. Their ultimate failure to officially record the war hampers collective memory today because archives lack the materials that spur public remembrance. Archival information intrigues and inspires academic historians to further research, encourages local historians to create displays at town halls, and captivates genealogists who connect with their ancestors by understanding the major events that shaped their lives. Hefty, leather-bound, gilt-edged memorials to the war effort, and the materials used to create them, would have served as continual reminders to researchers, librarians, local historians, and public officials that the war was worth remembering. Fortunately, New York, Virginia, and Kansas all retain the archives of information collected after the war. In some states, the material was forgotten as quickly as the war, and archives of information were lost. Ultimately, the sparse war service records collected in New York, Virginia,

Kansas, and other states are all that remain to document the service of millions of American soldiers after a fire at the National Archives in St. Louis in 1973 consumed the vast majority of World War I army personnel records, furthering the public's disconnection from the war.[132] War data are most accessible in Virginia, where all fifteen thousand soldier questionnaires are available through an online database. In Kansas, researchers can access an alphabetical index of soldier questionnaires. In New York, researchers must comb through microfilm to read the reports submitted by each local historian. As the one hundredth anniversary of the end of the war approaches, World War I will likely emerge into the public consciousness once again. These vital, yet incomplete, archives will serve as a starting point for understanding those who served, and why Americans have forgotten them and the war they fought.

2

War Memoirs

They Pour from Presses Daily

Most Americans would be hard-pressed to identify a single memoir from World War I, yet soldiers, volunteers, and civilians produced at least five hundred personal narratives between 1914 and 1941. The previous chapter demonstrated that scores of soldiers foiled the state's sophisticated efforts to secure their personal war histories, but many would write of their experiences on their own terms. Whether they served on the battlefield, in hospitals, in the diplomatic corps, as volunteers, or were accidental witnesses to war, these individuals' stories were recorded for posterity.[1] Why, then, is there such a disconnect between those who wanted their legacy known and our ignorance of the war today? The paradox is compounded by the fact that the prolific writing of World War I veterans represents a much greater outpouring of testimony than that produced directly after World War II, yet that war remains strongly entrenched in the American public consciousness.[2]

Common wisdom suggests that the audience for American war stories was weak because Americans experienced war for a shorter time, on foreign soil, and at a lesser intensity than other combatants. But generalizing the American experience in such a dismissive manner does a disservice to those who faced the full force of the war, often in very meaningful and painful ways. Furthermore, Americans may have experienced war for fewer years than the Europeans, but they were also given credit for winning it. It would seem that Americans would have a strong curiosity about a war in which they were the victors. It was the infusion of millions of Americans into the war that finally brought defeat to the Germans. Some of the stories of her conquering heroes, both good and bad, ought to have found a permanent place in the American collective consciousness about the war. Yet the thrilling exploits of Eddie Rickenbacker in the air, the story of a president's son on the exotic Mesopotamian front, or the bitingly critically report of a nurse serving the wounded in France, along with hundreds of other stories, never gained significant audiences and remain obscure today. Most Americans seem to have forgotten the war after the armistice, and encouraged the market for escapist fiction rather than the introspective writing of veterans.

Some historians have argued that American testimony about World War I is little known because the narratives were not compelling, sophisticated, or well written. However, the evidence fails to bear this out. Reviewers, literary critics, and others applauded the literary merit, complexity, and drama of many postwar American narratives. Books like Norman Archibald's *Heaven High, Hell Deep*, Elizabeth Shepley Sergeant's *Shadow Shapes*, Howard O'Brien's *Wine, Women and War*, Hervey Allen's *Toward the Flame*, and many more, were eloquent and cogent offerings to the reading public. Some of these books were hampered by poor marketing, others suffered because of the authors' lack of publishing bona fides, and almost all were victims of a fickle public's predilection for adventure stories of the West. There were captivating, sophisticated, and nuanced views of the war after 1918, but the public failed to take notice. Only established authors, government officials, and generals would be able to sell a respectable amount of war books in the solidly antiwar and isolationist America of the 1920s and 1930s. Unfortunately, their stories were often too dense, dry, or narrowly focused to gain any traction with the reading public. Because of this long delay in capturing the essence of the Great War from those who knew the story, a second, larger war effectively silenced the legacy of the first within a few decades.

Before the War

War memoirs generally fall into two categories: the prewar and war-years frenzy, and postwar reflections. Of the approximately two hundred books written before 1919, almost all lent credence to the sanctity of the cause, if not always the glory, of war. The early books represent a skewed view born of a potent mix of patriotism and censorship—they are more propaganda than literature. The Espionage and Sedition Acts, signed into law in 1917 and 1918, respectively, heavily constrained writers whose books had to toe the line with a fairly heroic picture of war if publishers were to print them without fear of legal repercussions. Victor Berger, a prominent socialist and publisher of the *Milwaukee Leader*, ran afoul of the law and learned just how serious the government was about censoring negative public opinion about the war. Berger railed about the cost of the war, cautioned about the likelihood of profiteering, and offered strenuous opposition to the draft in the pages of his paper—all sentiments that were considered deleterious to recruitment and as such violated the terms of the Espionage Act. A federal court found Berger guilty of hindering the war effort and sentenced him to twenty years in prison. It is therefore no surprise that books published during the war offered a rosy perspective of the conflict and championed one's duty to the nation as far outweighing any grim hardships of war.[3] To do otherwise was likely to get you thrown in jail.

There was more freedom to write before the war, but most of those writing pre-1917 were trying to encourage

American intervention. Civilians in the path of fighting gave Americans their first personal introduction to the war, and they had a vested interest in riling up opinion in their favor. Two of the earliest popular accounts were Mildred Aldrich's *Hilltop on the Marne* in 1915 and Frances Wilson Huard's *My Home in the Field of Honor* in 1916. Both American women lived a short distance from the fighting around the Marne River and wrote of a war that was, literally, taking place in their backyards.[4] Their firsthand accounts fed American curiosity about the war and went through several printings in short order. *My Home in the Field of Honor* was the top-selling war book by an American in 1917.[5] Both Huard and Aldrich penned subsequent volumes that were received with similar enthusiasm.[6]

Teddy Roosevelt's ex-press agent, Richard Harding Davis, joined the list of early writers in 1915 with the best-selling account of his experiences, *With the Allies.* Davis and other independent reporters like Irvin Cobb (American) and Sir Philip Gibbs (British) found large audiences for their books because American newspapers did not employ a stable of foreign correspondents who were able to bring the news back to the American market. The shortage of reporters in the field compelled people to buy books to get the latest news from journalists, government officials, and others who found themselves in the path of war.[7] Also in 1915, Leslie Buswell wrote a well-regarded book about his experiences as an American volunteer with an ambulance unit aptly titled *Ambulance No. 10: Personal Letters from the Front.* His account and *Kitchener's Mob* in 1916 by James Norman Hall, an American fighting with the British, were the first popular accounts of the war from the perspective of Americans on the front lines. These early books were almost universally supportive of the war effort.

The one glaring exception to patriotic conformity was Ellen La Motte's highly critical *The Backwash of War.* La

Motte demonstrated the most demoralizing aspects of the war in an unflinchingly negative account of her experiences as a nurse in France. She described how soldiers morphed into selfish, brutish men who abused the very women they were supposedly fighting to protect. She argued that the heroes that nations hold up as examples of strength and patriotism were actually glorified for actions born of fear or compulsion rather than courage and bravery. Those charging forward in the front lines were often running from the barrel of a gun pointed at their backs. She also highlights the butchery of the battlefield by recounting the story of eighteen-year-old Antoine, a boy who lost all his limbs, eyes, and facial features in the war. When his father picks him up at the hospital, the soldier begs in agony, "Kill me Papa!"[8] A newspaper reviewer noted that La Motte "exhibits with painful frankness the septic, gangrenous aspects of war, which are, after all, just as true as the inspiring red-blooded side."[9] Governments could not raise and maintain armies on such ideas, and the book was banned in Great Britain and France when it was published in 1916. The United States government followed suit upon entry into the war, and La Motte's book would not become available again until 1934, by which time antiwar memoirs had become relatively uncontroversial, if not often read.

La Motte's book, however, was well reviewed when it was published, even as prowar sentiment was building after the sinking of the *Lusitania*, demonstrating a public appetite for a more balanced depiction of the war. However, by the spring of 1917, war books in America were about to pick up the mantle for Uncle Sam without exception.

War Narratives of 1917 and 1918

American war writing began in 1914 as a trickle but quickly ramped up to a crescendo in 1917 and 1918. American writers produced almost 20 percent of the total oeuvre of personal war narratives in 1918, with just over one hundred published. So many hit the shelves, one critic suggested that he "fancies the modern soldier carrying a typewriter instead of a grenade."[10] Several books were best sellers based on sales expectations for the time period. Historians can track the reach of these successful war narratives through the monthly and annual best-seller lists that were produced by several publishing periodicals, including the *Bookman* (1895–1918), *Books of the Month* (1918–32), and the *Publishers' Weekly* (1872–).[11] The job gets much harder, though, when attempting to determine sales for less successful books. Publishers have always been secretive about book sales statistics and there is little public information beyond those that are worth bragging about.[12] Best-seller lists were based on sales reports sent in from a sample of fifty to one hundred bookstores.[13] The task of tracking popular war books was simplified in 1917 and 1918 as publishing periodicals began issuing separate lists for fiction, nonfiction, and "war books," which generally included personal narratives, humor, and poetry.[14]

Best-seller lists in 1917 and 1918 included several entries under the "war books" category, but only two memoirs written by Americans sold enough copies to join the ranks of best sellers for the decade, with total circulations of at least five hundred thousand copies. A top-tier best seller would have sales closer to the million mark, a feat that no American memoir inspired by World War I would achieve before World War II. Both Arthur Empey's *Over the Top* and Edward Streeter's humorous representation of army life, *Dere Mable*, however, *breeched* the five hundred thousand mark in sales.[15]

Streeter's *Dere Mable* sold just over six hundred thousand copies and was a pseudo-memoir based on the training camp and overseas experiences of its author.[16] The humor came mostly at the expense of the main character, army private William Smith, who was comically unaware of his deficiencies, both as a soldier and sweetheart, and inept at spelling and the French language. Streeter used humor to highlight some of the hardships faced by soldiers in a way that shielded readers from any of the grim realities of war. Soldiers faced many "inconveniences," but nothing that might hinder recruitment. Private Smith bemoaned army food, army bureaucracy, and the decisions of his superiors; these complaints might have gotten one prosecuted under America's harsh sedition laws, but this character's dim-witted persona diffused any hint of real criticism.

A typical letter from Private Smith to his sweetheart was filled with misspellings, misinterpretations of the French language, and a misplaced bravado. One letter began:

Chair Mable: Thats French. I didn't expect you to kno what it meant though. The Y.M.C.A. are learnin me French now . . . The only difference between French and English is that there pretty near alike but the French dont pronounce their words right. When I use French words Ill underline them. Thatll give you some idea of the language. When we get voila as the French say for over there itll come handy to be able to sit down and have a dosy dos with them poilus. (That means chew the rag in English.) A poilus Mable is a French peasant girl an they say that they are very belle . . . There crazy about us fellos. They call us Sammies. They named one of there rivers for us. You have heard of the battle of the Samme. But I dont suppose you have.

Dere Mable was more of an extended comedy skit than a personal war narrative, and its status as a best seller as doughboys were dying in France says a lot about the impressions many Americans had about the war.[17] The book had a brief but lucrative moment in the sun and then was entirely forgotten after the war.[18] Streeter followed up *Dere Mable* (1917) with two sequels, based on the original premise of a soldier writing letters home to his sweetheart. Each sold at about half the rate of the first.[19]

Arthur Empey's *Over the Top* was the only American personal narrative to achieve best-seller status either during or after the war. The timeliness of Empey's story seems to have been key, as most copies sold during the war— over 350,000 by January 1, 1918. Advertisements created to entice booksellers noted that it was selling at a rate of 250 copies every business hour for seven months.[20] Sales were helped by Empey's tour of the United States after he was sent home to recover from injuries sustained as a machine gunner. His book and lectures portrayed the war as thrilling, justified, and patriotic and encouraged other men to follow in his adventurous footsteps. *Over the Top* included a thirty-five-page dictionary of trench slang that helped the reader understand the new lingo of war and served as a primer for those contemplating service in the near future. Empey sought to inspire men to enlist and was critical of those who were drafted. He believed the true heroes were those who went to war of their own accord.[21]

Empey received a great deal of public acclaim for his book, which led to a series of speaking engagements in which he encouraged donations to the Red Cross, the Liberty Loan Program, and the soldiers' tobacco fund, but his fame was fleeting.[22] By the time he published a second book in late 1918, *Tales from a Dugout*, Empey's star had faded, and sales were weak. It is important to note that while both Empey and Streeter achieved strikingly strong sales, their success was relative. For war books, they did quite well, but their sales paled in comparison to the top-selling fiction book of 1918, *The U.P. Trail* by Zane Gray, which sold over 1.2 million copies.[23]

The following list includes eight additional war memoirs written during the war by soldiers, diplomats, and newspaper reporters that, while not achieving Empey's blockbuster sales statistics, either sold in significant quantities or gained acclaim from the literary set in 1917 and 1918.

PUBLISHED IN 1917

Over the Top, Arthur Empey, American soldier with British forces

Carry On, Coningsby Dawson, American soldier with Canadian forces

My Four Years in Germany, James Gerard, diplomat

The Land of Deepening Shadows, Daniel Curtin, war correspondent

High Adventure, James Norman Hall, American serving with Lafayette Escadrille

Journal from Our Legation, Hugh Gibson, diplomat

PUBLISHED IN 1918

The Glory of the Coming, Irvin Cobb, war correspondent

Outwitting the Hun, Pat O'Brien, soldier with Canadian Royal Flying Corps

Ambassador Morgenthau, Henry Morgenthau

Of the four memoirs written by soldiers, Empey's was, by far, the most popular. One library reported having seventy-eight copies of *Over the Top* in 1917. Every copy was checked out, and there was a waiting list of over one hundred people to read the book.[24] There were, however, two significant reasons that Empey's work may have had little staying power in the American imagination. First, and most importantly, his highly jingoistic tale was pure war boosterism. He coyly told American boys that the war was not all death and destruction, that there was a lot of fun to be had.[25] The government could not have invented a better war propagandist than Empey. Because he would always be associated with the propaganda that got America into the war, his credibility as a chronicler was suspect after the armistice. Second, he was not an American soldier fighting under the American flag. Technically, he had renounced his citizenship to fight in the British army. He was a charming soldier of fortune who filled the imaginations of young men on the cusp of war more than an icon of the American war yet to come.

James Norman Hall was one of the few commercially significant war memoirists who wrote from the perspective of an American soldier fighting under his own flag. He was an aviator in a time of great interest in the nascent technology, and, if any of these books might have captured the imagination of the reading public, it should have been his. Hall presents himself as a swashbuckling hero with the compellingly titled work *High Adventure*. Hall began the war with the British, moved to the French, and served with the Lafayette Escadrille (the name of the unit of American flyers serving with the French before the American army took over in 1917) before winding up as an American pilot when his country entered the war. He was also an experienced writer who had submitted work to the *Atlantic Monthly* and *Harper's* before the war.[26] He had both the record and the talent to tell an iconic American war story. Almost fifteen years after the war, his literary collaboration with fellow veteran Charles Nordhoff would result in the wildly popular *Mutiny on the Bounty*. *High Adventure* explores his many harrowing encounters in the sky during the war. Within months of entering active service Hall was shot down, and his plane plummeted into a frontline trench. His plane reportedly "fell into a corkscrew dive, its motor roaring at full revolution. The enemy pack hung on his tail and another round pierced his flight suit and creased his scrotum." Hall was greeted by friendly forces on the ground after his first crash, but he would not be as lucky in the future. He was shot down again in May 1918 by enemy antiaircraft fire. German soldiers captured him after he skidded to a stop across an open field and made him a prisoner of war for the last months of the conflict.[27] His thrilling adventures in the air secured an avid audience of young men, if not a wider audience. The same was true for the other aviator on the list, Pat O'Brien.

O'Brien was an American flying for the Canadians, and he had an even more thrilling story to tell. The Germans had captured him after he was shot down on a patrol mission behind enemy lines and brought him to a prisoner of war camp. O'Brien escaped from his captors by jumping from a moving train and making an arduous trek through hostile territory to safety through Germany, Luxembourg, Belgium, and Holland. His book was a vivid description of his experiences and paved the way for O'Brien's return home as a hero. After the war, he hoped to become the first man to fly across the Atlantic nonstop. Unfortunately, he met an untimely and controversial death at his own hand less than three years later. He shot himself in the mouth after his wife of less than one year left to live with another woman. She claimed he was abusive, and he made veiled references to her homosexuality. O'Brien's heroics were quickly forgotten after his suicide, and he was buried in an unmarked grave in Momence, Illinois, both the man and his book seemingly lost to history because of his ignominious end.[28]

The diplomats James Gerard, Henry Morgenthau, and Hugh Gibson would not offer such exciting fare, but they had direct experience with the situation in the war zone through their official posts. Gerard was ambassador to Berlin from 1913 to 1917, Morgenthau was ambassador to Constantinople from 1913 to 1916, and Gibson was the secretary of the American legation in Brussels from 1914 to 1917. All believed they were uniquely positioned to relay the "truth" about the war to the public, and Americans were hungry for news. Morgenthau believed that the Germans had set out to conquer the world and the American public needed to understand this fact in order to commit fully to the cause. In the preface to his book he argued, "all eye-witnesses to this, the greatest crime in modern history, should volunteer their testimony." Gerard argued that the sole motivation for his book was the enlightenment of the citizenry, stating, "It is only because I believe that our people should be informed that I have consented to write this book."[29]

Historians are well served by the writings of diplomats, but the stories lacked popular appeal as they were only memoirs in the loosest sense of the term. The books were more about providing education and historical context than a biographical testimony of war. Hugh Gibson's book was based largely on extracts from his private journal, and a colleague criticized Gerard's work as being "put together in a rather haphazard way; . . . contain[ing] unnecessary repetitions; carelessly written and appear[s] to have undergone little if any revision."[30] Neither the content nor the approach was likely to have garnered a sustained following in the years after the war. Diplomats wrote more like journalists in their approach than memoirists. They reported on conversations they had in diplomatic circles, offered information gleaned from prized sources, and analyzed some of the war's main characters, but these books by government officials were hardly page-turners for an American public that preferred novels to any other reading material. They served a practical purpose and were more akin to government reports than literature. They were "of the moment" and provided a curious public with information that it was unlikely to get anywhere else.[31] After their immediacy faded they were quickly forgotten.

Correspondents were able to sell their stories for the same reasons that diplomats could, the American public wanted reliable information about the war, and newspapers did not always provide the type of in-depth coverage they sought. Diplomats told their story from the heights of government, while correspondents told the story from the ground. Much like war reporting today, correspondents immersed themselves in the action to get an authentic story. Daniel Curtin and Irvin Cobb were American newsmen who spent a great deal of time abroad during the early years of the war, and both reported substantially on Germans and the German army, hot topics of inquiry for most Americans.[32] Curtin's *The Land of Deepening Shadows* covered his experiences in Germany beginning in 1915, and Cobb's *The Glory of the Coming* related his experiences with some of the first fighting by Americans in the spring and summer of 1918. Their books were more appropriately labeled as bound collections of articles, rather than literature, as much of what was inside had already been published, over time, in the newspapers. The book format provided a more comprehensive snapshot of the action, but the content was somewhat obsolete when new information became available. As such, these books did not withstand the test of time.

In fact, within a decade, most of the books published in 1917 and 1918 were derided by literary critics and writers as inauthentic portraits of war. They were criticized as the product of a war propaganda machine that was built on lies and exaggerated calls for patriotism. To some extent this assessment was accurate, but the critics failed to recognize that the war was many things to many people. Not all of the books produced during the war years were crafted as tools of public coercion. No one suggests that Coningsby Dawson, Arthur Empey, or a third popular memoirist, Harold Peat (Canadian), fabricated their stories in any way, or felt differently about the war than their words would seem to indicate. Their stories were authentic at the time they were written, but the passage of time would change the context through which authors, and the public, viewed the war.

Given time for further reflection, best-selling Canadian memoirist Harold Peat reconsidered his experience and wrote *The Inexcusable Lie* in 1924, well before it was considered fashionable to speak ill of the war or to expose the primal part of war that patriotic tomes were apt to leave out. He blamed the patriots for convincing youth that war is glorious.[33] Arthur Empey, on the other hand, retained the same patriotic ideas years after the war when he wrote *A Helluva War*. His third volume swam against a tide of antiwar books in 1927 by relaying the fictional, and amusing, war high jinks of an Irish American Private O'Leary. However, Peat's second book did not erase the validity of the first; it represented an evolution of thought over time. The narratives written during the war years represented a snapshot of American culture and could have survived as a commentary on their time just as well as some books representing postwar realism and the "lost generation."

There were other reasons, however, that these books failed to take hold in the American public consciousness. One could argue that the war-era books reflected a romantic and simplistic tone that attracted a fairly unsophisticated audience who believed in a traditional set of values. The early narratives fostered an idealistic view of good versus bad that sustained support since "the war was distant and exciting for most Americans, their reactions resembling those of a schoolboy reading *Ivanhoe*." The names of French, English, and German soldiers filled the casualty lists, not Americans, and the fighting was in distant lands. The intelligentsia, however, never bought these narratives because the cultural shift toward modernism placed the focus on realism rather than romanticism and it would be the culturally avant-garde who shaped opinion in the postwar years.[34] The ideas expressed in the early narratives would be considered naïve and ignorant within a year of the war's end. The "lovely buoyant optimism, the rawboned, good natured awkwardness that characterized the Adamic American in antique Europe" turned quickly into cynical and hardened pacifism.[35]

The continued marketability of war books came into question even before the armistice in November 1918. In an October 1918 advertisement for the book *The Winds of Chance*, large text proclaims that "This is NOT a War Book." The full-page ad contended that the author was proving his patriotism by offering readers a way to forget the war by championing the exploits of American prospectors during the Alaskan gold rush. The publisher suggested that it was a good book to send to soldiers on the front who might be transported from the bomb-pocked terrain to "revel in the atmosphere of this romantic story and feel that they too are among the gold-hunters of other days."[36]

Booksellers were forced to ponder the future of the genre. Most were skeptical that it would hold the public's attention in a postwar world. Why would books glorifying or justifying war sell in peacetime? However, the most optimistic among them argued that remaining inventories would be bought up by libraries and historical societies, who would want to preserve these stories for future generations because they were "first hand documents of the greatest period in world history." Soldiers, too, it was thought, would seek out those volumes that memorialized their war experiences. Bookseller optimism was probably more marketing ploy than unbiased observation, given the fact that war books were never particularly good sellers as a genre. Empey and Streeter sold hundreds of thousands of copies of patriotic and lighthearted books to a nation gearing up for war, but 90 percent of war books would not reach a second edition, and many sold less than two thousand copies each.[37] After the war, soldiers did not memorialize their war experiences by collecting the works of Empey and Dawson, they read books that might secure their future. The American Library Association reported a great demand for business and agricultural books on the Western front after the armistice but no war books, "the soldier does not read them."[38]

War Narratives of 1919

More than eighty war narratives were published in 1919, and it would be the last year that war books would get significant attention, as a group, for many years. One contemporary writer noted that during the war the public was motivated by "shocks of propaganda . . . with luscious stories of heroes. The end came; and then it felt as did the man the morning after the night before; it would not look at the bottle."[39] Magazines like the *Publishers' Weekly* stopped listing "War Books" as a separate category for sales, and the genre as a whole began a rapid decline. Most of the books published in 1919 were underway well before the armistice and reflected the patriotic sentiments of the war years. Since there is reliable sales data only for best sellers, and few of the interwar books even approached those heights, determining the popularity or visibility of postwar books is not a science. A creative plan of attack is necessary. I make educated guesses here about popularity based on the number of published book reviews, recommendations by the American Library Association, listings in the *Standard Catalog for Public Libraries*, guides for college reading published by universities, lists produced in compendiums of best books, bibliographies of personal narratives, lists of books in demand at public libraries, and holdings at select libraries.[40] Library holdings are important because this was the primary way many Americans accessed books in the 1920s and 1930s.[41] In 1925 a long-time book publisher estimated that only 0.8 percent of the population bought books regularly.[42] Bookstores were also few and far between, and libraries were free.

Using the aforementioned resources as a guide, the personal narratives listed below garnered significant attention in 1919.

Fighting the Flying Circus, Eddie Rickenbacker, ace fighter pilot

With the Help of God and a Few Good Marines, Albert Catlin

War in the Garden of Eden, Kermit Roosevelt, soldier on Mesopotamian front

Belgium: A Personal Narrative, Brand Whitlock, ambassador to Belgium

Catlin, Rickenbacker, and Whitlock's accounts were underway before the armistice and fully reflected the patriotic tone that was required of books published during the war years. Rickenbacker was motivated to write his book, at least in part, by financial problems and signed with a ghost-writer in late 1918 to capitalize on his flying record. His co-writer embellished Eddie Rickenbacker's flying career and crafted an elegant, if not entirely factual, account of his exploits. If Rickenbacker's motivation was profit, this was not an opportunity to voice antiwar sentiments, and the book was largely an adventure story with the flyer as an American hero. One reviewer noted, "If there is no more of the war in this story than there is of the world in a college freshman's letters home, no fault is to be found with the author on this account. Perhaps it is too much to ask to ask one man to fight a war and understand it too."[43] Given Rickenbacker's fame, the allure of the early fighter pilots, and his daring exploits, the book should have been a surefire hit even if the war was already becoming an uncouth topic by the time publishers released it in mid-1919. The book sold fairly well, earning Rickenbacker at least $25,000 in royalties, but it's hard to understand why this book did not do better. Rickenbacker was a successful race-car driver before the war, well known as an American flying ace with twenty-six confirmed "kills" of enemy planes—he was hero material at every level. The relatively flat reception his book received speaks to public apathy about the war that set in quite quickly.[44]

It is unlikely that Albert Catlin's memoir of service as a marine sold as well as Rickenbacker's high-flying tale of dueling fighter pilots, and it certainly had less staying power. Catlin's profile was not nearly as high as that of the dashing hero and flying ace. Catlin was almost fifty years old in 1917 and had been with the marines for twenty-five years. He was a first lieutenant on the battleship *Maine* when it was sunk in Havana in 1898, and in France was the commanding officer at the fateful battle of Belleau Wood. Thus, he had the credibility to get a book contract and potentially sell books. Catlin was shot through the chest at Belleau Wood and went home in July 1918.[45] While *With the Help of God and a Few Good Marines* received complimentary (and numerous) reviews, the book went through only one printing. The experience and the gravitas were there, but a portly and relatively old Catlin was not the voice of the young men who went to war. Catlin may have directed the lauded attack at Belleau Wood, but he was the voice of the older men who sent the youth of America into harm's way. His romantic notions of war may have left him solidly in the camp of discredited propagandists as the peace movement gained steam.

Catlin's and Rickenbacker's memoirs were typical soldier fare by 1919, but Kermit Roosevelt's story was different on two accounts. First, he was the son of American military royalty, and second, his brother Quentin had died a war hero when his airplane was brought down by a German pilot.[46] Quentin Roosevelt was arguably the most grieved casualty of the war. Dignitaries named airfields, a town, and a ship in his honor after his death on Bastille Day in 1918. Thousands of French and American soldiers and civilians flocked to his grave on the Western Front, quickly making it a shrine.[47] Kermit also dedicated his book to his father Theodore, who died eight months before it was published, certainly fortuitous timing in terms of potential book sales. Second, Roosevelt spent more time describing the exotic Middle East than he did explaining warfare. His *War in the Garden of Eden* contained a great deal of "narrative comment on the peoples and places that made the 'cradle of the world' so picturesque," and was one of only a few books that would look at the war from this perspective.[48] His story of an exotic land was compelling, but it served as a poor representation of the American experience because it described the Mesopotamian front, which few Americans ever saw, and he primarily fought with the British Expeditionary forces. Only a small portion of the book covered his service with the American army. Roosevelt's book gained widespread publicity more because of who he was and the unique perspective he offered of a far-off land than because his tale of World War I resonated with the American public. His status as a president's son, a hero's brother, and an exotic traveler ensured attention but not stellar sales. The book saw a second printing in 1920, then disappeared.[49]

The last of the four 1919 war narratives, Brand Whitlock's story of life in Belgium was the sole diplomatic account that gained acclaim in 1919, and arguably one of the most talked about. He followed in the footsteps of Gibson, Morgenthau, and Gerard. In fact, he was Gibson's superior in Brussels throughout their tenure in Belgium. Gibson had beaten Whitlock to the punch by publishing his story almost two years earlier, but Whitlock dismissed Gibson's *A Letter from Our Legation* as an account of "foreshortened perspective." He insinuated that Gibson had taken too much credit for American diplomacy in Belgium and that it was important to demonstrate a more balanced and thoughtful view given the benefit of time. Whitlock was also clearly pushed by the slew of other memoirists on the horizon. He noted that there were hundreds of other Americans in Belgium who were writing manuscripts, many who were, no doubt, succumbing to the lure of easy money. Publishers were still eager for new war stories when Whitlock was writing his book and offered large sums to secure them.[50]

Whitlock was a compelling target for publishers. He was a four-term Ohio governor, a novelist, and newspaper reporter, and he had firsthand war experience as the minister to Belgium during the war, having been appointed to the post by President Woodrow Wilson in 1914. Because of the scope of human suffering that would occur in Belgium, he administered many relief activities sponsored by the government and through donations from Americans. His journal during the war years served as the basis for *Belgium: A Personal Narrative.*[51] Whitlock's work reflected his personal experience, but it was printed with the active support and advice of men like Newton Baker, secretary of war under Wilson, and George Creel, director of the Committee on Public Information, men who were later criticized for force-feeding the American public patriotism through propagandistic writing, films, and posters. Whitlock was part of Creel's propaganda machine, wittingly or not. While the government clearly saw Whitlock as a vehicle for the party line, his letters indicated that he believed he was bucking the trend of sensationalist war stories because he did not focus on atrocities committed by individuals but on the juggernaut that produced the acts of violence. He wanted Americans to understand the power of the German government, the failings of a system that had run amok. Whitlock believed that it was his patriotic service to expose "the long slow torture, the systematic attempt not only to corrupt but to assassinate a nation's soul." Officials at the Department of State liked what they saw and granted permission for Whitlock's book, chapter by chapter.[52] As such, *Belgium* was much more a product of 1918 than 1919.[53] In fact, Whitlock began work on his book in the summer of 1917, just after the publication of Gibson's work.

Given the fawning reception the book received from numerous quarters one might expect that the book was a retail success, but Whitlock notes only that it "made [him] some money, but no fortune."[54] Whitlock was enriched by the sizeable fee he was paid up front, but royalties were probably meager in comparison. He had been courted by many publishers, newspapers, and magazines, including the *New-York Tribune* and *Harper's Magazine*, Macmillan, Doubleday, Page and Company, and D. Appleton and Company for a book deal and serial rights. Ultimately, he gave serial rights to the magazine *Everybody's* at the recommendation of George Creel. *Everybody's* offered early support for American involvement in the war, publishing an article by Theodore Roosevelt encouraging entry, "America-On Guard!," in 1915.[55] The magazine offered Whitlock the substantial sum of $41,000. D. Appleton and Company published the book at the tail end of war book marketability as a two-volume set in the summer of 1919, and Whitlock's plans for a revised second edition and a third volume were quickly dashed. By June 1920, the publisher was decidedly negative about future editions or a third volume as the country faced a growing tide of antiwar book sentiment.[56]

The year 1919, the first year since American entry in which writers could freely express themselves about the war, brought few publications that might persevere as iconic war memoirs. Of course, Americans were not looking for an iconic representation of the war, but were hoping to put it behind them. Writers in 1919 provided nothing that would jar them out of their avoidance of everything war related, and the tolerance for war stories was about to drop precipitously. The following poem by prominent novelist Carolyn Wells, published in 1919, demonstrates this point well:

Ballade of War Books

I seem to wander in a world of books,
    With titles such as, "'Neath the Trumpet's Blare",
And "Sammy Fire-Away!" and "Private Snooks",
    And Hank, the Yank", and "Danny Do-and-Dare"
    And though the war is over, Over There,
Yet must be published books already penned:
    They pour from presses daily! I declare
Of making many war books there's no end!

And, somehow I opine—the way it looks–
    That for an aftermath we must prepare:
Adventure yarns of wartime cranks and crooks,
    And lives of heroes who have done their share.
    True tales of noble deeds of courage rare;
Histories of events, as yet unkenned;
    Journals and diaries, and such small ware–
Of making many war books there's no end!

And there'll be messages from soldier spooks,
    Transmitted through a wily medium's care;
Telling of waving trees and limpid brooks
        Where rove the souls who've climbed the Golden Stair:
        And poems! "Lyric Lines to France, the Fair",
"Red Poppy Fields", "My Faithful Four Years' Friend",
        "Heroic Feet", "A Lock of Lemuel's Hair"–
Of making many war books there's no end!

L'Envoi

Publisher, Printer, Editor, forbear!

Nor longer than you must, your lists extend:

Do let this gushing output stop *somewhere!*

Of making many war books there's no end![57]

War Narratives of 1920–41

The year 1920 began a dramatic decline in the publication of war books, from more than eighty the year before to less than forty. The number dropped to thirteen in 1921 and eight in 1922. Publishing would remain at roughly that level through the interwar years, with only a slight uptick between 1927 and 1929, when a flood of European war books hit the market, including Erich Maria Remarque's *All Quiet on the Western Front.* Not only books, but the number of magazine articles plummeted as well. Some might expect that the trend would have gone the other way around. Veterans would require time to reflect upon their experiences. As Samuel Hynes put it, "imagination must wait on memory to reveal itself."[58] However, many publishers believed that the story had been told already and the market was saturated. "Stern, hard headed publishers were grim and silent at the mention of any book dealing with combat, and the booksellers—well, the booksellers had plenty of war books that they could not even give away."[59] The few that reached the war-weary public faced an uphill battle, some finding a niche that other authors had not yet explored, others breaking through because of personal connections or literary credentials. Using the same criteria for analysis as for 1919, the personal narratives of war enumerated below were most visible from 1920 through 1941:

That Damn Y, Katherine Mayo

Leaves from a War Diary, James Harbord

Fix Bayonets!, John Thomason

One Man's War, Bert Hall

My Experience in the World War, John J. Pershing

Katherine Mayo published *That Damn Y* in 1920, and it became an interesting coda on the war years' stream of personal narratives. Aside from Aldrich and Huard, Mayo was the first woman to attract widespread attention for her war writing, and she was one of the few who had both experience near the battlefields in France and the writing ability to compile a readable and credible narrative. Mayo was already well known in the literary world by 1917 for her influential *Justice for All,* which profiled the success of the Pennsylvania State Police, and reformers have credited her with spurring the development of the State Police in New York. Theodore Roosevelt was impressed enough with Mayo's findings to write the introduction to *Justice for All.*[60]

In *That Damn Y,* Mayo set out to profile the YMCA and its activities in Europe to assist American servicemen. She was prompted by some soldiers' claims that the YMCA and other war organizations like the Red Cross and the Salvation Army were self-serving and greedy. Mayo was predisposed to believe the charges, as she imagined these groups made up of "hard, cold religiosity—a lot of rich, old women, male and female, with nasty minds, tying strings to their dollars and buying cheap hypocrites to play watchdog against live and wholesome pleasures in mausoleums to unburied cant."[61] Essentially, soldiers and some French citizens criticized the YMCA for proselytizing and profiteering. They were trying to convert a captive audience with one hand while picking their pockets with the other. Soldiers seemed to care less about the proselytizing than the profiteering. They were highly critical of the prices they were charged for grocery items they believed had already been paid for by the American taxpayer. Mayo made it her mission to research the activities of the YMCA and report back to the American public. She was strident in her desire to be objective and financed the trip herself in order to claim independence from influence while she traveled across the war zone with leaders of the Y as her guides. Mayo fully vindicated the YMCA in the end, suggesting that the Y provided wholesome entertainment with little taint of religious propaganda. She also believed that the concerns over the prices charged at commissaries could be blamed on Americans' poor understanding of the situation on the ground in Europe. Mayo argued that the Y was making a profit off of young soldiers, but was also struggling to stay financially viable in a tough, war-ravaged environment.[62]

The book was well reviewed, and Mayo was lauded for her writing skills as well as her refreshing look at a stale war. The 424-page book was really a compilation of thirty vignettes that were supposed to represent the war and the Y's part in it. Mayo not only redeemed the Y in the eyes of the nation by clarifying their role in Europe, she painted soldiers as self-sacrificing and heroic in a manner that was neither cloying nor hyperpatriotic. In this respect, she set her work apart from propagandistic memoirs or state-sponsored war histories. The reviewer for the *New-York Tribune* thought she could have been the voice of the war, even as a woman, because she had a "manifest ability in handling drama in a stirring way . . . that feminine something that is able to get further down toward doughboys' souls than a man ever may."[63]

Mayo's publisher reported that sales were brisk for the first six or seven months the book was in print, exhausting the first edition of twenty-five hundred copies and spurring a second printing of an additional one thousand copies. Of course, those are not the numbers for a book that is flying off the shelf. Her total royalties for the first year of publication were probably less than $2,000. A book about the war, regardless of its reception by literary critics and the leadership of the YMCA, faced an uphill battle in a country that would have liked nothing better than to forget. Mayo, however, drew a significant subset of readers, most of whom had ties to the Y or other aid organizations. *That Damn Y!* made appearances twice in the *Bookman*'s list of books in demand at public libraries, and ranked as the fifth book most in demand in the United States in January 1921, according to statistics compiled by the American Library Association. But its popularity was short-lived, disappearing from the lists just two months after it appeared, a mere drop in the bucket compared with the longevity of true best sellers for the time period. Americans would not remember her book on the war. Literary critics most remember Mayo for her controversial book arguing against independence for India, *Mother India*, written in 1927.[64]

The four other standout books were from soldiers—a marine, a pilot, the commander of all American forces, and his chief of staff. The pilot, Bert Hall, appeared to have the most saleable story as a dashing daredevil with the Lafayette Escadrille. Hall published his second book, *One Man's War*, in 1929 as a follow up to his first, *En L'Air*, published in 1918. The first book told a thrilling story of air warfare that appealed even to the war weary because pilots were much more than soldiers, they were pioneers in a new world with no boundaries. Pilots were risking their lives as guinea pigs to advance a bold new technology; their war service was ancillary to the awe they inspired "in the air." The appeal of pilots built to a frenzy from the time of the war until Charles Lindbergh became the most famous man on earth after his solo flight across the Atlantic in 1927. Hall's story painted the picture of a swashbuckling adventurer flitting from one escapade to the next. Some would argue that he fabricated much of what he wrote, but he had always had a predilection for bravado.

Hall ran away from home in his teens and joined the circus as a human cannonball, oddly foreshadowing his career in the air. After the circus, he left the United States on a merchant ship and settled into a career as a taxi driver in France. When the war broke out he was one of the first Americans to join the French Foreign Legion, an organization that would provide several of the first American war pilots, and eventually was part of the flying unit known as the Escadrille Americaine. The Escadrille Americaine, renamed the Lafayette Escadrille in honor of the sacrifices of the Marquis de Lafayette during the Revolutionary War, was a high-profile organization during the effort to bring the United States into the war.[65]

Hall's service record and the reports of his fellow pilots make him out to be half hero and half scoundrel. The French army awarded him the Médaille Militaire and the Croix de Guerre, and he racked up several "victories" in the air, bringing down nine German aircraft. However, his superiors ultimately transferred him out of the squadron because he was "an habitual liar, a check kiter, and a card sharp."[66] Shortly after his dismissal from the squad, Hall was granted permission to visit the United States. Several of his fellow pilots have suggested that he never returned to the service, and French aviation records listed him as a deserter. Hall argued that he had come back in January 1918 and joined another outfit when he could not immediately locate his old squadron. His writings never identified that unit by name or location, but he was in Paris in April 1918 when he married a French entertainer. *One Man's War* contained much of the same information from his first book but also included his exploits with the Russo-Romanian army, although he embellished his earlier tale to a much greater extent. Some historians have called both *En L'Air* and *One Man's War* "unreliable fabrications."[67] It might have been hard for Hall to have become the poster boy of war stories given this questionable background, but the public was largely unaware of his storied past. While much of his appeal was as a pilot, not a soldier, his testimony as a member of the Lafayette Escadrille was vitally important. Of the approximately 210 Americans who flew as part of the Escadrille, only 28 survived until December 1917, when American pilots were taken into the fold of the United States Army.

The *New York Times Magazine* called Hall a "real D'Artagnon" in 1930, and he managed to maintain his reputation as a soldier of fortune after the war through exploits like training and directing air forces in the Chinese Nationalist Army. Hall became the commanding officer and took the moniker "General Chan."[68] It was his dealings with the Chinese government, though, that would land Hall in jail and brought the seedier side of his reputation to the forefront. In 1933 the United States government sentenced Hall to two and a half years in prison for taking money from the Chinese government for firearms that he never delivered.[69] Hall's credentials as a soldier of fortune may have increased, but his status as a hero was definitely tarnished. It is also important to note that Hall never served in American uniform. It seemed he was a soldier for almost everyone but the United States in his storied career.[70] All of these factors, lack of integrity most notably, may have played a role in dampening the long-term appeal of his writing.

On a sliding scale of author credibility, we move from the ridiculous to the sublime. Major General James Harbord began the war as the chief of staff to the American Expeditionary Forces under John J. Pershing, commanded the Second Division at Belleau Wood, and then moved on to become the chief of services of supply for American forces. He was a man with pedigree when it came to the war. His book, *Leaves from a War Diary*, published in

1925, was the journal that he kept during his service and sent home to his wife at regular intervals. Literary critics noticed the book more for Harbord's frank, offhand assessments of some of his high-ranking colleagues than for any commentary about the war. In fact, he acknowledged his arm's-length view of the fighting when he argued that his diary was not really in conflict with regulations aimed at the security of military operations because his distance from the front lines ensured the enemy would never capture it.[71] As such, his experiences were interesting to those who appreciated gossip about war leaders, but hardly illuminated the typical American war experience. Harbord's war was one of warm, hospitable accommodations and dinners that would have made a trench soldier salivate. He wrote about boarding at French chateaux and the beauty of the strawberry blossoms and lilies of the valley outside his window and seemed oddly removed from the brutality of the front lines. Harbord's insider view of military politics was no doubt attractive to publishers, so was his stature as the president of the Radio Corporation of America, but his story remained the reading domain of those who preferred their wars to be civilized.[72] As one reviewer noted, it was a "vivid and readable story of experiences at the war front, with the horrors of war not overemphasized . . . as well as on the pleasanter incidents of [the] campaign."[73] He, too, bucked a trend toward pacifism.

Coming just one short year later but from the same division and battlefield was *Fix Bayonets!* by Capt. John Thomason Jr. Thomason was a marine who had seen action at Soissons and Belleau Wood and became an author by a circuitous route. He started out as a visual artist who crafted haunting images of soldiers and the wreckage of war using burnt matches and spare paper. During the course of the war his images drew the attention of the prominent writer Laurence Stallings, who used his pull in the literary world to bring awareness to Thomason's drawings.[74] Soon after, Thomason began putting words with his images, and Stallings claimed that "not in Hugo nor in Stephen Crane nor in any author that he knew were there such accounts of men in battle as in these typewritten pages from Captain Thomason." From such lofty praise Thomason ultimately wrote *Fix Bayonets!*, a collection of partially fictional short stories based on his experiences at war. Thomason, a lifelong marine, wrote sympathetically of the Old Breed, and his prose showed little emotion about the brutality it depicted. His first book saw modest sales, and Thomason went on to write more on the war, as well as other topics, for which he earned himself fleeting fame for his dual talents as a writer and artist. A multipage spread in the June 1925 issue of *Vanity Fair* furthered his career and played into a mild renaissance of war writing that would build on Stalling's earlier success with the play *What Price Glory* and the semiautobiographical novel *Plumes*, both written in 1924.[75]

The last of the successful American war memoirs of this period, and arguably the definitive narrative for historians up to that point, was Gen. John J. Pershing's *My Experiences in the World War* (1931). Publishers pestered Pershing throughout the 1920s to write his memoirs, but the general was slow and deliberative in both deciding to write a memoir and actually penning one. His book was not published until 1931, after Erich Maria Remarque's *All Quiet on the Western Front* (1929), which critics suggest represented the height in the resurgence of interest in the war.[76] In Britain, the years 1928–32 were considered the boom years for memoirs and saw the "flooding of the booklists with 'war books.'"[77] This was not really the case in America. Remarque's book did very well: almost 150,000 copies sold in the United States in its first six weeks of publication, and more than 300,000 copies sold in the first seven months.[78] It was the first time a war book sold in quantities comparable to Empey's *Over the Top*, but little of enduring value emerged from American authors' attempts to ride its coattails. Fifteen American war memoirs were written in 1929, the majority of which were put out by obscure publishers. None of the titles produced during this resurgence of war writing were particularly noteworthy except Pershing's memoir.

There was a fierce competition to bring Pershing's experiences during the war to the market. Twenty book publishers, eleven magazines, and sixteen newspapers vied for the rights. Pershing also signed away the serial rights, and the story appeared in American newspapers before publishers issued the expensive two-volume set. This free preview, along with the worsening economic crisis, hampered sales of the book. Priced at ten dollars, it was a luxury largely out of reach for the vast majority of Americans. The publishers had lofty sales goals and printed fifty thousand copies as a first run and expected a second run equally as large. Their expectations were overly ambitious. Within three months the book was selling at half-price, and by 1933 it was being sold at the embarrassingly reduced price of two dollars, with twenty-five thousand sets of the first run still on the shelves.[79]

Sales were poor, but critical reaction was mixed. On the one hand, Pershing was a horrible writer. Pershing's tedious focus on giving equal attention to each unit and commander meant that the finished product emerged reading more like a military report than a narrative. George Marshall, who would gain renown in the next war, said, "the Meuse-Argonne account was too detailed for the general reader and not detailed enough for the military student . . . the battle has been made to appear a confused mass of little events, and from my point of view the big picture was lost."[80] On the other hand, historians were eager for the "official story" of the war to come out and lauded Pershing for his effort. This explains, in part, why the book was a commercial and critical failure yet Pershing won the Pulitzer Prize for his work in 1932.[81]

Strikingly absent from the list of the most visible interwar books are two books that gained attention for different reasons. The first is arguably the book most associated with American World War I writing today—Hervey Allen's *Toward the Flame* (1926). The second documented the wartime heroics of the most decorated American soldier of World War I, Alvin York. The book *Sergeant York: His Own Life Story and War Diary*, would later serve as the basis for the incredibly successful film *Sergeant York*, starring Gary Cooper.

Allen's work is most often mentioned as the token American example in any international review of significant war memoirs. Allen is often cited because he was one of the few American writers who experienced the war, had the talent to artfully paint a picture for the American public, and had the credibility with the literary set to gain attention. He did an admirable job capturing the essence of the war through a very narrow lens at the front line. The book covered only a few months' time and focused on Allen's experiences in combat until he was wounded at the Battle of Fismette. Allen challenged those who wrote about the war in romantic tones by sharing experiences that demonstrated the brutality of war. He wrote about "a little German boy, some fifteen years old, who, desperate with thirst had lingered behind at a spring only to have his back broken by a rifle butt in the hands of an advancing American."[82] Reviewers shared almost universal praise for the book and Allen's writing skills. His writing talent, combined with his combat experience, could have placed him in the same company with war writers like the Englishman Robert Graves or the German Ernst Jünger.[83]

Allen, however, is best known as the author of a bestselling novel that debuted in 1933, *Anthony Adverse*. It was a twelve-hundred-page piece of historical fiction that captured readers so completely that it sold three hundred thousand copies in the first six months after publication and eventually over one million copies.[84] Book buyers picked up *Toward the Flame* at the rate of five thousand copies per year for the first six years after its debut, a successful book by the standards of the time, but a far cry from the reception for *Anthony Adverse*.[85] And by 1946, *Toward the Flame* was out of print in America, not to appear again for over twenty years.[86] A 1937 compilation of the best books of the decade between 1926 and 1935 cited Allen twice, once for *Adverse* and once for *The Life and Times of Edgar Allan Poe* (1926). Editors failed to mention the work that would gain him entrance to the pantheon of World War I memoirists, *Toward the Flame*. The compilation measured the number of times authorities cited a book on "best book" lists, including the American Library Association, Yale Alumni reading lists, and almost one hundred other literary sources.[87] So, while the academic community may have come to value Allen's contribution to war literature, popular contemporary reaction was decidedly less enthusiastic.

If Allen's highly nuanced book was a bit too sophisticated for the masses, York's was not. Alvin York had become a certified folk hero during the war. General Pershing reportedly called him "the greatest civilian soldier of the war."[88] Sergeant York was a farmer from Tennessee who had rarely ventured outside the boundaries of his home county until he was drafted by the United States Army in 1917. York went to war a reluctant soldier, after having been denied an exemption on religious grounds, but decided that if violence was a prerequisite for peace, he could fight the Germans.[89] He earned the Medal of Honor for his exploits in the Argonne Forest, charging a machine gun nest and taking more than 130 Germans prisoner. York was the quintessential American hero: a God-fearing, hard-working, red-headed backwoods boy who whipped the Germans with his frontier shooting skills. This single American had rescued over one hundred of his fellow soldiers in a shoot-'em-up fight to the finish.

Upon his return to the states York was feted from the port of New York to Fentress County, Tennessee. He was, without a doubt, the most famous American soldier of the war. But, York was as reluctant a hero as he was a soldier. Corporations and literary agents vied for his attention, promising tens of thousands of dollars for his story or his endorsement of their product.[90] York turned them all down, as he believed that he could never really explain war and that it was unseemly to profit from killing. He reconsidered his position in 1927, when he realized he needed funding to support his Alvin C. York Institute to provide better education for Fentress County youth. The author Tom Skeyhill reworked York's diary into *Sergeant York: His Own Life Story and War Diary* in 1928, earning a $10,000 advance that York and the author split equally. Where Allen's book presented the violence and debasing nature of war, Skeyhill presented York as a hero in the romantic mold of traditional warriors. The book may have sold well when it was first released but provided little lasting monetary support to York, whose financial situation was precarious, at best, for the rest of his life.[91] The time for war books backed with slick ad campaigns had passed. Had York succumbed to the pressure to sell his story in 1918 it's possible that the book would have been quite successful.

York's and Allen's books clearly had different audiences, but both could have been a bookseller's dream. Allen was a polished, skilled, and successful writer whose book was timed well to take advantage of a lull in the unofficial ban on war books. Additionally, he was telling a story that dovetailed well with the newly fashionable perspective that war was hell. York's book was also issued at a potentially lucrative time, although with an old-fashioned message of heroism. But, neither book attracted significant attention from buyers or libraries. The American experience at war never achieved sustained or significant public interest, not even for the literary set's acclaimed voice of the war or a heroic Medal of Honor winner.

American apathy about the war seems to have run deep. However, it is interesting to note that York, Thomason, Allen, Mayo, and Pershing all earned hefty fees for allowing magazine editors to serialize their books. The large investment suggests these issues were popular with the public, which may have dampened book sales. If one could read the story relatively inexpensively in a weekly publication, there was little incentive to buy the book. Moreover, weekly and monthly magazines were much more ubiquitous in rural America than books. In their seminal work *Middletown: A Study in Modern American Culture*, Robert and Helen Lynd studied the "average" American town and noted that carriers delivered 20,000 periodicals to the 9,200 families that lived in "Middletown" in 1923. Seven in ten working-class families subscribed to at least one magazine, and nine of ten business-class families subscribed to at least three.[92] It seems that the postwar generation may have read war narratives in magazines, but there are several reasons why it is problematic to use magazines as an indicator of public interest in a topic. First, while it is possible to track the reach of a given periodical, how does one determine which articles were read? Second, if readers did gain exposure to war stories through magazines, their experience may have been incomplete because they may have only had one issue of the magazine and read one installment of a serialization, only a small fraction of the entire book. Third, the ephemeral nature of this medium made it unlikely to influence a second generation of readers, since magazines, unlike books, were made to be thrown away and were not reprinted. Finally, if soldiers' war stories in magazines had gained a particularly strong following, one might expect that this popularity would either be evident in discourse about the war in the late 1920s and early 1930s or would have spurred remembrance about the war that led to discernible actions, like greater efforts at commemoration. However, this does not appear to have happened.

Books, too, can be problematic memory vectors. In 1920, experts estimated that no more than between 0.8 and 5 percent of Americans were regular book buyers, and libraries served as a source of books for approximately 40 to 50 percent of the population.[93] People accessed books much more often through lending libraries than through booksellers because of both cost and possibly convenience since there were only approximately two thousand bookstores in America in the 1920s.[94] Libraries had a much greater potential for reaching a larger audience with only one copy than bookstores did with many. So, this begs the question, what books did libraries make available to their patrons? While there is little data documenting the specific inventories of libraries at any given time—card catalogs were fluid entities—there is a significant amount of information about what books experts recommended for libraries. Buying guides began appearing in the early 1920s, about the same time that libraries began to extend their reach into many communities. These guides were generally created under the aegis of the American Library Association and were a compilation of librarian recommendations from around the country. While lists of recommended books for libraries provide a separate focus for research, the lists were heavily influenced by sales. Libraries with limited resources and time were typically precluded from purchasing books with limited print runs, or those that were out of print. As such, the guides relied on cheaper editions of books that remained in print, a set of circumstances that generally favored books with good sales statistics.[95] So, the fact that American war narratives were poorly represented in book buying guides published during the interwar years may simply be an extension of their poor sales, but it is still worth noting, because it demonstrates what books librarians were making available to the large portion of the population who could not afford to buy books.

Editors produced several guides specifically for high school librarians, and they included recommendations based on the opinions of librarians as to what *should* be read as well as their experience with student borrowing interests. More often than not, these parameters resulted in a very limited pool of war books on the lists. Earlier guides tended to contain more references to war books. A 1924 guide for high school libraries includes Rickenbacker's *Fighting the Flying Circus* (1919), Vernon Kellogg's *Headquarters' Nights* (1917), and R. D. Paine's *Fighting Fleets* (1918). However, the compilers of this guide found none of the three "most essential" based on their rating system.[96] In 1929 a similar list included only two narratives, Aldrich's *Hilltop on the Marne* (1915) and Hall's *High Adventure* (1918). Publishers had reissued *Hilltop* in 1927 and *High Adventure* in 1929, which explains why these two seemingly random titles were chosen. Again, neither book was "recommended for first purchase."[97] A 1930 list of five hundred essential books, prepared specifically for senior high school libraries, included no references to American war narratives.[98]

The *Standard Catalog for Public Libraries* issued in 1940 contained an annotated list of twelve thousand books that were most appropriate for small- and medium-sized libraries. Editors once again chose Aldrich for this list, along with Allen's *Toward the Flame* and Harvey Cushing's *From a Surgeon's Journal 1915–1918*. None of these books, however, was recommended as a first purchase for libraries with limited resources.[99]

Personal guides to reading for the individual were also published, but here too, editors made only limited recommendations of war books. When they did recommend a memoir, it was usually written by a foreigner.[100] In 1928 Trinity College in Hartford, Connecticut, produced a widely circulated list of books that college students should read to open their horizons and better prepare them for their studies. It included a recommendation for John Masefield's *Gallipoli*, which was part memoir and part history of the Gallipoli campaign. Masefield was a well-known British author, and poet and literary critics praised his work as some of the best to come out of the war. The American authors John Thomason (*Fix Bayonets*) and Thomas Boyd (who wrote the fictive, but semiautobiographical *Through the Wheat*) were also mentioned in passing.[101] A 1934 guide for college students and adult readers listed nine hundred books "worth knowing, enjoyable to read, and largely available in inexpensive editions." It included references to *Under Fire* by the Frenchman Henri Barbusse and Remarque's *All Quiet on the Western Front*, but included no narratives by Americans.[102] The same publication also listed the fifty books that college students most frequently recommended, which included *All Quiet on the Western Front* at number twenty-five.[103]

A 1929 study by two prominent interwar experts on adult reading behavior, Douglas Waples and Ralph Tyler, offered a wider perspective on reading interests. They conducted an extensive survey to determine what subjects interested people and if their reading habits reflected those interests.[104] Interest in the "next war" was particularly high, but interest in biographies about "military and naval heroes" was only of middling interest to most men and of very low interest to most women. The most pronounced interest was evidenced by high school boys and young men in their first year of college.[105] Women, on the other hand, actually rated biographies of military and naval heroes among their least-liked potential reading topics. In fact, it was the number one most-avoided reading topic for women in college.[106] Interest was also related to the number of hours one spent reading. Those who read less than four hours per week evidenced a strong interest in military and naval heroes, and those reading eight or more hours per week registered little or no interest.[107] However, the study also reported that these books were in demand at public libraries, that demand presumably coming from young men reading less than four hours per week, a small subset of the reading population, but also a group most likely to get its books from libraries.[108]

George Moreland conducted a follow-up study in 1940, *What Young People Want to Read About*, to provide school and public librarians with empirical data from which to base future book purchases. Not surprisingly, information about the "next war" was at the top of the list for young men. Study organizers asked students to rate their interest in "Why certain soldiers and sailors became heroes." The results were very similar and based on gender, as in the previous study. Boys were much more likely to express an interest than girls, ranking number twelve for boys and close to the bottom for girls. Overall, however, both sexes rated their interest as only slightly higher than they had in 1929.[109] The interest that boys expressed in this topic was probably based on the fact that these books would be adventure stories and they saw the men portrayed in them as role models, rather than an indication of an abiding interest in World War I and its repercussions. Young men were likely not absorbing these narratives as written cues to a past war, but as vehicles for an escape from their everyday reality.

Publishers as Gatekeepers

Outside of young men, the public's reception of war memoirs was muted at best, but was it muted because the right book was not offered to them, or because any war book was a reminder of a troubling episode to be forgotten? Was there no interest or no defining story? Many writers, including Coningsby Dawson and Gertrude Atherton, thought the latter might be true and argued that publishers deserved the blame for the paucity of war-related books after the armistice because many refused to print them.[110] Dawson bemoaned what he called the "unharvested literature of the war." By December 1919 Dawson thought there would have been an outpouring of honest expression, penned up by years of censorship, presenting a nuanced picture of the hell men endured. He dismissed the earlier work of men like Arthur Empey as "stuntbooks." Dawson asserted that, after the war, publishers turned veterans away when they submitted their war stories for publication. In doing so they silenced those who would bring meaning to the war. Publishers squandered an opportunity to benefit from the war's lessons because they, mistakenly, believed there was no market for war books. Dawson believed that some persistent authors might eventually find a way to get their words into print. Others, unfortunately, would retreat, never to speak of the war again. It could be one of these rejected men who told the story that would lay bare the sacrifices of the common soldier and resonate with the public.[111]

The English novelist William J. Locke concurred with Dawson's assertion.[112] He believed that both British and American authors were "met with the barring hands of publishers, editors, managers, cinema people, holding up the placard: 'No War.'"[113] Locke pled his case in the August 1920 issue of the *Atlantic Monthly* and sparked a heated debate. One writer, agreeing with Locke, protested that publishers were given too much credit for their ability to judge the public mood. Just as fashion designers were unable to predict what may strike women's fancy for a season, neither could publishers delve into the human mind and determine what the public wanted. However, even if one was to concede the fact that the public was war weary, another writer argued that publishers should have considered the larger societal costs of silence. Publishers should have felt obligated to disseminate the lessons of war. "To play up war-books one year and forbid them the next is to encourage levity, superficiality, and fickleness and to cater to the weaknesses of democracy."[114]

A journalist from the *New-York Tribune* believed that publishers, or the "intelligentsia," catered to socialism by blocking war stories. The intellectual elite who made the reading decisions for the rest of the American public was unhappy with the way the war evolved and wanted to ensure that no further mention of the unpalatable mess came out. According to this writer, publishers, for the most part, were bolshevists at heart. He argued, "For centuries literature was reproached for being a Tory; now it is a roaring radical."[115] The *Tribune* reporter's comments were consistent with the anticommunist hysteria that dominated much of the public discourse in postwar America. His suggestion that leftist radicals were hindering the publication of war books would likely have been supported by the leadership of the American Legion. The legion was formed right after the war to advocate on behalf of veterans, and its leadership quickly endorsed a militant stance against the perceived Red Menace threatening the country. Communism was simply un-American. The legion's stance against socialism was so strident that in 1927 the American Civil Liberties Union suggested that it had "replaced the [Ku Klux] Klan as the most active agency of intolerance and repression in the country."[116] The legion would have supported Dawson's plea for books that brought meaning to the war as long as they inspired admiration for the veteran and nationalist sentiment. Other writers defended publishers for exhibiting restraint by not printing much of the same type of book that the American public was served in spades during the war. Critics argued that if a masterpiece had materialized it would have been published, but no masterpiece had yet been written. Booksellers backed up publishers as well, claiming that "to offer a purchaser a war book damaged [their] trade and produced an exodus."[117] A blurb in the *Publishers' Weekly* noted, "A publisher's salesman dreamed that his House had sent him a new war book and told him to push it, and he woke up in his berth in a cold sweat."[118]

Robert Graves, the well-known British poet and fiction writer, tried to quantify the mood for war writing in 1924 and found an unreceptive environment. He agreed with those publishers who argued that the public simply had no appetite for war. In fact, he would argue that there was a downright hostile attitude toward it in England. According to Graves, the war "may be emotionally and personally discussed behind closed doors between intimates, preferably at night; or it may be written about impersonally and historically in a three to five-dollar textbook . . . But any other treatment is considered vulgar, anti-social and disgusting."[119]

It is quite possible that one or two of the many novice writers who were turned down by publishers could have produced the definitive piece of literature on the war—a book that would have withstood the onslaught of a second world war that would appear to be more noble and heroic, and would see greater sustained American involvement than the first. However, this assumes that no American testimony of the war was good enough to capture attention and enshrine its lessons in the American consciousness.

This is not true, although many publishers and literary critics argued over the veracity of this statement in the 1920s and 1930s. Those who argued that there was nothing worth reading are supported by contemporary authors like Paul Fussell and Samuel Hynes. Fussell believes that American writing during and after the war was "spare and one-dimensional." He argues that America's lack of literary depth and Americans' unfamiliarity with great literature in general was such that they were unable to produce great literature. He derides the best-known American World War I poet, Alan Seeger, as an amateur when compared with the likes of Wilfred Owen. "It is unthinkable that any American poem issuing from the Great War would have as its title and its last two lines a tag from Horace familiar to every British schoolboy," because Americans were ignorant of literary canons.[120] His opinion of the quality of American writing aside, it's unlikely that specific references to ancient writers were the key to generating American interest in Great War literature. Such techniques may have impressed British literary snobs, but they would not have encouraged book sales in Peoria.

Writing over twenty years later, Samuel Hynes, an influential writer and World War II veteran, was equally strident in his belief that few American World War I memoirs were memorable. He attributes this void to the duration of doughboys' service on the front lines and the fact that few, if any, men who became great writers in the postwar generation actually served in the trenches. Ernest Hemingway, William Faulkner, and F. Scott Fitzgerald all served in uniform, but did not see combat. Hynes believes that if these great writers had been in the thick of the fighting, a truly memorable "soldiers' tale" might have emerged from the experience.[121] In fact, it is more likely that Americans chose not to remember at all. They avoided war books after the war and denied would-be classics attention.

Although many doubt the existence of enduring World War I literature by Americans, some contemporaries of postwar writers highlighted the quality and significance of their work. American critics wrote of the superlative quality of several war narratives, including those mentioned above by Allen, Thomason, Sergeant, Hall, and Archibald, as well as others. *War Birds,* Elliot White Spring's editing of the pilot John McGavock Grider's diary after his death in combat, was singled out for particular praise, as was Howard O'Brien's *Wine, Women and War.* Reviewers lauded many of these books and claimed that they were destined to become valued treatises on the war. *Fix Bayonets!* and *Toward the Flame* were predicted to become classics. A reviewer for *Toward the Flame* noted that it "will be read as long as the World War is remembered."[122] And that turned out to be true.

Cyril Falls wrote *War Books* in 1930 to analyze the "floods of ink" that had been expended on commemorating what was then the largest conflict to roil the world. Falls was a well-respected British scholar on the war and a soldier who earned the Croix de Guerre for his service in France. As a veteran of the Royal Inniskilling Fusiliers, one might expect that his analysis of war books would reflect a bias toward British writers, but he also demonstrated a great admiration for many American books.[123] Falls divided war books into several categories, including war fiction and war reminiscence, and awarded select books praise according to a three-star system he devised. One star was given to "good" books, two stars for "very good" books, and three stars for books of "superlative merit." In the category for war reminiscence he was fairly effusive in his praise of American writers. Five American books were highlighted within his star system. *Personalities and Reminiscences of the War* (Major-General Robert Lee Bullard), *Leaves from a War Diary* (Major-General James G. Harbord), *War Birds* (Elliot White Springs), and *A.E.F. Ten Years Ago in France* (General Hunter Liggett) all received one star. *One Man's War: The Story of the Lafayette Escadrille* (Bert Hall and John Niles) received two stars. These ratings were all the more impressive considering that such classics as Robert Grave's *Goodbye to All That* and Paul Lintier's *My Seventy-Five* received one star.[124]

Ernest Hemingway weighed in on the quality of American war prose in his 1942 anthology, *Men at War*. He was very critical of most writing during the war years. He believed that poets had more success because their talent obscured their meaning just enough to avert censorship. He also believed that there was some good postwar writing, although none of it was done by established writers because most of them had lost their credibility by participation in the propaganda machine that existed during the war. Only amateur writers, mostly soldiers, had the perspective and the credibility to tackle the subject accurately. One of the amateur writers that Hemingway presumably admired the most was John W. Thomason. *Men at War* contains four selections of Thomason's work (one from *Fix Bayonets!*), more than any other writer represented. He also included selections from the Americans Laurence Stallings and James Norman Hall and Charles Nordhoff.[125]

Hemingway and Falls differed on what they considered great works about the war, but both found something to celebrate, and in Falls's case, compare favorably with some of the best war writing ever produced. They were writing, however, from different environments. During the renaissance in war writing in the late 1920s and early 1930s the reception of war memoirs in the United States contrasted starkly with that in Great Britain. Gaging public consumption of war books can be even trickier in Great Britain than in the United States because the British did not maintain best-seller lists until well into the second half of the twentieth century. Even though concrete evidence is elusive, circumstantial evidence indicates that war book sales were relatively stronger than those in America. A 1934 analysis of British books between 1830 and 1930 estimates a minimum sale of one hundred thousand copies to be considered a true best seller. The same analysis lists ninety-four books that not only sold one hundred thousand copies but "took the country by storm," or sold into the six figures in a relatively short period of time. While no British war books are listed in this compilation, Remarque's *All Quiet on the Western Front* does make the cut. The analysis is useful, however, in providing a contemporary measure for successful books.[126]

Using this standard, the well-known war memoirs by British writers Siegfried Sassoon, Robert Graves, and Edmund Blunden fare quite well. Sassoon's fictionalized autobiography, *Memoirs of a Fox Hunting Man*, the prequel to his book about his experiences at war, sold more than 60,000 copies. Sales of the second installment, *Memoirs of an Infantry Officer*, were more than 25,000.[127] Graves's *Goodbye to All That* sold no fewer than 50,000 copies in 1929 and 1930 alone (with up to 20,000 copies selling the first week after publication).[128] The first impression of Edmund Blunden's *Undertones of War* sold out in one day and went through four impressions in two months, then seven more impressions in the next twenty months.[129] Assuming a minimum first run of 5,000 copies, total sales by September 1930 could have been in excess of 50,000 copies. R. C. Sherriff's 1928 play, *Journey's End*, was even more successful. The play was based on Sherriff's experiences as a captain during the war and sold well over 100,000 copies in book format.[130] Aside from Sherriff's theatrical work, the most widely recognized British memoirs were not runaway best sellers. They did, however, sell admirably well and far exceeded relative sales of American memoirs written during the same time period. This is, perhaps, where the Americans' shorter time at war made a difference in perceptions of the war. Graves, Blunden, Sassoon, and Sherriff all wrote stories of disenchantment, and that interpretation found a more receptive audience amongst war-weary Brits than it might have in the United States. Most American memoirs from the late 1920s and early 1930s were not tales of disenchantment. It may be that stories of embitterment and a "lost generation" have more appeal than rehashed adventure stories.

The book considered by many to be the quintessential American memoir of World War I, Hervey Allen's *Toward the Flame,* embodied the disenchantment expressed by Graves and Blunden but included at least a touch of Arthur Empey's fascination with war. Allen's work could be read as an antiwar tract because it directly confronted the romance of war with some of the ugly realities of the battlefield. It also, however, demonstrated the idea of war as an action-adventure, with soldiers courageously persevering in the face of unfathomable danger. This had the effect of glamorizing the war in the minds of some readers. So, in one sense, *Toward the Flame* is truly the archetypal American memoir of the war in that it reflects the duality of thought prevalent at the time. Much of what was written on the war can be broken down along two poles of thought—patriotism and adventure versus a slaughter of innocents. This was particularly true of the fiction I present in the next chapter.

Allen's book, along with books by Eddie Rickenbacker and Alvin York, were some of the most visible works in the American portfolio of personal war narratives, but they all were and are still relatively obscure in the larger literary canon. The fact remains that the average American could not have recalled any of these titles if asked about the war. The legacy of the war was not carried forward through the critically acclaimed writing of Allen, the high-flying adventures of Rickenbacker, or even the folksy heroism of York. It was also not advanced by the early narratives from 1917 and 1918, which are regarded much as Dawson suggested almost a century ago—as stunt books. Maybe Coningsby Dawson was correct in asserting that publishers effectively squelched war books and silenced the writer who might have spoken for the war generations, but probably not. Although only the most visible books are described herein, there are hundreds of others written by thoughtful young men and women who carefully pondered the war and the world it created. Plenty of writers laid bare their experiences, and they were mostly ignored. An American classic may have been produced between the years of 1920 and 1941, but without contemporary acknowledgment, it is hard to determine which spoke loudest on behalf of the war generation. There was not only no consensus on what message or messages about the war should have been passed down in American collective memory, but there was no attempt even to forge a consensus. Biographical war writing was simply not engaged with on any level by most Americans during the interwar years.

This dilemma may be a twist on the question of a tree falling in the forest: If a great book is published and no one reads it, does it make a sound? A *Washington Post* reporter conducted a well-known experiment in a Washington DC, subway station in 2007. He arranged to have Joshua Bell, an internationally acclaimed violinist, play to a rush-hour crowd of commuters at the L'Enfant Plaza stop. Bell was selling out venues with seats costing over $100 each at the time of the experiment. He dressed as any other street performer might and played one of Johann Sebastian Bach's most challenging pieces on his $3.5 mil-

lion Stradivarius violin during his forty-five-minute performance. The reporter wanted to know if "a great musician
plays great music but no one hears . . . was it really any
good?" Joshua Bell never gathered a crowd, and only a
handful of people even paused momentarily to glance his
way as he played as only a virtuoso could. His violin case
served as a receptacle for pennies and quarters, as well as
the occasional dollar, and contained just over thirty-seven
dollars when he was done.[131] One of the world's top vio-
linists had serenaded thousands of Americans and wasn't
heard by any of them. And these people had not made
a conscious decision to tune out classical music as many
postwar Americans had decided to tune out the war. Just
like Bell, war writers had little chance to demonstrate the
beauty of their work, or the meaning of their words, in
an environment of indifference.

3

War Stories

Fiction Cannot Ignore the Greatest Adventure in a Man's Life

The real World War I failed to hold readers' interest, the fictive war, however, was more fashionable.[1] Fiction was the reading material of choice for Americans during the interwar years, and popular authors sold millions of books to meet this demand. One of the hottest writers of the 1920s and 1930s, Zane Grey, catered to an escapist mentality with his stories of cowboys and the American frontier. Other best-selling authors like John Galsworthy, Booth Tarkington, and Harold Bell Wright told stories that illustrated the struggles of the times, often through the lens of the upper middle class. Sinclair Lewis offered a more satirical view of life in the 1920s in his best-selling books *Main Street* (1920) and *Babbitt* (1922), both of which skewered middle-class conformity and challenged romantic notions of small-town America. From fantastic tales of the old West to biting social commentary, fiction of all stripes captivated American audiences. And, although there was no stampede of writers focused on telling stories about the war, it had touched so many facets of life that it was almost impossible to exclude it from contemporary narratives. Novelists would incorporate the "thousands and thousands of manifestations of human character revealed by the war" into their work to different degrees and varying levels of success.[2] Readers showed interest in tales about the war, but they preferred stories that used war as a backdrop for passion, heroic exploits, and journeys of redemption. Reading a soldier's memoir might have seemed like a civic duty, but reading war fiction was immersing oneself in a martial adventure.

The best-known and best-selling American war novels from this period include Ernest Hemingway's *A Farewell to Arms* and Willa Cather's *One of Ours*, but the canon of popular books includes many others that are virtually unknown to readers today. Appendix 2 contains a selected bibliography of more than one hundred of the more prominent titles. In general, war fiction typically hewed to one of two perspectives that roughly mirrored the approach taken by Hemingway and Cather in their famous works. Hemingway's *A Farewell to Arms* epitomizes the "all war is futility" perspective on war, while Cather's *One of Ours* suggests that war can be a redemptive experience. This duality of thought is reflected in Michael Kammen's work on American collective memory, *Mystic Chords of Memory*. He notes that some scholars call the interwar era a time of "debunking" of many of the myths that permeate American history. This would seem to suggest that Hemingway's vision of war was predominant. However, he notes that it was a time when "romantic patriots and apologists were responding quite vehemently to cynics, highbrow critics and academic skeptics."[3] That dynamic is evident throughout the discussion in this chapter.

The first of the two approaches mentioned above, the "all war is futility" attitude, was tied closely to Gertrude Stein's concept of the "lost generation." The term was meant to convey the idea that the war generation was somehow unmoored by the chaos and violence it lived through. F. Scott Fitzgerald described a generation that "found all Gods dead, all wars fought, all faiths in man shaken."[4] Ernest Hemingway popularized the term "lost generation" when he used it as an epigraph for *The Sun Also Rises* in 1926. *A Farewell to Arms,* published in 1929, fully reflects this loss of faith and sense of disillusionment throughout.

Those authors like Cather who presented the war as having purpose typically saw military service as a patriotic duty and painted the conflict as either an emancipative or adventurous experience. While war was certainly not good, it was sometimes necessary to protect a valued way of life, and the men called to service might find their purpose in life by defending democracy. In other words, fighting a war could bring out the best in a man. Claude Wheeler, the protagonist in Willa Cather's *One of Ours*, is a great example of a life redeemed by sacrifices on the battlefield. This theme ultimately found full fruition on the screen in the *Fighting 69th*, with James Cagney playing a soldier who redeems his life of petty crime by sacrificing himself to defend his fellow soldiers

The redeemed or adventurous warrior was found in many novels but also proliferated in war stories found in magazines. War stories appeared in many mainstream periodicals of the day but also became their own genre in the mid-1920s in pulp magazines devoted solely to the war. Between 1926 and 1941 pulp publications like *War Novels*, *Under Fire*, and *Over the Top* specialized in stories about the Great War, reaching millions of readers every month. The large number of Americans reading these magazines, many more than would read any of the popular war books, suggests that they understood the war as a redeemable experience rather than completely futile. This runs contrary to the more dominant myth of the "lost generation" perpetuated by Hemingway's iconic book. Part of the reason for this is that, until very recently, most scholars dismissed pulp fiction as popular culture—a trivial pastime of the masses—rather than a medium that could serve as a telling indicator of collective memory.[5] I explore in this chapter war-related pulp fiction, in tandem with mainstream novels, as an understudied phenomenon that may shed greater light on American memory of World War I.

The novels studied in this chapter were selected based on the weekly best-seller lists prepared by the editors at the *Publishers' Weekly* and the *New York Times*. Weekly lists are useful because, although war fiction was relatively popular, it was not popular enough to have launched many books onto the annual best-seller lists. War fiction was never a sales contender against the most widely read fiction of Zane Grey or Sinclair Lewis. A Grey novel about the American frontier could easily sell one million copies, placing it in the ranks of the most widely sold books in the twentieth century. There are several compilations of best sellers that track the books that fall into this elite class of sales: one of the most popular, by Alice Payne Hackett, classified any book with sales beyond five hundred thousand as a best seller.[6] Using this measure, only Hemingway's *A Farewell to Arms* was a true best seller in the interwar era. Scouring the weekly lists, another five strong sellers come to the forefront.

Table 1. Best-selling books of fiction about war

Title	Author	Year of publication	Time on charts
One of Ours	Willa Cather	1922	Debuted at no. 7, peaked at no. 6 (8 weeks), 28 weeks total
A Farewell to Arms	Ernest Hemingway	1929	Debuted at no. 3, peaked at no. 2 (12 weeks), 20 weeks total
The Deepening Stream	Dorothy Canfield	1930	Debuted at no. 7, peaked at no. 3 (4 weeks), 16 weeks total

Paths of Glory	Humphrey Cobb	1935	Debuted at no. 7, peaked at no. 5 (4 weeks), 12 weeks total
Ramsey Milholland	Booth Tarkington	1919	Debuted at no. 9, peaked at no. 7, 8 weeks total
War Birds	Elliot White Springs	1927	Debuted at no. 5, peaked at no. 5, 8 weeks total

The Deepening Stream, Paths of Glory, Ramsey Milholland, and *War Birds* earned critical accolades when published and spent significant time on the best-seller lists but are largely forgotten today. Table 1 ranks Willa Cather's *One of Ours* first because, although it sold fewer copies, it remained on the weekly best-seller lists much longer than Hemingway's *A Farewell to Arms.* However, *A Farewell to Arms* vastly outsold *One of Ours* over time, based largely on Hemingway's emerging stature as an author during the 1940s and 1950s. Hemingway's fame, bolstered by legions of adoring critics and scholars, made *A Farewell to Arms* the seminal American book about World War I long after it was first published. Because of this acclaim, and total sales, my analysis will begin with Hemingway's book, followed by Cather's, and then the others, per the number of weeks spent on the best-seller lists.

Hemingway's war story, about the doomed love of an American soldier and an English nurse, sold 1,842,000 copies by 1965, classifying it among the best-selling novels of all time.[7] Most "top" lists of American literature include *A Farewell to Arms,* and educators at the high school and collegiate levels have made it required reading about World War I. However, there is little to suggest that most Americans recognized it as a book about the war, much less a cue for remembrance about the American war experience.

One of the problems with holding up *A Farewell to Arms* as the American story of World War I is that Hemingway had little credibility as a documentarian of the war. He volunteered for service in an ambulance unit as part of a wave of young men, most relatively wealthy and well educated, who sought adventure in the American Field Service before the United States entered the war. More than 120 universities sent men into the Field Service, including 325 volunteers from Harvard, 187 from Yale, and 181 from Princeton. Many of these educated men became the chroniclers of the war as the "lost generation," including E. E. Cummings, John Dos Passos, William Slater Brown, Harry Crosby, William Seabrook, Robert Hillyer, Julien Green, Malcolm Cowley, and Hemingway.[8] Hemingway, however, did not spring from such lofty heights as Harvard or Princeton. He was just out of high school and working as a reporter for the *Kansas City Star* when he signed up to go to the Italian front in 1918.[9] After his first few weeks of service, anxious to get closer to the fighting, Hemingway volunteered to work with a Red Cross canteen. After just thirty-four days in the service, an Austrian *Minenwerfer* (a mortar launching artillery shells) wounded Hemmingway in both legs as he was delivering cigarettes, chocolate, and postcards to soldiers along the Piave River. He staggered toward safety and was hit again by machine-gun fire that tore into his right knee. An American Red Cross volunteer nursed him back to health, and their brief romance serves as the basis for the love story in *A Farewell to Arms*.[10]

While Hemingway served admirably, his service was hardly the experience one would anticipate of the man who would write the definitive American novel about the war.[11] He served just over a month, on a front that was little known to most Americans, before the country officially entered the war, as a volunteer handing out chocolate and cigarettes. These are hardly the bona fides expected of the voice of the war generation. Hemingway struggled with this perceived inadequacy, both personally and as a writer, and frequently made vague or misleading statements about his war experience. Consequently, numerous sources suggested that Hemingway served with the Italian "Arditi," a special-forces fighting corps, and the author did little to dissuade people from this belief, even though it was patently false.[12] Hemingway never served in a combat role during the war. Most of what he writes about the war is knowledge gained through other soldiers' accounts. In a satirical article he wrote in 1920, Hemingway is forthright about the ease with which one could fake firsthand knowledge of the war. He argued that any would-be hero could:

> Buy or borrow a good history of the war. Study it carefully and you will be able to talk intelligently on any part of the front. In fact, you will more than once be able to prove the average returned veteran a pinnacle of inaccuracy if not unveracity. . . . With a little conscientious study you should be able to prove to the man who was at first and second Ypres that he was not there at all.[13]

Hemingway fooled many reviewers, and presumably readers, into believing that A Farewell to Arms was a thinly veiled autobiographical account of his experiences at the front, but he was merely channeling the war experiences of others. Of course, this does not disqualify Hemingway as a voice of the war. Stephen Crane became a voice of the Civil War, even though he was born long after Gen. Robert E. Lee's surrender at Appomattox.

A second problem with associating A Farewell to Arms with the American war experience is that it was primarily a love story. One reviewer claimed that "Mr. Hemingway comes as near as a novelist can to making unmixed, lyrical love his central theme."[14] Most critics and reviewers described it as a story that explores how war can both facilitate and hinder romance. Hemingway had much more personal insight to offer on this subject than he did on war, and he played into public demand for love stories. Hemingway argued against the book being marketed as a war story, especially in light of the other war books that were being published at the same time. He told his publishers that they "should start hammering it as a love story—i.e. Farewell to Arms—A Gt. Modern Love Story [*sic*]. It most certainly is a love story and most of the reviewers called it so."[15] Many readers likely came away from the book contemplating the complexities of modern love, not modern war. Hemingway's other popular classic *The Sun Also Rises* used the same pretext of a love story that is touched by war, but this book is not touted as a war novel. In *The Sun Also Rises*, published in 1926, Hemingway presents the prototypical member of the lost generation, Jake Barnes. Barnes, the protagonist, suffered a war wound that left him impotent, suggesting the frustration felt by a generation that had been inalterably changed by war. Critics championed the novel in later years, as they would *A Farewell to Arms*, as being far more influential in the 1920s than it may have been, attributable mostly to the cult of Hemingway that arose in later decades.[16]

A third reason that *A Farewell to Arms* failed as an iconic representation of America at war was the fact that Hemingway's protagonist, Lt. Frederic Henry, was an American out of context. Henry fought for the Italians in Italy. He served with an army that engaged in a disastrous retreat from Caporetto and suffered humiliating defeat. Lieutenant Henry also committed the unfathomable sin of desertion from the army. Retreat and desertion are not themes traditionally associated with American war stories, even in those that demonstrated strong disillusionment with the war. Neither the setting nor the actions encouraged American readers to make a national identification with the war.

If anything, the success of Hemingway's novel engrained the idea that it was a distant, foreign, *European* war.

Two of the most commercially successful war novels in the decade after the war, *All Quiet on the Western Front* by Erich Maria Remarque (1929) and Vincente Blasco Ibáñez's *The Four Horsemen of the Apocalypse* (1919), also advanced the concept of the war as a "foreign war." Remarque's novel sold approximately six hundred thousand copies in the United States in the postwar period, and Blasco Ibáñez's around five hundred thousand.[17] *All Quiet on the Western Front* is the most widely known story of the war and is presented entirely from the perspective of a German soldier. Remarque vividly portrays the physical and mental horrors that befell young men at war through the main character, nineteen-year-old Paul Bäumer. *The Four Horsemen of the Apocalypse* is, at its core, a romantic novel about love, honor, and fighting for a just cause. Secondarily, it is about the longstanding rivalry between two nations, France and Germany, and the stereotypes that categorized their people. Both stories were translated into smash hits on the screen, and I explore those films in greater depth in chapter 4. One reading the works of Remarque, Blasco Ibáñez, and Hemingway, and there were literally millions who did so, might have thought that the English and Americans had no part in the war. The war was a distant, foreign rivalry gone terribly wrong.

Some of the appeal of *A Farewell to Arms* was no doubt born of controversy. For starters, it was one of the books most frequently banned from American classrooms.[18] It was considered scandalous at the time because of Hemingway's allusions to sex and his blunt descriptions of bodily functions. A famous critique by Robert Herrick of the *Bookman* labeled *A Farewell to Arms* "dirt" for what Herrick considered unseemly eroticism and scatological frankness. Both factors were, in his mind, justification for the book being banned in Boston.[19] Herrick's review, and the appeal of the forbidden in Boston and elsewhere, no doubt drummed up additional interest in the book that may not have existed absent a scandal. Hemingway's reputation, too, was a factor in generating book sales, particularly in later years. His persona as a womanizing, drunken, moody philosopher only lent credibility to his reputation as a disaffected writer and served to increase academic and popular interest in his works. A cult of personality unnaturally boosted sales of many Hemingway books years after their first release dates.

While *A Farewell to Arms* racked up sales over time, Cather's *One of Ours* had strong sales upon publication that faded in the face of a poor critical reception from many of her literary colleagues. The lack of critical support only makes Cather's success more telling, especially given that she published her war story at a decidedly inopportune time for such a tale. Hemingway rode the coattails of the phenomenally successful *All Quiet on the Western Front* in 1929. The public's lack of tolerance for the genre in the earlier 1920s led Cather's publisher, Knopf, to forgo serializing the book because magazine editors feared a drop in circulation. Cather was puzzled by this because she never saw her book as a war story; she believed it to be the chronicle of a boy's life—a coming-of-age story. The war was just a means by which Cather fully explored the life of her main character, a frustrated farmer who endures a life of disappointment and failure until he finds redemption on the battlefields in France. Cather's biographer, James Woodress, notes that Burton Rascoe of the *New-York Tribune* said war was "the deus ex machina which solves in ironic fashion the perplexities of the main character, Claude Wheeler. It is war which offers him adventure, release for his pent up energies. The body of the story is concerned with the frustration of those energies."[20]

Fully half of the book was dedicated to Wheeler's early life in the Midwest, but magazine editors were not convinced. They found the Nebraskan portion too provincial and the war portion too taboo.[21] Cather modeled Claude Wheeler after her cousin G. P. Cather, whom she had cared for from time to time and loved as one must love family, but always considered him rather depressive and dull—a disappointment to the family name.[22] His death in the war was compelling to her because it demonstrated that sacrifice could redeem a life of mediocrity in a split second. G. P.'s letters home indicated that he had become more confident about himself and the purpose of his life while in France, and Wheeler's experience would be quite similar. Wheeler left for war a frustrated midwestern youth and died in the trenches a redeemed man. He found his life purpose in duty to country. "For him the call was clear, the cause was glorious. Never a doubt stained his bright faith."[23]

The war chapters were critical to Wheeler's evolution, but they hampered the perceived marketability of *One of Ours* and opened Cather up to withering criticism for presuming to write a "war book." Some of the most influential critics of the day argued that her prose was riddled with errors, and found her presumption to explore emotions on the battlefield a reach at best. Some of the era's literary elite, including Malcolm Cowley and H. L. Mencken, pilloried Cather for presenting a romanticized image of war and suggesting that Claude Wheeler found purpose and a life's fulfillment by dying in France. Cather was part of an older generation of writers who believed the war was morally significant, while Hemingway represented a group of more modern, disaffected writers who believed the war had no redeeming value. Some critics, like Mencken, were much kinder about the portion of the book set in the Midwest but believed her writing on the war "dropped to the level of the *Ladies' Home Journal.*" Their display of male chauvinism was a stinging rebuke for Cather.[24]

Cather's supporters rallied around the book, and she received about twice as many positive as negative reviews, but the bad reviews were incredibly harsh. One reviewer called it "deadly dull," and another "a pretty flat failure." Much of the criticism was a backlash against Cather's rejection of the prevailing idea among the literary set that John Dos Passos's version of the war in *Three Soldiers* was correct and Cather's was hopelessly outdated. Dos Passos's work was the first significant American book that reflected themes of disillusionment about the war. Critics effectively discredited her interpretation of the war by suggesting that a woman had no perspective from which to judge the situation accurately. Cather had, in fact, made a concerted effort to learn about the war from several sources, including the letters of the cousin who had been killed in France, the diary of a troop ship doctor, and experiences gained on an extended visit to postwar France. However, forgetting Stephen Crane for a moment, her critics argued that because Cather did not experience the war, she could not speak cogently about it. Ernest Hemingway even joined the fray by privately suggesting that Cather had gotten her ideas of war from highly suspect sources. He claimed that she had taken her cue from the film *Birth of a Nation* and told a colleague, "I identified episode after episode, Catherized. Poor woman, she had to get her war experience somewhere."[25] This was a bold statement from someone who gathered most of his war experience from books.

Cather wrote *One of Ours* at the wrong time if she had hoped to get support from "the intelligentsia" who pronounced the war a tragic failure and did not want "one of theirs" to suggest otherwise. While many castigated Cather for glorifying war, one of her most esteemed biographers, James Woodress, defended the perspective she gave Claude

Wheeler by arguing that his experience mirrors that of one of the most famous World War I veterans—Harry Truman. David McCullough's acclaimed biography reminded Woodress of the similarity. Truman's early years operating a family farm in the Midwest mimicked the experience of Wheeler, and he too left for war based on a patriotism that also allowed him to escape the drudgery of farm work. Truman wrote to his fiancée from the war, bragging that he looked "like Siam's King on a drunk when I get that little cockeyed cap struck over one ear, a riding crop in my left hand, a whipcord suit and a strut that knocks 'em dead." McCullough found this reminiscent of a line from *One of Ours*: "That was one of the things about this war; it took a little fellow from a little town and gave him an air and a swagger." Truman was luckier than Wheeler because he escaped death, but he came home from the war with the same sense of accomplishment and growth that Wheeler might have. He was not one of the demoralized veterans who found nothing but futility in war.[26]

The perspective Cather gave to her main character may not have been popular with all literary critics, but the reading public received it well, including many young men who identified with the experiences of Wheeler. *One of Ours* went through seven printings, sold fifty-four thousand copies its first year in publication, and curried favor with ex-soldiers who believed that Cather had told their story well. While some critics may have found her book trite, many young American men saw themselves in Claude Wheeler. When the Pulitzer Prize Board honored Cather with the Prize for the Novel in 1923, the *New York Times* editorial staff seemed to echo the sentiment of many farm boys when it suggested that Cather "knows as well as any of them that war has 'horrors,' and doubtless she hates it as much as any of them, certainly she does not laud it as among the more commendable of human activities. But she is as little of a pacifist as a militarist; she is a sane woman who understands that there are worse things than war."[27]

Critics and supporters of *One of Ours* continue today to write articles and books examining Cather's motivations and message. Some remain convinced that Cather was hopelessly behind the times when she wrote it. Others defend her approach by suggesting that her views were not the same as Wheeler's, she merely used Wheeler as a vehicle for demonstrating the irony of the actions of those who romanticized war. Stephen Trout, a prominent Cather scholar, suggests that *One of Ours* was an example of "novel as war memorial." Cather's book was a monument to its war hero, Wheeler (and indirectly G. P. Cather), and also demonstrated the irony of his actions, capturing the ambiguity of American commemoration of the war. Trout points out that the proliferation of memorials and postwar literature suggested that, while the dominant narrative about postwar America was one of disillusionment, there were many competing perspectives on the war. While Cather may have wished to highlight the irony of Wheeler's romanticized notions of war, at the same time she joined other Americans in trying to understand the meaning of the war and to commemorate the sacrifice of so many young men.[28]

However, Cather's critics in the 1920s, some of the most prominent writers of the era, gained more attention than her supporters. Their denunciations probably contributed to the fact that *One of Ours* garnered less attention and commercial success than *A Farewell to Arms*. She was given only passing mention when literary critics discussed enduring works about World War I.[29] Cather's message ran counter to that of the literary giants of the time, and it was easy to cut her down based on her gender and lack of military credentials. The Pulitzer Board's decision to award Cather its annual prize for best novel only stirred the controversy surrounding the book. Before 1929, the Pulitzer Prize for the Novel was guided by the specification that it best presented "the wholesome atmosphere of American life, and the highest standard of American manners and manhood," with emphasis on *wholesome*. This constraint, and the often conservative nature of the selection committee, deeply affected the outcome of the early awards.[30] Two years before Cather won, the committee awarded the fiction prize to Edith Wharton for *The Age of Innocence* over Sinclair Lewis's more cynical *Main Street*. One of the committee members found *Main Street* "depressing . . . vicious, and vengeful," certainly not in keeping with wholesome American life.[31] In 1923, the committee considered Lewis's *Babbitt*, a critical commentary on American business and the middle class. Cather's work met the prerequisite of "wholesome" much better than Lewis's, and she took home the prize. For most of the 1920s, the Pulitzer Prize Committee avoided writers who criticized what many considered sacrosanct American values.[32]

Dorothy Canfield Fisher, a friend and confidant of Cather's, was another of America's wholesome writers and later a contender for the Pulitzer with *The Deepening Stream* (1930).[33] In *The Deepening Stream*, Fisher explores a woman's struggle to overcome the fear of intimacy she acquired while watching her parents bicker and spitefully "one-up" the other throughout her childhood. Her aversion to a life spent in a constant grudge match is overcome incrementally through a relationship that is fulfilling and comfortable in ways she never imagined possible. The novel demonstrates the "deepening stream" of a relationship, part of which took place during the war. The storyline was considered a loose autobiographical account of Fisher's life, including her wartime experiences in France.[34] It was Fisher's second book about the war. Her first, *Home Fires in France*, which was published to some acclaim in 1918, was a collection of stories about the suffering of the French people that she witnessed while in France.

Cather and Fisher were roughly the same age, around fifty, when each wrote about the war, and had been friends since Fisher's brother and Cather attended the University of Nebraska. Their reactions to the war and their war writing were similar in many ways.[35] Both hated war but also believed in the righteousness of fighting for a cause and the validation that the fight might bring. Both Cather and Fisher portrayed the war as a necessary, or inevitable, evil that drew out the best in some people, but Fisher also hinted at the more sinister aims of profiteers and pointedly suggested that Americans never met the lofty expectations of the French in terms of postwar reconstruction. Both were also marginalized as women writing about a man's game, but Fisher had stronger credentials than Cather. Fisher moved her family to France at the height of the war because of a strong conviction that Americans should help in any way possible. In France, Fisher worked with several relief organizations, including aid to the blind, and wrote of her experiences for the American market. Her husband, John, worked with an American ambulance unit.

Like *One of Ours*, *The Deepening Stream* is about the struggles of an individual, Matey Gilbert, that happen to coincide with the war. The war scenes were almost entirely set on the French home front, and information about the war was gleaned through dispatches from a volunteer in the ambulance corps, with brief vignettes of soldier life offered by French men on leave from the front. The war was a milestone in the main character's life, but clearly not a turning point or the focus of the book. In fact, the reviewer for the *Saturday Review of Literature* wrote over one thousand words and never mentioned that half the book is set in war-torn France. He focused instead on the evolution of the main character through marriage.[36] Fisher, like Cather, also received a warm welcome from the reading public. She reported receiving supportive letters by the "baskets-full."[37] Fisher had connected with readers mostly through the protagonist's father-in-law, a Civil War veteran who never talked about the war because he believed war was something that could not be explained. People who went through war understood it, but that experience could not be conveyed with mere words. This sentiment struck a chord with many who had been to war and came back home to a world that never comprehended their experiences. The book was one of Fisher's best-selling titles, and she chose it for inclusion in the Modern Library, a series that publisher Boni & Liveright developed to provide inexpensive versions of popular and classic works of literature.[38] While the Modern Library edition widened the audience for *The Deepening Stream*, it remains one of Fisher's lesser-known works today, perhaps because she lacked cachet as a female chronicler of war.

A female perspective may also have hampered the war books of Edith Wharton (*The Marne*, 1918, and *Son at the Front*, 1922), and Ellen Glasgow (*The Builders*, 1919). Both women, like Fisher, were well respected and commercially successful writers of the era, but their war-related writing is among their least remembered, even though some of their war stories sold quite well. In a pocket volume of the "world's essential knowledge" on literature published in 1929, a New York University professor, Gerald SeBoyar, listed the era's best American novelists, including Cather, Fisher, Wharton, and Glasgow. All four had written war stories by 1929, yet SeBoyar's review did not mention any of these works. Of course, SeBoyar may not have been neglecting their war writing because of their gender, because he also discussed the works of Booth Tarkington but failed to mention his best-selling war novel, *Ramsey Milholland*.[39] SeBoyar may have been one of the intelligentsia who preferred that war novels promote pacifism, and chose to ignore those that were not stridently antiwar.

Booth Tarkington wrote *Ramsey Milholland* in 1919, a time when, according to one critic, Tarkington might have been forgiven for adding a dose of heroic patriotism. The cynicism and regret that would take hold in the early 1920s was still in its nascent stages, so feelings of patriotism were not out of place. However, the same reviewer also accused Tarkington of being a literary profiteer by using teenagers and a melodramatic love story to sell more books.[40] The criticism seems unfair, since most of Tarkington's books contained a melodrama of some sort. Ramsey Milholland, the titular character and the grandson of a Civil War veteran, spent many summers watching military parades at his grandfather's knee and learned about the righteousness of the cause for which Civil War soldiers fought. Milholland eventually enlisted to fight in World War I because of the convictions passed on by his grandfather. The story, however, takes a meandering path between the boy's first military indoctrination and his enlistment as a young man. That path includes a drawn-out flirtation with a well-spoken girl who grew into a pacifist young woman. *Ramsey Milholland* is part puppy-love story and part flag-waving patriotism. The pacifist girlfriend abruptly turns patriotic supporter when her love interest makes it to the Western Front, and the story ends with all in agreement about the necessity for the war.

Tarkington was an energetic supporter of the war and wrote numerous articles supporting preparedness and suspicion of German Americans.[41] Because he was too old to serve in the armed forces, Tarkington saw his writing as an alternative way to contribute to the war effort. He told a friend, "I have a feeling of shame . . . that I'm not carrying a gun."[42] Tarkington was an unabashed propagandist, and this would forever shadow his war story in the eyes of some literary critics. Other critics either agreed with Tarkington or were still caught up in the patriotic war frenzy. A *New York Times* critic believed that Tarkington had captured the essence of "a typical American soldier" and as such gave readers "a wider and clearer understanding" of the war.[43] What readers saw in Tarkington's war story clearly depended on where they sat, but the popularity of his work was certainly not enduring. Tarkington's book was the subject of critical commentary for only a short time and seems to have been quietly relegated to the dustbin as a relic of the wartime propaganda machine shortly after its brief success. Almost no reference to the book appeared after 1919. Had it not been for Tarkington's stature as one of the most popular writers of the era, the book might have received little notice when published.

Author Humphrey Cobb entered the war with the conviction of a Ramsey Milholland and left it bitterly disillusioned. Cobb was the only American veteran who saw active duty in the trenches to later write a best-selling novel, but his status as an American came with some qualifications. He was born in Italy to American parents, went to school primarily in England, and enlisted to fight with the Canadians at the age of seventeen after being expelled from an American school.[44] Cobb entered the service in 1916 but managed to escape the war largely unscathed. He was superficially wounded by flying shrapnel more than once and was "slightly gassed" a couple of times. Physically, Cobb was luckier than most, but emotionally he emerged contemptuous of the military. He held a series of jobs after the war, none of which he liked, traveled the world for a while, and worked at an advertising agency before writing *Paths of Glory*.[45] A great buzz surrounded the book's publication in the summer of 1935, and more than twelve thousand advance copies were ordered before it came out.[46]

Cobb's story was a composite of his experiences at the front and a series of French court cases that challenged the execution of a group of soldiers who were accused of mutiny. In the 1930s relatives of the executed men petitioned the French government to erase the stain left by the charges, and their stories were well publicized in the international press.[47] The incident began when a highly respected military unit was ordered to attack a salient at Saint-Mihiel. As the first wave of men went over the top, German machine guns fired a deadly barrage and, as Cobb described it, "The dead from the preceding attack were piled one upon the other, and there was not a foot of ground on which there was not a corpse." After the first few waves, some soldiers failed to move forward to their inevitable slaughter, and commanders charged the company with mutiny. In Cobb's version, a particularly haughty officer, who believed he might earn the "Grand Officer of the Legion of Honour" for taking a position deemed almost unattainable, sought retribution for the failure. Ultimately, each of four squadron leaders was charged with selecting one man who would be sacrificed to pay for the sins of all the suspected mutineers. One squadron leader refused the order and hid in the woods until after the executions. Three others each put forward a man using a variety of means to choose the most appropriate sacrifice. In one squadron they drew lots, as in the case of the real-life story Cobb mirrored. The second squadron leader chose a man out of spite, and the third selected a man he believed to be the most "uncivilized." None of the three men were guilty of mutiny, but all were killed by firing squad to satisfy the vanity and insanity of men at war.

Cobb deftly humanized each of the men who were executed, making their pointless deaths more meaningful to the reader. War has always been cruel, combatants kill, rape, and maim in an all-or-nothing race to victory. However, in *Paths of Glory*, the enemy was within. Cobb demonstrated that war led to senseless death in many ways, and he encouraged readers to rethink the righteousness of their own armies. He made it painfully clear that armies were run by fear. It was the type of story that haunted readers for days after they finished the last, heart-wrenching pages. *Paths of Glory* received a great deal of prepublication praise from critics and sold very well for a few months, helped along by the fact that it was the Book of the Month Club's selection for June 1935. Publishers, literary agents, and film companies began a bidding war for subsidiary rights, and Hollywood eventually adapted the book for the screen. Its reign at the top of the charts was short lived, though, for a much-anticipated book. It may have suffered from poor word-of-mouth recommendations because it was so very depressing to read. One reviewer noted that "You emerge from reading this war book a little shell-shocked." Some speculated that it was too unreasonable, too primitive, to be embraced by the general reading public.[48] It was a book that made Remarque's *All Quiet on the Western Front* "seem merely sentimental."[49] Humphrey Cobb believed that *All Quiet* was a failure as antiwar propaganda because although the characters demonstrated a hatred of war, "Christ, how nobly they suffer."[50] *Paths of Glory* was supposed to strip war bare of any semblance of virtue.

Book sales slid very quickly after publication, and the play adaptation of *Paths of Glory* failed. The book was also a relative failure, having gone through only one printing before World War II. It was relegated to library bookshelves, where it has remained for over seventy-five years, largely untouched.[51] Even if readers had been more willing to confront the bleak story Cobb presented, it had the same flaw as *A Farewell to Arms* in spurring remembrance: it represented a foreign war experience. Unlike Hemingway's work, which at least has an American main character,

Cobb's story is about foreigners, on French soil, caught up in a drama over mutiny—a concept alien to most Americans' understanding of the war. *Paths of Glory* was an instant success in 1935 that had flamed out by 1936. Interestingly, Penguin Books issued a new edition of the work in 2010.

Cobb's story of the darker side of human nature in the trenches was a world away, literally and conceptually, from Elliot White Springs's tale of heroes in the sky. Springs was an ace pilot during the war, serving with the Aviation Section of the United States Army Signal Corps. By the end of the war he ranked third among pilots in the number of German planes he took down over the Western Front, and earned both the American Distinguished Service Cross and the British Distinguished Flying Cross for his efforts. *War Birds* was a composite of the experiences of many of the men he flew with and was partially based on the diary of a fellow pilot who died in service, John MacGavock Grider.[52] Critics lauded Springs for his fresh approach to the war, which laid bare the real lives of pilots, including their pranks, drinking, and womanizing. The diary entries that made up the book alternated between dramatic dogfights in the sky and drunken escapades on the ground—the latter clearly the salve for the former. One of many tense battle scenes involved a German plane closing in on an American fighter, whose pilot "put in a good burst from both guns right into his cockpit . . . the Hun burst into flames and went down in a dive. The pilot must have fallen on his stick and I saw him go down like a comet. As he hit the ground a pillar of flames and smoke shot up."[53] The pilots fought hard and they played hard in an environment that had few of the constraints of home. Another entry tells of a girl who had been living with one of the pilots and found herself pregnant with his child. She had "the sort of past that wouldn't sound well at home but doesn't seem to make much difference over here. At home every woman that isn't a virgin has a past, while over here they've got to shoot somebody, be divorced by somebody who is somebody or get run over by a train." War provided an environment in which the constraints of American society no longer applied and the background for a book that would titillate American audiences. Publisher George Doran promoted *War Birds* as "the book of flaming youth, the men who fought and lived and laughed and died at the swiftest speed life could offer."[54]

The wine and women sprinkled throughout the book lent an air of scandal and helped overcome the apathy among readership for war stories in the years before the release of *All Quiet on the Western Front.* Springs had inaugurated an action-adventure format that would captivate young men for several years both in novels and pulp-fiction magazines. *Liberty* magazine paid him the biggest fee ever for a serial story, and their money was well spent. "War Birds" was a major hit for *Liberty* in 1926, and circulation skyrocketed. George Doran published the manuscript as a book the next year, and Metro-Goldwyn-Mayer purchased the film rights for $25,000.[55]

The book was well received by critics and veterans. T. E. Lawrence, the famed British soldier who fought in the Middle East, congratulated Springs for one of "the sharpest, reddest, and liveliest" books about the war yet written.[56] *War Birds* and two other publications in 1927, *The Red Knight of Germany* (by Floyd Gibbons, about the German war ace Baron Manfred von Richthofen) and *We* (Charles Lindbergh's autobiography), set off a frenzy of interest about war aviators. Lindbergh's book remained on the best-seller lists through 1928 and sold more than five hundred thousand copies.[57] More than thirty aviation fiction magazines were launched shortly after the success of this trio of aviation stories. Known as "pulp fiction" for the poor quality of their paper, they focused on general aviation, sometimes mixed with science fiction, or war stories. Those in the last category followed the formula set out by Springs and included "German barons—complete with sneers and monocles—and slit eyed American pilots, but each and every one was provided with devastating French girls who always were on hand to bind up a wound, bestow the Legion of Honor or adjust a carburetor while the air hero staggered away to show his despair over the loss of a comrade."[58] The same storyline also ran through many popular movies of the era, including *Wings* and *Hell's Angels*, which I discuss in chapter 4.

In addition to launching a wave of war aviation literature and films, *War Birds* was a commercial success and was reprinted nine times through 1988.[59] Springs "officially" retired as a writer after the book came out to continue working his way up the ladder in his father's cotton business in South Carolina, but he continued to publish new work for the rest of his life.[60] His second novel, *Leave Me with a Smile* (1928), was an autobiographical exploration of the rough transition from aviator back to civilian after the war. Springs's success with *War Birds* guaranteed interest in this second novel, but it sold only five thousand copies. Springs found success with an air adventure, but apparently far fewer people were interested in the emotional and psychological scars that pilots faced after the crowds stopped cheering.

The Presumed Preeminence of *A Farewell to Arms*

Of the six war novels examined, Hemingway's has gotten the most attention and generated the most sales. But Hemingway's sales figures are misleading. While the book sold moderately well, it was hardly flying off the shelves. *A Farewell to Arms* did not rank among the top ten sellers the year it was published. The top three sellers in 1929 were *All Quiet on the Western Front* (Erich Maria Remarque), *Dodsworth* (Sinclair Lewis), and *Dark Hester* (Anne Douglas Sedgwick). Remarque's World War I classic sold three hundred thousand copies in the United States in its first year, Lewis and Sedgwick both hit it big with stories about marital infidelity. Lewis, also American, was much better known than Hemingway and, arguably, the most popular novelist of the 1920s. A 1933 survey of libraries found the breakdown shown in table 2 of inventory for both Lewis's and Hemingway's books.[61]

Table 2. Books by Sinclair Lewis and Ernest Hemingway in three public libraries in 1933

Library	Copies of books by Lewis	Copies of books by Hemingway
St. Louis Public Library	472	30
Newark Public Library	310	101
Boston Public Library	290	3

Hemingway's poor showing is attributable partially to the fact that he had published only half as many books as Lewis.[62] Nonetheless, the numbers are still in Lewis's favor, and yet Lewis is not nearly as well remembered as Hemingway. While *A Farewell to Arms* is the seminal American story of World War I today, much of that may be due to the mystique that began to surround Hemingway many years after he wrote it. The book did not resonate as much with contemporary culture in 1929 as it did with academics and critics in the 1930s and 1940s. *A Farewell to Arms* was reprinted as part of the Modern Library in 1932 and was not reissued by another major publisher until Scribner's came out with a new edition in 1948. Modernist critics championed Hemingway's works in the decade after his war novel was published and "turned [him and others] into academic industries in the 1950s and 1960s."[63] A significant portion of the over 1.8 million copies bought by 1965 sold long after the book was published. Bantam published the first paperback edition in 1955, after Hemingway's preeminence had been established in the cultural hierarchy and in academia, and it was this version that accounted for the lion's share of sales (over one million) that made *A Farewell to Arms* a top-selling novel of all time.[64]

In contrast, the immediate appeal of Cather's *One of Ours* continued unabated for several years after its first publication in 1922. It was reprinted in 1923, 1926, 1931, 1934, and 1937, but critics were not as kind to authors who mired their writing in the lives of the bourgeoisie—chronicling the lives of the middle class and the challenges they faced. Gordon Hutner, the founding editor of the journal *American Literary History*, argued that so-called middle-brow literature was given short shrift in the early and mid-1900s. He believed that critics and scholars formed and promulgated their own ideas of taste and literary quality, something that is detrimental to historians, both literary and otherwise. Middle-brow novels "clued readers to the way their fellow citizens were thinking, believing, and acting."[65] In other words, they spoke for the clear majority of Americans in their analysis of a host of topics, including war. He pointed out that "Countless copies were given as birthday and Christmas gifts—enjoyable yet serious, . . . a tacit social imperative—read and ye shall understand; taken as a group, these books create a whole storehouse of evidence for determining the history of American middle-class taste and cultural anxieties."[66]

But scholars steered well clear of middle-class literature, partly because it needed no analysis or dissecting. The scholar could add very little to the average reader's understanding of *Ramsey Milholland* or *The Deepening Stream.* So, they consistently focused on a group of writers who would become the literary elite, writers who wrote abstractly or with ambiguity and thus required an academic guide to be thoroughly understood. Authors like Hemingway and

John Dos Passos, another significant war writer, would fall into the latter category. According to Hutner, scholars and critics bore a great deal of the responsibility for the fact that Tarkington and Fisher, and their depictions of middle-class ideals in the 1920s and 1930s, largely faded from literary consciousness. Reviewers, on the other hand, were much more egalitarian in their approach because they remained tied to the publishing businesses in a symbiotic way—part of their mission is to sell books—and reviewers were often much less critical of middle-brow works.[67] They often congratulated writers for the ability to capture the lives of the middle-class, a huge slice of the book-buying public. In 1921, a reviewer for the *Bookman* called Tarkington "the most faithful portrayer of American life as our generation has lived it." Tarkington spoke for the mass of people in the middle, those who might have found Hemingway coarse and alien. One editor noted that novelists like Tarkington "think like the people, not for them."[68]

Literary historians have contributed to the diminishment of writers of middle-class fiction by continuing the focused study of a few select authors and a handful of anointed books. Hemingway and *A Farewell to Arms* is clearly among the anointed. The author and title are perpetual contenders for spots in any list of laudable American writers or fiction. The *Saturday Review of Literature* sponsored a poll in 1944, and *A Farewell to Arms* was ranked number ten among reader favorites.[69] In 1998, the Modern Library launched a readers' poll of best-loved novels written since 1900, and *A Farewell to Arms* remained in the top one hundred (at ninety-one).[70] Writing about Hemingway, and any one of his many well-known books, is a cottage industry unto itself. There have been no fewer than 130 essays, book sections, and articles; 2 books; and 6 book-length collections of essays written about *A Farewell to Arms*.[71] The reputation of Hemingway and *A Farewell to Arms* has affected collective memory of the war in several ways. First, as discussed earlier, it emphasized a Eurocentric view of the war. Second, its popularity from midcentury until today has insinuated that most Americans embraced Hemingway's modernist, antiwar commentary. Last, it overshadowed other war novels that presented a different American perspective.

Other Critically Acclaimed War Books

All of this is not to say that Hemingway did not strike an authentic note with a significant segment of the population, because he did. Those writing both before and after Hemingway's seminal book was published reflected strong disillusionment with the war. Several books stand out as representative of this attitude, including three books by men who were, or would become, acclaimed authors who served in France during the war—John Dos Passos, Thomas Boyd, and William March.[72] Boyd and March served on the front lines in active combat, and Dos Passos was a volunteer ambulance driver. Their status as veterans infused their work with legitimacy and increased their stature with critics. Dos Passos's politics may have ultimately hampered his marketability, but Boyd and March might have been more commercially successful if the "lost generation" perspective truly represented the views of large segments of the reading public.

Dos Passos wrote several books on the war and was the first major author to publish a thoroughly negative portrayal of the war in *Three Soldiers*. The book, which presents realistic images of trench warfare as experienced by three soldiers from diverse backgrounds, garnered a moderately good sales record and was also one of the first war books to break out of the trend of eyewitness, or journalistic, accounts of the war toward a more nuanced and sophisticated approach. Many critics hailed Dos Passos's pacifist writing as a much-needed antidote to the prose of the war years. H. L. Mencken, a leading critic of the 1920s, said, "At one blast it [*Three Soldiers*] disposed of oceans of romance and blather. It changed the whole tone of American opinion about the war; it even changed the recollections of actual veterans of the war. They saw, no doubt, substantially what Dos Passos saw, but it took his bold realism to disentangle their recollection from the prevailing buncombe and sentimentality."[73] Others were outraged at what they considered an unconscionable insult to the American army and the men that served. Coningsby Dawson wrote a scathing review, claiming that "the book fail[ed] because of its unmanly intemperance both in language and in plot. The voice of righteousness is never once sounded; the only voice heard is the voice of complaint and petty recrimination."[74] The *Chicago Tribune* ran an article that proclaimed that *Three Soldiers* was "branded as textbook and bible for slackers and cowards."[75]

His writing was not traditional American fare, and he had faced an uphill battle to get it published. Dos Passos claimed that he was rejected by thirteen publishers before Doran ultimately accepted the manuscript.[76] Dos Passos was in Damascus when the book came out, and friends wrote to tell him that the novel provoked "a 'grandiose rumpus' and was 'talked about noisily in subways and churches.'" However, all the publicity failed to get the book on the major best-seller lists.[77] Dos Passos was selling a virulent antiwar message, a new phenomenon at a time when the public was apathetic to almost anything war related. Additionally, the postwar "Red Scare" probably influenced public reception of Dos Passos's work. In a time of heightened governmental and social scrutiny of ideological radicals, consumers may have steered clear of any book whose purchase might have branded them as a socialist.[78]

In later years, Dos Passos's works might have become more prominent had he been less upfront about his evolving political leanings. He moved from the Far Left of the political spectrum in the 1930s to supporting Barry Goldwater in the 1960s.[79] His metamorphosis to the Right, including support for communist witch hunts conducted by Sen. Joseph McCarthy in the 1950s, may have estranged him from the literary elite, and by extension readers, in the later years of his career.[80]

Thomas Boyd believed that his war story, *Through the Wheat* (1923), shared the quality and uniqueness presented by *Three Soldiers*, and critics agreed. Boyd's manuscript was originally rejected because of the perceived postwar disinterest in war stories, but he was firm in his conviction that "the belief that people are sick of war books is false. They are tired of books which use war as a background. The same thing was said when *Three Soldiers* was published. But it went, and well. Because it was a different kind of war book. And so is this again."[81] In fact, were it not for the intervention of F. Scott Fitzgerald, it is unlikely that publishers would have taken a gamble on *Through the Wheat*, penned by an unknown author at the time.[82] Soldiers championed Boyd for his portrayal of the average soldier in the book, essentially a fictionalized account of his war experiences. Where Dos Passos presented the story of the frustrated American soldier who spent more time waiting than acting during the war, Boyd detailed a soldier's exploits in several of the major American offensives. Veterans of all stripes praised his novel as authentic. One critic even believed that Boyd had "rewritten *The Red Badge of Courage*," picking up the mantle from Stephen Crane for the edification of the war generation.[83] However, as is often true, compelling writing and strong reviews did not translate into stellar sales. *Through the Wheat* sold modestly well for a book in general, just over thirteen thousand copies through several printings, but considerably well for a war book published in 1923, a few years before war writing would gain any real footing in the market. Yet his book has been largely forgotten since the 1920s.[84] Some thought the main character, William Hicks, was a difficult character to sympathize with and the author's approach was too journalistic, making it tough for readers to warm up to it as a work of fiction.[85] More likely, readers were not about to warm up to any war book, regardless of the main character's disposition. Critics were unkind to his second war novel published in 1935, *In Time of Peace*, a postwar continuation of his earlier book and a statement about the evils of capitalism.[86]

William March, like Thomas Boyd, saw the tribulations of war up close. He fought in some of the battles most associated with American persistence and achievement during the war, like Belleau Wood, Saint-Mihiel, and Mont Blanc. He was wounded at both Belleau Wood and Mont Blanc and was awarded the Croix de Guerre and the Distinguished Service Cross for heroics at Mont Blanc.[87] He also claimed to have suffered grievously from exposure to gas during his service and left the war with the trauma of his wounds and the haunting memory of having bayoneted a blue-eyed, blonde German soldier in face-to-face combat. It was these demons that he seemed to be exorcising in *Company K* (1933), which was an unflinching criticism of the rigid bureaucracy of war and what it made men do to each other. *Company K* met, for the most part, with rave reviews both for content and March's allowance for a variety of perspectives through his episodic format. Many scholars considered *Company K* a classic, but March is much better remembered for his 1954 *The Bad Seed*, which was turned into a popular movie in 1956.

Company K was not a strong seller, having sold approximately five thousand copies several months after release. One left-leaning publisher thought the novel was the only true picture of war he had encountered and suggested that it might fail to find an audience because it was so harsh in its portrayal of war, without any pretense of "false idealism," that readers would be disgusted by it.[88] One scholar suggested that it was the intensity of the ideology expressed by March, and others like Boyd, Humphrey Cobb (*Paths of Glory*), and later Dalton Trumbo (*Johnny Got His Gun*) that deterred readers. Hemingway and Dos Passos approached the war from a much more artistic, and in the case of Hemingway, romantic perspective. The spoonful of sugar made some books more palatable to readers, but the authors still conveyed strong antiwar sentiments.[89]

The visibility of books by men like Dos Passos, Boyd, and March, men who found no honor or glory in war, suggest that there was a strong vein of support for the lost generation theory in America, but their sales figures don't suggest that it was a dominant theme. The critical acclaim they garnered means that books by Dos Passos and March likely appeared on college reading lists in the 1920s and 1930s and will be studied by generations of students to come, but it doesn't mean that these books reflected the predominant opinion of contemporary society. They found a niche market but likely did not represent the views of most Americans. As we see later in the chapter, there were stronger currents of thought reflected in the mass sales of pulp-fiction magazines.

Several African American writers also wrote critically acclaimed novels, and it took a brave black man to write about the war in 1920s and 1930s America.[90] David Davis, who has written extensively about African American postwar literature, called black war writers rebels because "A military uniform on the body of an African American person symbolized the moral and ethical necessity of social equality, so literary representations of the African American soldier constituted acts of creative dissent on the part of African American writers."[91] They were also rebels because they were unafraid to demonstrate their service at a time when merely standing on the street in your uniform was enough to get a black man flogged in some parts of the country. African American writers might just have likely ignored the war, just as many black veterans refused to participate in the war histories explored in chapter 1. Instead, men like Walter White, Claude McKay, and Victor Daly did write about the war, and they used their bully pulpit to expose the realities of the black soldiers' experience on the battlefields in France and the reception they received upon returning home to the United States.

Walter White, best known for his long tenure at the head of the National Association for the Advancement of Colored People (NAACP) and his civil rights work, was one of the first black writers credited with realistically presenting the wartime race situation in the South. H. L. Mencken encouraged his friend White to share his insight into Southern race relations through fiction. White met the challenge when he published *The Fire in the Flint* in 1924.[92] The book's main character, Kenneth Harper, was a physician who went to war believing that his service would buy him a modicum of respect when he returned to the South. The story explores the fallacy of this idea, ending tragically with Harper's lynching. It sold somewhere between five thousand and ten thousand copies, and went into at least a third printing after an initial run of three thousand copies. White called it "a modest best seller," and with sales comparable to that of *Company K*, the book deserves a place in the canon of significant literature of World War I.[93] Sinclair Lewis called *The Fire in the Flint* one of the two best novels produced in 1924.[94] White utilized a strong network of NAACP supporters to spread the word about the book, which bolstered visibility and probably helped sales. White also was an adherent to the philosophy that there is no such thing as bad publicity and pointedly sent review copies to newspapers with strong ties to the Ku Klux Klan. Their outrage, including the reviewer who argued, "I cannot see any truth in a book which depicts every negro character a hero and a noble creature, and every white man a rape fiend, a coward, or a scoundrel," offered free publicity.[95] *The Fire in the Flint* was one of only a handful of novels by black authors to which critics paid any serious attention in the mid-1920s.[96]

Along with White, Claude McKay figured prominently in the Harlem Renaissance. He was a poet first and a prose writer second. His first novel was *Home to Harlem* (1928), in which a young longshoreman enlisted to fight the Germans but deserted when he realized that black soldiers were expected to work as laborers, not combatants. He went home to Harlem, as the title suggests, and struggled with some of the grimier aspects of life for working-class blacks in New York City. The book was considered a raw representation of life for many African Americans after the war, a departure from novels that presented an idealized version of the black middle class. It was the first novel that presented a working-class black man and included no ancillary characters, like a wife or children, to soften the picture of barrooms and street brawls presented by McKay.[97] Reviewers for most major outlets took notice and discussed the vivid picture of Harlem life McKay painted, not his depiction of war. Many African Americans criticized McKay for presenting characters that were crude and hedonistic, suggesting that all blacks lived similar lives. W. E. B. Du Bois declared the book nauseating, and another black reviewer believed that whites "think we are buffoons, thugs and rotters anyway. Why should we waste so much energy to prove it?" It made the best-seller lists in New York City, and its appeal to the "prurient interests in white people" may have attracted readers of both races.[98] It is considered the first novel by a black writer to achieve signifi-cant commercial success.[99] As such, it likely had a wider reach than White's *The Fire in the Flint.*

Of the three black-authored novels under discussion, Victor Daly's *Not Only War* (1932) deals most directly with the war, and he is the only one of these authors who served in uniform. Daly was a first lieutenant in the famed 367th Infantry of the 93rd Division, also known as the "Buffaloes." His short novel is about two men, one white and one black. Their lives intertwined on the home front because of their desire for the same black woman, and their paths coinci-dentally intersect on the battlefield as well. Both at home and abroad, the white man, Robert Casper, held the bal-ance of power throughout most of the book and treated the black man, Montgomery Jason, with derision. Casper had Jason court-martialed in France for having the temerity to socialize with a white Frenchwoman in the home where he was billeted. Later, after being seriously wounded, Casper is at Jason's mercy for survival. Even given the opportunity for retribution, Jason made the compassionate decision to save his tormentor. Sales statistics are not available for the book, but it is still substantially represented in librar-ies across the country, suggesting its appeal.

While Daly's book is set primarily on the battlefield, and as such was the most direct representation of African American war experiences, none of these three books are, at their core, about war. All three were written to under-score the racial situation in the South. The title of Daly's book refers to William Tecumseh Sherman's famous quote about war being hell. In his forward Daly explains, "The Hell that Sherman knew was a physical one—of rapine, destruction and death. This other, is a purgatory for the mind, for the spirit, for the soul of men. Not only War is Hell." White and McKay wrote about the same battle for the soul of men and used the war to strengthen their claim for equality by demonstrating that blacks fought and died for their country, yet failed to reap the rewards of citizenship.

The aforementioned titles are just a small sampling of novels written about the war; an expanded, but certainly not exhaustive, bibliography is available in appendix 2. As the bibliography demonstrates, there was no shortage of war books at any time, but the American Legion still felt compelled to sponsor a competition to encourage further war-related writing in 1928. The editors of *American Legion Monthly* put out a call for the "big novel of the war," arguing, "Hitherto many authors and publishers have been doubtful of war fiction as a publishing venture, yet public interest in the war as a theme for fiction has been steadily increasing. The time is ripe for a novel or group of novels that will endure as the best record of the great years between 1914–1918." To the legion, the best record would have to reflect themes of patriotism, service to country, and national unity. The American Legion was the largest veterans' organization formed after the war, and they sought to trumpet their achievements and crush any semblance of radicalism that might undo the unity brought by war.[100] The magazine's editors offered a $25,000 prize and a book contract with Houghton Mifflin to the novelist who best encapsulated the war for the benefit of the American reading public.[101] Writers sent in approximately five hundred manuscripts for consideration.

Two novels split the judges' favor: Mary Lee's *"It's A Great War!"* and William Scanlon's *God Have Mercy on Us!* Lee's work was decidedly antiwar and referenced some of the seamier aspects of life in the army, including the lax morals of many soldiers who frequented prostitutes. Scanlon's work was a straightforward glorification of the marines in the war. Two of the five judges, representing the Authors' League of America and Houghton Mifflin's literary director, voted for Lee, two judges, representing the army and the *American Legion Monthly*, voted for Scanlon, and the fifth suggested that the competition be extended because none of the submissions were worthy of the prize. The legion's attempt to solidify a collective memory of the war that centered on comradeship and duty was being hijacked by a woman who focused on filth, promiscuity, and fear.[102]

The debate mirrored the public's split allegiance between books like Cather's *One of Ours* and Hemingway's *A Farewell to Arms*. Did the war have some redeeming value for America and those that fought, or was it just an unmitigated waste? Just like the public, the prize was split, and Houghton Mifflin published both Lee's and Scanlon's books. American Legion officials exacted payback by revoking Lee's membership from a Boston-area post. However, Lee was astute enough to play up her expulsion in the press, and the resulting publicity boosted sales. Ultimately, Lee's book sold twice as many copies as Scanlon's and may have topped thirty thousand copies in America and England combined.[103]

This dichotomous judgment was evident among literary critics as well. Malcolm Cowley and Archibald MacLeish, both veterans, poets and critics, had differing perceptions of the war. MacLeish unleashed his perspective of the war's memory in a somewhat critical review of Laurence Stalling's *World War I* in 1933. He criticized Stallings for offering a one-sided view of the war that he called propagandistic. He chided Stallings's fashionable line of thought that all those who died in the war did so in vain. MacLeish argued that some men truly believed that they were fighting for a cause and to discount their convictions, and their sacrifices, was unfair.[104] He suggested, "Is it perhaps conceivable that to die generously and in loyalty to a believed in cause, regardless even of its validity, is to die in vain?"[105] Cowley responded to MacLeish's review by arguing that presenting the war in any positive light was only an incentive toward further war. He staunchly believed that Stallings needed to present the starkest picture of war possible, one that left no question that American soldiers died in vain, as history had proven true. The fact that these "loyal" soldiers were not around to learn of the futility of the war did not somehow redeem their deaths.[106] MacLeish certainly abhorred war and espoused pacifism in his writing, but he believed that one could write about war using some of the taboo terminology like "patriotism" and "loyalty" and still present a valid viewpoint. Men fought with the information they had at the time, and if belief in a cause or an obligation to duty guided their actions, those actions were honorable and needed to be part of the record and legacy of the war.

This duality of thought is evident in the hundreds of personal narratives surveyed in chapter 2 here as well as the reminiscences of many veterans. Frederick Pottle, a veteran writing fifty years after the war, believed that his war experience was "the best-invested years of his life." He recalled the thrill of "the first time in a foreign country. . . . The joy of frank, unreserved male friendship." While this veteran had not reached the battlefield, he knew many who had and suggested that most believed that the "cause was just and, well, heroic."[107] Another soldier who did see action at the front lines, Amos Wilder, a poet and scholar, backed up Pottle's contention. Wilder argued that soldiers were "willing actors in a necessary drama and one inseparably linked with the meaning of the American story." He disdained that American writers like Hemingway and Dos Passos saw little of the real war and chose to write about deserters and slackers. He suggested that both writers were reaching for different goals, both only superficially related to the war. Hemingway had a "heroic code," and the war was a pretense for his protagonist. Dos Passos was an avowed socialist who was presenting propaganda for an eventual revolution.[108] Pottle's and Wilder's views stood in contrast to veterans like Boyd and March who presented the war as one of complete futility. The divergent views of veterans, novelists, and critics no doubt mirrored a similar confusion on the part of the general public.

By the mid-1920s and early 1930s, modern ideas of the complete futility of war had generally taken hold in higher-brow literature. This made many later World War I novels distinctive from those written about World War II. Writers like March, Cobb, and Trumbo predominantly focused on the senselessness of the war and its futility and suggested that nothing was accomplished for all the bloodshed. They also expressed disdain for the values that supposedly sent Americans to war—patriotism, democracy, and sacrifice. After World War II, writers certainly did not embrace war, but they believed that they had accomplished something very important by stopping the advance of fascism. They won a war against an evil foe, and if patriotism and sacrifice helped them do it, so be it.[109]

The antiwar writers after World War I also strongly criticized their leaders, both military and government, and blamed their ineptness for unnecessary bloodshed. Novelists after World War II were, generally, much more sympathetic to military leaders. They were writing during the Cold War, and their government was still engaged in a battle against evil.

One scholar has called World War II novels an "affirming flame."[110] They told the story of a war that had to be fought, not by gung-ho patriots, but by men who fought hard to defeat a threat to American freedom and then got back to their families. This sense of duty is reflected in World War II authors often focusing on the teamwork of a bomber crew or infantry platoon, not the individual feats of pilots or heroes like Alvin York.[111] Of course, not all writers shared this view; some reflected the disillusionment prevalent in doughboy accounts as well. There were a dozen best-selling war novels written by Americans between 1940 and 1965, including *The Naked and the Dead* (Norman Mailer's first novel), *The Young Lions* (Irwin Shaw), *Don't Go Near the Water* (William Brinkley), *From Here to Eternity* (James Jones), *The Caine Mutiny* (Herman Wouk), and *Battle Cry* (Leon Uris).[112] All six of these books not only dominated the best-seller lists in the year they were published, but sold in large quantities for many years. Except for *Don't Go Near the Water*, which was a comedic novel, these books sold over two million copies each by 1965, placing them in an elite level of sales.[113] By comparison, only one book about World War I sold over two million copies (*All Quiet on the Western Front*).[114] The closest American competitor to Remarque was Hemingway's *A Farewell to Arms*. It is important to note that the inexpensive paperback had become ubiquitous by the 1940s, making books more accessible to a wider portion of the populace. Most of the sales of the books mentioned above were in paperback format. Publishers began producing more paperbacks in the 1930s, and while this did improve sales of some World War I novels, very few were issued in cheaper editions, presumably because of lack of demand.[115] But if paperbacks were the dominant mode of transmitting war stories after World War II, readers after World War I had pulp fiction.

Pulp Fiction and the Great War

Pulp-fiction magazines had the largest audience of any written publication at the height of their popularity during the interwar period. Publishers have estimated that ten million issues of pulp fiction circulated monthly. By comparison, the *Saturday Evening Post* and *Ladies' Home Journal*, two of the highest circulation magazines in the 1920s and 1930s, had circulations of approximately

2.5 million.[116] "Pulp" fiction referred to the inexpensive rag paper that was used to produce the magazine versus the slick paper used in the more traditional magazines. Most pulp magazines sold for ten cents, taking the place of the dime novel from an earlier generation, and by the middle of the 1930s over two hundred separate pulp magazine titles were on sale at newsstands across America.[117] The pulps drew in audiences from all socioeconomic levels, but appealed mainly to the uneducated, particularly juveniles or the working class. The pulps traditionally contained fiction in the short story, novelette, or serialized novel format and critics called them "cheap thrills" for their portrayal of detectives, cowboys, soldiers, or science fiction aliens.

In 1926, Dell Publishing produced the first Great War pulp, *War Stories* (see figure 2), and it became an instant hit. The timing was fortuitous, as several other war books, movies, and plays were issued around the same time, including Hervey Allen's *Toward the Flame*, Leonard Nason's *Chevrons*, Elliot White Springs's *War Birds*, Eddie Rickenbacker's *Fighting the Flying Circus*, Floyd Gibbons's *The Red Knight of Germany*, Laurence Stallings's play and film *What Price Glory?*, and the blockbuster silent film *The Big Parade*. *War Stories* focused mainly on stories of adventure and heroism or comedic shenanigans, steering clear of mood-dampening death and destruction. In the inaugural issue of *War Stories* the editor noted that enough time had passed to allow soldiers and citizens to look back at the war and remember the tremendous role it played in the lives of millions of men and women. However, the magazine hoped to trigger only positive memories:

> Bloodshed, the actual sorrows and horrors of war, will in no way be played up in this magazine. There will be nothing that might rouse resentment, bitter thoughts, or set

the mind aflame. We want to assure the wives, mothers and sweethearts of America that they can pick up this magazine with no fear of having their hearts wrung, their fears aroused. . . . Writers who think that bloodshed and horror make entertaining, profitable reading, writers who do not know that the war is over—men of this type will not get their stories into this magazine.[118]

Almost immediately, literary critics derided the new magazine as an inducement to war. As one put it, by only portraying the "vin-blink, and the girls, and that crazy sergeant, and the exercise in the open air," pulp-magazine editors were encouraging readers to forget the war, or at the very least its lesson. Covering up the gangrene, executions, shell shock, lice, and mutilations was to the great detriment of future generations. The literary elite had supported and publicized the war stories of Hemingway and John Dos Passos because of their anti-war messages. War stories in pulp magazines were far removed from pacifist thought, and critics feared they would be devoured by millions of young men and boys who would see war only as a great adventure.[119] The editor of *War Stories* pointed this criticism out to his readers, who generally responded that there was nothing wrong with presenting the human side of war. A Canadian captain wrote, suggesting that:

> *War Stories* is not a defense of no [*sic*] argument for war. The magazine is a monument to all ex-servicemen, a "book of memory" where we again meet those of our comrades who have passed from the sight of man by the blood-drenched path of duty and self-sacrifice. In its pages they live again. . . . Memories are reborn that cannot but make us better citizens, because they take again from our nature that taint of selfishness that was burned out in the fiery furnace of war.[120]

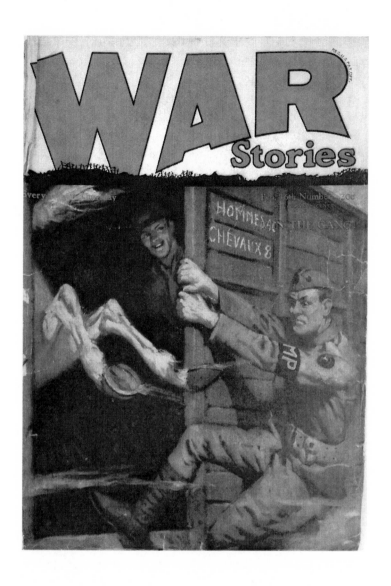

FIG. 2. *War Stories*, February 16, 1928. Dell Publishing Co., cover artist unknown.

War Stories was successful and quickly moved to publication twice monthly. It also made war pulps trendy until the early 1930s. Competing pulp publishers put out their own war magazines, beginning with *Battle Stories* (see figure 3) in 1927, and *Under Fire* and *Over the Top* in 1928. The short-lived *Love and War Stories* tried to combine two successful genres, but folded after only one issue. The first issue of *Battle Stories* insinuated that interest in war stories was long overdue, noting that "several years of disinterest has been particularly discouraging to the boys who came back to civilian life," but now "all America seems eager to hear and read stories of the part her soldiers and sailors played in that great conflict." Although the editor believed "all America" was eager for these stories, he suggested that they would be most interesting to former enlisted men, officers, Civil War veterans, and young boys—the presumed audience for most of the war pulps.[121]

Dell tried to build upon its success with *War Stories* by issuing a slew of copycat publications, including *War Novels*, *War Birds*, *War Aces*, and *Navy Stories*. *War Novels* followed basically the same format as *War Stories*, but included full-length novels to combat the complaint that serialization required buyers to purchase more than one issue. *War Birds* and *War Aces* capitalized on the popularity of Charles Lindbergh and American fascination with aviation, and *Navy Stories* (which alternated between that title and *Submarine Stories*) met the demand for stories set at sea. *War Birds* was the first in a long list of aviation-based pulps, most of which contained at least some articles on the war and fighter pilots.

In total, there were at least forty-eight pulp titles that were either solely or partially dedicated to war stories. A partial list of those most directly related to the war is given in table 3.

FIG. 3. *Battle Stories*, December 1930. Fawcett Magazines, cover art by George Rozen.

Table 3. War-related pulp-fiction magazines

Name	Publisher	Years of Publication
WAR PULPS		
Battle Stories	Fawcett Publications	1927–36
Love and War Stories	Good Story Magazine Company	1930
Navy Stories/ Submarine Stories	Dell Publishing Company	1929–30
Over the Top	Street & Smith Corporation	1928–30
Soldier Stories	Fiction House	1929
Under Fire	Magazine Publishers	1928–29
War Novels	Dell Publishing Company	1928–30
War Stories	Dell Publishing Company	1926–32
World War Stories	Ramer Reviews	1929?
AVIATION WAR PULPS		
Aces	GlenKel Publishing Company	1928–40
Air Stories	Fiction House	1927–39
Air Trails	Street & Smith Corporation	1928–31, 1937–39
Battle Aces	Popular Publications	1930–32
Battle Birds	American Fiction Magazines	1933–34, 1940–44
Dare-devil Aces	Popular Publications	1932–35
Flying Aces	Magazine Publishers	1928–42
G-8 and His Battle Aces	Popular Publications	1934–44
The Lone Eagle Flying Ace	Better Publications	1933–41
Sky Aces	Magazine Publishers	1938–41
Sky Birds	Magazine Publishers	1929–35
Sky Devils	Western Fiction Publishing Company	1938–39
Sky Fighters	Assorted	1932–50
Sky Riders	Dell Publishing Company	1928–31
Squadron	Adventure House	1934
War Aces	Dell Publishing Company	1930–32

| *War Birds* | Dell Publishing Company | 1928–35 |
| *Wings* | Wings Publishing Company | 1928–52 |

Some magazines only ran for one or two issues while others became staples of the newsstand. Two longstanding titles were *Battle Stories* and *War Stories*. Battle Stories ran for sixty-six issues between 1927 and 1936, and *War Stories* had the same number between 1926 and 1932. Americans were most fascinated by the aviation war pulps, and thirty-seven of the forty-eight titles were air war magazines.[122] Aviation was the new frontier, and men like Calbraith Rodgers, who flew across the country in forty-nine days, and Charles Lindbergh, who crossed the Atlantic, were idolized, along with war flying aces Eddie Rickenbacker, Billy Bishop, and Manfred von Richtofen.[123] According to one author, they were "honored as demigods, objects of an unparalleled secular holy cult."[124] The pulps glorified every aspect of the holy cult of flying, including air pioneers, war pilots, model plane enthusiasts, and aspiring pilots. Their diversity of subject matter was clearly a key to success, but the war stories provided the most fertile scenarios for adventure and heroism and played a significant role in marketing efforts. Magazine covers often depicted brightly colored warplanes (see figure 4).

The stories in the pulps were close in tone to those written during the war in that they often focused on adventure and camaraderie rather than the horror of the trenches or the tragic loss of life. In fact, Arthur Empey, who wrote *Over the Top*, was a frequent contributor to many war pulps. Empey created the famous war hero Terence X. O'Leary, who graced the pages of several pulps, including *War Stories, Battle Stories*, and, eventually, *Terence X. O'Leary's War Birds*, which shifted to a science fiction format. O'Leary

FIG. 4. *Sky Aces*, February 1941. Magazine Publishers, Inc., cover artist unknown.

was a stereotypical fighting Irishman who evolved over time from a bumbling fool to a skilled and feared soldier and pilot. O'Leary would be a staple in many different titles and was one of the best-known serial characters in the war pulps. Empey was only one of many ex-servicemen who wrote for the pulps, including ex-officers, and their motivations were varied. One contributor to *War Stories* told readers that he wrote stories "based on all the brave things I would have done in this war if I had just thought of them at the time."[125] Using veterans as storytellers was an astute move, as letters to the editor often commented on how well the writers understood what American veterans had experienced during the war.

In many ways, postwar pulps and the patriotic books published during the war years offered readers something very similar, yet there was a distinct lack of patriotic jingoism in the pulp stories. A soldier from Indiana wrote the editor of *Under Fire* with praise because the authors were realistic about the men they portrayed and did not take themselves too seriously. He argued that, in his experience, "if anyone had tried to make heroic speeches or give vent to patriotic phrases he might have turned into a first rate casualty right on the spot."[126] Soldiers in the stories were constantly complaining and rebelling against the system, not proclaiming loyalty to flag and country, but they still managed the task at hand. They presented an image of the American experience with which many veterans of the American Expeditionary Force could identify.

Stories in the war pulps could be strictly for laughs, nail-biting dramas, or slightly more nuanced stories about life in a war zone. Articles with titles like "Dummy's Cruise De Luxe," "Three Mugs of Beer," and "Ride 'Em Plowboy" kept the tone light, and soldiers also appreciated the liberal use of humor in pulp stories. Humorous stories were relevant to the soldiers' experience because, as one veteran said, "at the most trying moments there was always some dumb-bell who would do something or say something that furnished a laugh and lightened up the situation."[127] Other stories like "Beyond the Last Outpost" and "The Dawn of Death" provided more action. American soldiers engaged with the enemy in a desperate life-or-death struggle of some sort, and the Americans always emerged victorious. Stories could also confront incorrect perceptions of those who stayed on the home front. A short story in *War Stories*, "Men: Pink tea ideas didn't count in that red horror at the front," explored how a charity worker from an American agency slowly recognized that the war was very different from the image presented at home. Sent to convince soldiers of the error of their smoking, drinking, and carousing ways, the naïve worker discovered that smoking, drinking, and carousing were three of the most effective coping mechanisms for dealing with the business of war.[128]

Pulps were primarily an American phenomenon. Although British publishers participated in the pulp craze during the interwar years, British pulps don't appear to have been as popular as pulps were in America. There were two significant British war pulp magazines, *War Stories* and *Air Stories*, both of which were latecomers compared to American war pulps. *Air Stories* was first published in 1935, with a primary focus on World War I aviation. Most of the contributors were former pilots, many of whom flew with the Royal Flying Corps. Arch Whitehouse, British by birth but American by residence, republished several of his American pulp articles under a pseudonym in *Air Stories*. There was little difference in the type of fiction story in both countries, but *Air Stories* also included a regular feature on World War I flying aces and book reviews. *Air Stories* ran for a respectable five years. The British *War Stories* was launched five months after *Air Stories* but was very short lived, running only five issues before folding in 1936.

At the height of their popularity in the late 1920s and early 1930s, a conservative estimate is that at least five hundred thousand copies of war pulp magazines were circulating monthly. The Dell publications (*Sky Riders, War Stories, War Novels, War Birds,* and *Navy/Submarine Stories*) alone were selling over three hundred thousand copies monthly in 1930.[129] *Aces, Air Stories,* and *Wings,* distributed through Fiction House, added at least another one hundred thousand, and possibly two or three times that amount. Figures are not available for all titles, but there were at least a dozen more war pulps that would have had circulations of at least thirty thousand copies monthly at any given time.[130] Magazines selling less than seventy-five thousand copies were considered failures, and one commentator estimated that the average circulation was two hundred thousand copies.[131] Sales were strong, but the magazines' reach was much wider than sales suggested. A survey of vocational school students in Milwaukee, Michigan, in 1932 found *Air Stories* to be the eleventh most popular magazine among young men, a decent showing toward the tail end of that magazine's popularity, but not the most interesting aspect of the study. Interviewers also determined how students acquired the magazine—either through subscription, on the newsstand, or borrowing a copy from a friend. For *Air Stories,* five students reported having a subscription, seventy-nine purchased it on the newsstand, and eighty-eight responded that they borrowed copies from friends, indicating that circulation might be as high as twice that suggested by the circulation numbers issued by the publisher.[132] In fact, pulp publishers estimated that each issue was seen by three readers, greatly expanding its reach. It is likely that over one million readers were exposed to World War I stories in the pulps every month in the late 1920s and early 1930s.[133]

The pulps' circulation was phenomenal when compared with the reach of traditional novels discussed earlier in this chapter. The fascination with pulps might have translated into acts of remembrance in later years had a second war not intervened. Samuel Hynes's *The Soldiers' Tale* explores how the stories of World War I both horrified and intrigued men as they prepared to fight in World War II. The mixed message propagated by books, films, and monuments suggested that "war may be terrible, [but] it is also great, the greatest experience most men will have."[134] As World War II crept into the public consciousness in the late 1930s, it temporarily revived interest in World War I, but stories of the new war would quickly displace it. The boys who were avid students of World War I fought their own war, and their memories, and acts of remembrance, were reserved for their generation.

The pulps were also a poor vector for long-term memory and remembrance for more tangible reasons. First, by nature they were ephemeral. Printed on a low-quality wood-pulp paper to facilitate cheap sales, pulp magazines were considered disposable, and those that were retained disintegrated over time. A contemporary remarked about their longevity, "No library files copies of wood-pulp. Of the millions of words the wood-pulp writer grinds out, of the hundreds of plots he concocts, nothing remains but ephemera, shadows—dead wood-pulp with an old date on the cover."[135] The pulps quickly faded during World War II in the face of paper shortages. When paper was more plentiful again, comic books and paperbacks overshadowed them. Existing copies of war pulps are brittle and too fragile to be read. Pulp enthusiasts have ensured the preservation of many issues, but their enduring appeal seems to be a campy worship of vintage stories and over-the-top graphics, primarily from the science fiction and detective genres.

Pulp fiction influenced the collective memory of significant segments of the population, yet it has been largely ignored in historical and literary analyses of the war. In the past, many scholars marginalized it as a source because pulp writing was considered neither a valid literary pursuit nor a credible barometer of public attitudes because of the class of people it served. Yet, war pulp magazines were the most widely read works of fiction in postwar America and therefore likely had the most, or at least broadest, influence on memory of the war. Pulp war stories of heroism and camaraderie encouraged young Americans to look at the war as a boys' adventure, complete with guns, planes, and high jinks. These stories also allowed older Americans to separate some of the redeeming experiences from the disillusionment and anger that colored the perceptions of many in the immediate postwar years. The pulp version of war was most consistent with that presented by those who considered the war experience redemptive, but by significantly downplaying the violence and focusing extensively on humor, to some extent the pulps are a caricature of that perspective. They present an excessive version of the more nuanced perception of writers like Willa Cather.

Sales figures for the pulps, along with the popularity of similarly themed books by Cather, Tarkington, Canfield, and Springs, suggests that many more Americans imagined the war as an adventure or redemptive experience. The war was not good, but it was not entirely bad either. Many veterans agreed with this premise because the war gave them an opportunity to leave the confines of small-town America and cross the ocean to a different world where wartime definitions of propriety ruled. The war also offered many a chance to prove themselves on a scale unthinkable on the streets of rural America. However, this is not the memory promulgated by Hemingway's *A Farewell to Arms*, the book that emerged from the postwar era with the most potential to shape collective memory because of the esteem accorded it by literary scholars. This book might have dominated American ideas about the war, but it was only half war story, and that half was Italian, and was too complex for many readers to absorb fully.

Ultimately, however, the dichotomous visions of war presented in American fiction reflected the general public's inability to agree about the legacy of World War I as they would about World War II and the Civil War. World War II was a victory over pure evil, and thus easily reconciled as being just and good. The redemption of Civil War memory in the late nineteenth century reconciled the war as both tragic and affirming. The loss was monumental, but the preservation of the Union was vital. Through a creative manipulation of the truth, the North granted the South a nobility of purpose that brought the country back together. The legacy of the Great War, however, remained caught between two poles of thought. It had either wrecked an entire generation of American youth or made them stronger as they passed through its trials. Moreover, a pervasive apathy, demonstrated in part by the relatively weak sales of American war fiction, seems to suggest it was simply easier to forget the war than reconcile the two perspectives. After all, there was no imperative to foster a common memory or myth about the war to reunify the country, and there were no readily evident economic and social consequences brought about from the breech in thought. Forgetting the war was the path of least resistance. Americans were content to agree to disagree about the war and put the whole affair behind them.

4

War Films

Shootin' and Kissin'

World War I fiction was more popular than war histories or memoirs, but the audiences for movies dwarfed the readership for them all. The market for Willa Cather's books was numbered in the thousands, but the market for popular war movies like *The Big Parade* was in the millions. Films had a much greater potential than writing to mold public consciousness about World War I by delivering war stories to Americans whether they were rural or urban, literate or illiterate, rich or poor. Audiences needed only to invest the relatively cheap price of admission and a few leisure hours. Film also has a powerful ability to present a compelling visual narrative that transcends the written word in reach and vibrancy. This is true today and demonstrated by the fact that movies like *Apocalypse Now* and *Saving Private Ryan* influence contemporary memory about Vietnam and World War II much more than any other medium. Director Ingmar Bergman summed up the power of film well, arguing that "No art passes our conscience in the way film does, and goes directly to our feelings, deep down into the dark rooms of our souls."[1]

American movie theaters were the most popular form of entertainment in the 1920s and had grown from being a largely working-class activity to a mainstream leisurely pursuit that attracted all classes. In their study *Middletown*, Helen and Robert Lynd determined that during the peak months of 1923 ticket sales exceeded four times the total population of the town, and admissions at movie theaters rose steadily as the decade progressed.[2] By 1934 it was estimated that more than seventy-five million people were going to the movies weekly in the United States, with only the Bible and the Koran having "an indisputably larger circulation [worldwide] than that of the latest film from Los Angeles."[3] Americans were primarily enthralled by tales of adventure, love stories, westerns, and war stories, all of which were typical movie fare. With World War I, film studios had the opportunity to present the narrative of an adventure, frontier, or love story against the backdrop of a familiar war, one that had personal resonance for many Americans.[4]

The potential for movie theaters to create indelible images of the war, for better or worse, was almost limitless. War movies trickled into theaters beginning in 1914, deluged theaters in 1918, and then, as did war books, fell into a slump immediately after the war. A Hollywood producer noted the change as early as Armistice Day when he overheard a conversation between a group of boys and girls who went to the local movie palace. Upon reading the title of the film on the marquee, one of the girls exclaimed, "Oh! It's a war picture! We're fed up on war—and it's over anyway. Let's go somewhere and see a *real* picture."[5] This attitude proliferated for several years and encouraged screenwriters to steer clear of war films until "the horror of war had faded a little and the color and romance began to appear," which happened in the mid-1920s.[6]

Hollywood studios produced hundreds of popular war films during the interwar period, and, as with my examination of literature, I focus here on those that achieved the greatest potential reach, or the greatest potential to foster a collective memory of the war. Only the highest grossing films remained in distribution for months or even years after their release, gradually increasing visibility further over time. Readers could easily acquire an old edition of most books through used books shops and libraries, but not so with film. Only those films that were popular and thus profitable stayed in circulation. Determining which films were most popular is a much easier task than for books because box office receipts are generally much more accessible than book sales figures.

Of course, because a particular film sold millions of tickets does not necessarily mean that patrons supported its message, but commercial appeal is usually a pretty good indicator that a film resonated with audience perceptions. People look for validation of their own ideas by associating with similar-minded people or reading books and watching movies that reflect their views, and Hollywood generally played into the wants, needs, and opinions of their customer base. This is probably why, as we will see, the message about war in many films was malleable, and audiences could take from the "screen war" what they wished. Those who championed the literary vision of war presented by Willa Cather and Booth Tarkington and those who found the version presented by Ernest Hemingway and John Dos Passos more accurate could still like the same war films. War could be presented as patriotic, adventurous, and tragic all at the same time. Film historian Michael Isenberg argues that war "could be applauded and excoriated at the same time" by viewers of the biggest war movie of the 1920s, *The Big Parade*, and this would be true of many other war films as well.[7]

Producers created, and audiences flocked to, films that often had no clear message about the war, which demonstrates the same apathy about the war and lack of interest in investing it with clear meaning and importance that was seen in the inability to create war histories and the poor sales of war books. Hollywood films also failed to capture the American war, often using foreign armies and generic battles to take advantage of the drama of armed conflict without being bound to the reality of the dough-boys' experience. Even those films that depicted American armies left no distinctive film testimony to the exploits of the marines at Belleau Wood or the army infantry at the Meuse-Argonne, two of the most important battles in which Americans fought. Hollywood used war more as a plot device than as a focal point of the narrative. Film-makers refreshed stale story lines with the excitement and adventure of combat. War scenes allowed producers to bring spectacle to romance, skirt the boundaries of impropriety by portraying the "real" lives of badly behaved soldiers, and add pyrotechnics and aviation feats of wonder to thrill audiences. Some movies studios did this quite successfully, as seven war-related films (listed in table 4) topped box office charts between 1921 and 1941.[8]

Table 4. War-related movies and studio revenues

Film	Year	North American Rentals to Exhibitors
Sergeant York (wb)	1941	$6.1 million
The Four Horsemen of the Apocalypse (Metro)	1921	$4.5 million
The Big Parade (mgm)	1925	$3.5 million
What Price Glory? (Fox)	1926	$2.0 million
Seventh Heaven (Fox)	1927	$1.8 million
All Quiet on the Western Front (Universal)	1930	$1.5 million
The Fighting 69th (wb)	1940	$1.5 million

Source: "Box-Office Hits 1914–1986," in Finler, *Hollywood Story*, 276. Finler grouped films in categories according to year of issue. The groupings for the films shown were 1914–31, 1932–40, and 1941–50. Inflation and population growth likely elevated the numbers for the later films, in comparison to the earliest films. Sales figures are based on North American rentals only.

Sergeant York takes the top spot on the list as a film that benefitted immensely from the war panic that engulfed the United States in late 1941. Warner Brothers released it just months before the Japanese attack on Pearl Harbor, and many argue that Alvin York's World War I exploits were appropriated to encourage military support for a second European war. Its success throws a chronological wrench in what is otherwise a list that charts the most successful war films beginning in 1921 and slowly fading in profitability through 1940. As such this analysis will begin in 1921 with *The Four Horsemen* and address *Sergeant York*'s timely release last.

The Four Horsemen of the Apocalypse

The Four Horsemen of the Apocalypse, by the Spaniard Vincente Blasco Ibáñez, was a wildly popular novel that topped the best-seller charts in 1919. The title refers to the New Testament prophecy that four riders, symbolizing conquest, war, famine, and death, would presage God's final judgment of humanity. It was the story of a Frenchman, Marcelo Desnoyers, who immigrated to South America during the Franco-Prussian War to avoid service in the French army. Desnoyers became a wealthy cattleman in Argentina and, with a German brother-in-law, returned to Europe just before World War I. Desnoyers went to France, and his brother-in-law to Germany. Both had sons who would fight in the war. The story perpetuated stereotypes of militaristic, rigid, and colorless Germans, and artistic, emotional, but brave Frenchmen. Desnoyers's son, Julio, was a carefree artist living off his father's largess, while the German's three sons studied to become a professor and soldiers. The German sons joined the war as single-minded aggressors, and Julio eventually enlisted to impress his lover. Once in uniform, however, Julio conducted himself heroically and won the respect of his father and the nation before dying on the battlefield, having fought righteously on the side of justice.[9]

The book combined the exoticism of adventure in foreign lands, a love story, and the heroics of war, and was phenomenally successful. Its status as a runaway best seller in the months after the war ended is even more impressive because it faced several obstacles to success, including the fact that it was a translation from a foreign language, was over 475 pages long, and sold for the relatively expensive price of $1.90.[10] Americans were historically cool toward translations of foreign works, and Ibáñez was an unknown author. In the end, the story Ibáñez crafted overcame cultural bias, cost, and length, and more than 170 editions were printed by the time the film came out, with over three million copies sold.[11] The book in 1919 and the film in 1921 also overcame a decidedly poor time period for discussion of anything war related.

After the armistice war books were seen as taboo, and producers were wary of war films for the same reasons. A glut of war films saturated the market during the war, including films produced by George Creel's Committee on Public Information (CPI). The CPI's propaganda juggernaut enticed publishers to produce war books and also influenced Hollywood studios through the CPI's Division of Films. The division independently produced patriotic films like *Pershing's Crusaders, America's Answer,* and *Under Four Flags.*[12] The films were distributed like any other feature to movie houses nationwide and did fairly well at the box office.[13] The division also oversaw domestic film production and strong-armed film companies into producing cheerful and wholesome films that would inspire those at home and appropriately represent Americans abroad.[14] With European film companies virtually out of business because of the war, American film companies actively sought new markets in Europe but were forced to seek export licenses from the CPI for each film sent overseas. Creel used this leverage to dictate the terms for film production during the war and censored any films that portrayed the war in a negative light.[15] Between 1914 and 1918 producers released more than three hundred films related to the war, the vast majority of which presented the war as an unfortunate necessity. Moreover, it was also depicted as an endeavor motivated by patriotism and likely to bathe its soldiers in glory.[16] After the war some commentators argued that Americans had had their fill of war movies, propagandistic or otherwise, and would be ready to move on to lighter fare. One industry analyst argued that amateur scenario writers were told, "Don't write stories dealing with the World War! The public doesn't want them."[17] The editors at *Moving Picture World* advised the motion picture industry to "use after-the-war characters . . . avoid harrowing scenes of human destruction . . . carry our thoughts brightly and encouragingly forward."[18]

The owners of Metro Film Company spared no expense in bringing *The Four Horsemen* to the screen. Blockbuster sales in print often translated into strong sales at the box office, and the studios saw this as a sure hit. The director, Rex Ingram, reportedly spent $1 million to complete the film, more than any film made at the time. He claimed to have used more than 12,000 extras, shot 450,000 feet of film (of which only 12,000 feet made the final cut), and built an entire French village using over 100,000 tons of steel, concrete, and lumber.[19] Producers invested much of the money recreating the second Battle of the Marne and in pre-release publicity. Aside from military displays at theaters, the film had unprecedented exposure through the storefront windows of no fewer than seven major retail establishments, including Lord & Taylor, Macy's, and Gimbels. Retailers clearly believed that this film would appeal to a large segment of the population who, perhaps, would be inclined to purchase the book at their stores.[20] Their hunch paid off, as the film was wildly popular with audiences. Opening nights in cities nationwide sold out weeks in advance at ticket prices that were higher than usual, and reviewers were almost unanimous with their praise. The film ranks third in rental revenues of all films produced between 1914 and 1931, behind *Birth of a Nation* and *The Singing Fool*, a part-talkie film with Al Jolson that followed his success with *The Jazz Singer*. It grossed $4.5 million in exhibitor rentals in North America alone and remained popular long after its original release.[21] In 1923 researcher Clarence Perry polled high school students in seventy-six American cities about their favorite films. Two years after the film opened, boys still selected *The Four Horsemen* as their favorite, and girls chose it second only to another movie featuring Rudolph Valentino in the lead, *The Sheik*.[22]

Valentino, who played Julio Desnoyers in the film, is another reason the film has had enduring appeal. The early film historian Terry Ramsaye noted that the film's success was "not, after all, a triumph of a war picture. It was a triumph of a new Don Juan on the screen (Rudolph Valentino), a victory for Latin love and suppressed desire among movie millions."[23] The film is regularly shown at retrospectives of his work, and Valentino's brief career on the screen makes each of his films that much more studied. He rocketed to fame after *The Four Horsemen* premier and quickly appeared in several more films that built up his persona as a mysterious and romantic hero. Women stampeded at his public appearances to get close to him. One scholar contended that "The Box-office horde swallowed *The Four Horsemen and* [*sic*] *the Apocalypse* to get a sex thrill" from proximity to Valentino.[24] His early death only heightened the public's fascination, and his name is still synonymous with magnetic appeal and sexuality.[25]

Because of the perceived ennui with war films, reviewers often downplayed the war angle in *The Four Horsemen*. The film's program encouraged owners to promote the film as the "greatest picture since 'The Birth of a Nation.'" It would leave one "gasping through its marvelous collection of thrills . . . inspire you with its dramatic moments . . . fascinate you with its beautiful romance and its colorful adventure. . . . Adventure, drama, romance, humor, pathos, thrills, suspense, action, sentiment. These are the elements which compose 'The Four Horsemen.'" It was touted as everything *but* a war picture. One reviewer noted that it "cannot be called a war picture. It is more a study in racial traits with adventure, romance and the effects of war used to give it color."[26] Another noted, "There is a certain amount of war in the picture, but not enough to work to its disadvantage."[27]

The producers, however, hedged their bets to include some references to war in their publicity on the chance that there was still a market for the genre. While highbrow literary critics and, by extension, theater critics, might look down their noses at war as a theme for great art, producers seemed optimistic that war films would still appeal to segments of the audience. Promoters publicized the use of war veterans as extras in *The Four Horsemen* and used military equipment to stage a faux artillery bombardment outside Hollywood during the film's premiere.[28] A reviewer for the *Sun* newspaper in New York City argued that "it must be confessed that the first-nighters gave more applause to the militaristic side of the big picture than they did to the symbolic spirit represented by the Four Horsemen of the Apocalypse."[29] In an era of silent movies, war allowed for dramatic settings and pyrotechnics that at least visually represented the sounds of war and thrilled moviegoers.

To the extent that *The Four Horsemen* survives in the public consciousness, it does so because it was a great film based on a popular novel that also featured a heartthrob actor who, tragically, died young. Historians include it in the pantheon of influential silent films, but the war aspect of the film seems to have contributed little to its long tenure in cinematic memory. High school students who listed it as their favorite film also noted that their favorite film genres were western and frontier stories (boys) and love stories (girls), and that is how many saw *The Four Horsemen*, as an adventure/love story.[30] Reviewers downplayed the centrality of the war theme, and few people, scholars or otherwise, would connect the film inextricably with the war. Furthermore, if Americans did connect this top-selling silent film with the war, they would tie it to a European conflict, in much the same way as with Hemingway's novel *A Farewell to Arms* or Remarque's *All Quiet on the Western Front*, because the focus is on foreign armies. The four horsemen were triggered by the offenses of the Germans, which brought France and England into a bloody and otherworldly war. Americans, at best, were witnesses from afar.

The Big Parade

The Big Parade (1925) was the first successful American-focused film about World War I. Valentino may have made female audiences swoon in their recollection of a European war in *The Four Horsemen*, but another screen matinee idol, John Gilbert, made them swoon while remembering an American version of the war. *The Big Parade* marked a resurgence of interest in the war as a film plot, and its genesis traces back to Laurence Stallings's theatrical production of *What Price Glory?*[31] The play was released to acclaim and strong ticket sales in 1924 and was the first indicator that the public was ready for a serious treatment of the war. The success of the play prompted Jesse Lasky, one of the founders of Paramount Pictures, to consider dipping a toe into the war-film waters. He rationalized that the young audiences filling movie theaters were old enough to appreciate a war film, yet young enough to have little firsthand knowledge of the conflict. Lasky sought out a script that was not as serious as *What Price Glory?*, and one that could incorporate a wartime romance between a soldier and a French girl. He signed Stallings to craft a perfect mixture of love and war, something that was neither bitter nor depressing, but still true to the American war experience.[32]

King Vidor, one of the most celebrated directors of the silent-film era, directed the movie. Vidor brought the idea for a war film to Lasky to combat the ephemeral nature of most of the films he had directed before. Movie studios produced films quickly and cheaply that would play a community theater for about a week before the next feature began showing. Vidor wanted to create a film with staying power, one that would reach a wider audience because it was spectacular enough to be held in theaters long enough to enjoy a solid run nationwide.[33] Vidor originally envisioned a film about war, wheat, or steel, but settled on war.[34] His boss, Lasky, thought war was perfect material for a big feature film, as it lent itself well to the use of thrilling effects, dramatic footage, and bold musical interludes.[35]

Vidor's goal was to create a film that was "not overly in favor of war, nor abnormally belligerent against it."[36] He explored the experience of the average American soldier, someone who did not necessarily want to go war but got caught up in the excitement and ended up in France. Once abroad, the soldier reveled in the camaraderie of his fellow soldiers and enjoyed the French wine and women before finding out what war is really all about. Vidor wanted to present the perspective of a lowly foot soldier, someone who had no control over his destiny but had to accept whatever the war dished out.[37] John Gilbert, who portrayed the prototypical American soldier, was a charming romantic lead who tempered the war theme and appealed to both male and female audiences.[38] Reviewers praised his performance, along with that of his female love interest, the

French actress Renée Adorée. An Irish bartender (Bull) and a steelworker (Slim) accompanied Gilbert on his journey and added comedic interest to the film.

The film was a war story, a love story, and a comedy. John Gilbert, as Jim, was from an affluent family but soon falls in with Bull and Slim, demonstrating the great equalizing effect of war. Jim and his newfound friends drink and made the most of life in a foreign land while drilling and preparing to be sent to the front. Jim, though engaged to a woman back home, falls for a French peasant girl, Melisande (played by Adorée), who lives in the town where his unit is billeted. After several amiable scenes that suggest Jim and Melisande's growing affection for one another, Jim's unit is called to the front. Melisande is frantic to see him one last time before he leaves and catches up with him as the soldiers were being driven to the front. In one of the most memorable scenes of the movie, she runs up and grabs Jim's leg, hugging it closely as the truck pulls out. Once they are separated, Jim throws her a boot as a final memento. Jim, Bull, and Slim receive a baptism by fire at the front and endure a withering barrage of artillery as they advance through the woods. By the closing scene, Bull and Slim are both dead, and Jim is seriously wounded in the leg. At the height of the battle sequence, Jim shoots a German soldier, and both end up in the same shell hole. Jim is about to seal the German's fate with a bayonet when he is overcome with the realization that the enemy is no different from him, both are stuck in a dreadful war. Instead of killing him, he tries to comfort the German soldier by offering a last cigarette.

Did Vidor convey that war was folly because of the senseless deaths of Bull and Slim and Jim's experience in the shell hole with the enemy? Although the main character balks at killing a German soldier at point-blank range and comes out of the war as an amputee, it is difficult to label this film antiwar.[39] Jim realized the true nature of war while fighting in the French woods, but he may not have regretted the experience. After all, he had experienced a new and exciting world, demonstrated his fighting prowess, and found Melisande. In this respect, the story is much like that of Claude Wheeler in Willa Cather's novel *One of Ours*. Claude suffers a worse fate in the war but finds redemption in the end. Jim returns home a wounded hero having earned the undying respect of his once disapproving father. He also finds that his girl at home had taken up with his brother, but this allows him to return to France to be with Melisande, ending the film with great optimism about his future. The camaraderie between men of diverse backgrounds, Jim's newfound confidence, the respect he earned from others, and the promise of a life with the right woman may have been acceptable trade-offs for the indignities of war. Michael Isenberg argues that it is Jim's success that takes the focus away from the relatively muted antiwar aspects of the film. He notes, "As long as individuals stood apart from the mass and were made *special* through devices of romance or action, the cinema could never come to grips with the nature of twentieth-century warfare."[40]

Vidor certainly had not set out on a mission to convert Americans to pacifism. He set out to make a film that would have longevity at the box office, and war had seemed a strong vehicle for the sweeping drama he hoped to create. His partner, Stallings, had written pacifist themes into his book *Plumes* and the screenplay for *What Price Glory?*, but *The Big Parade* was much more ambiguous. Vidor worked diligently on the war scenes to ensure accuracy and demonstrate an appropriate tone, creating what he called "a bloody ballet, a ballet of death," but he had no overt intention of making a political statement about the war.[41] What viewers took away from the movie seemed to depend on where they sat. Veterans were largely supportive of Vidor's effort. One called the movie "a war film. . . . And when I say 'war' I do not mean a sham battle in the suburbs of Peekskill either." The war scenes "were so obviously true that if you forgot for an instant you were only looking at a picture you caught your breath and wondered how [they] did it."[42] The United States Army loved it. Walsh told a reporter that the marines "had more recruits after that picture than they'd had since World War I. It showed the boys having fun, getting broads. Young fellers saw it, they said 'Jesus the Army [*sic*] is great.'"[43] Audiences might also have been so enamored with Gilbert's smoldering looks and Adorée's French charm that they may not have seen the war as anything more than a vehicle through which Vidor connected the two lovers.

The film succeeded beyond anyone's expectations, including Vidor's. A veteran wrote that "Soldiers themselves, though feeling forgotten, had almost begun to put the war beyond remembrance when 'The Big Parade' came marching along and drew those who beheld it back into the swinging stride of that man's old army again."[44] Reviewers heaped accolades on the film, calling it the best film of 1925, and it would ultimately be one of the most successful silent films ever produced. Opening week sales were phenomenal, and box offices could not fulfill the demand for advance ticket sales. The Astor Theatre in New York City reported ticket holders standing "six deep" to see the show its first weekend.[45] In 1925 most films ran for a week or so, but *The Big Parade* ran for an astonishing two years at the Astor Theatre in New York City and six months at Grauman's Egyptian Theatre in Hollywood. Within a few years it grossed $15 million, which would equate to almost $175 million today (the film only cost $245,000 to produce), and it quickly ranked among the top-five-grossing films ever.[46] Its long run and box office success meant that a significant segment of the American population saw this film, but it was unclear if the movie left viewers with an impression of the war that was pacifist or patriotic.

The film was successful in Europe as well. Some reports indicated that the British were insulted by the fact that it "overplay[ed] America's part in the war," but others reported unqualified British enthusiasm for the movie.[47] The French seemed to be enamored with the film, and French veterans praised its accurate presentation of battle.[48] Germans also seemed to embrace the film. German reviewers believed that it should be required viewing for mothers, wives, and sisters because it "destroys once and for all the heroic legend of the war; it shows war in its real repulsiveness and inhumanity and from pure sentiment calls upon men to cease butchering each other."[49]

The success of *The Big Parade* paved the way for many war features. By 1927 there were nineteen war films on the screen or in some stage of production.[50] The next big war movie hit was *What Price Glory?*, based on the play of the same name that debuted in 1924. Critics championed it as one of the best plays of 1924 and the most realistic portrayal of the war to date. Literary critic Heywood Broun called it "the best use which the theatre has yet made of the war, and it is entirely possible that it is the best American play about anything."[51] The film would meet with equal acclaim.

What Price Glory?

Stallings played a key role in bringing *What Price Glory?* to the screen, just as he had *The Big Parade*. His close involvement in the production of both films, and the fact that one came so quickly on the heels of the other, led some to believe that the second film might be a stale rehashing of Vidor's smash success. There were inevitably many comparisons of the two films, but some critics believed that *What*

Price Glory? emerged as a more authentic picture of war, not because it was pronouncedly more antiwar or included more graphic detail of life on the battlefield, but because it was a much less sanitized depiction of American soldiers.

The original theatrical production followed two hard-boiled marines on their military adventures in a blunt and uncensored manner, and critics championed it for its realist approach to soldiers and war. Captain Flagg and Sergeant Quirt, the two lead characters, had an ongoing rivalry over the women they encountered on the job, first in Shanghai, then the Philippines, and finally on the western front in France during World War I. Charmaine, the beguiling daughter of the local tavern owner, Cognac Jack, was the object of their affection in France. The quarrelling and maneuvering necessary to win Charmaine was the comedic relief that dominated much of the movie. Drinking and womanizing were the soldiers' release from the wickedness of war, which interrupted the comedy only twice. Each battle sequence demonstrated the violence and destruction wrought by war, the unpredictable nature of death on the battlefield, and the resolve of the marines to see things through. War was not glory, and men were not fighting for democracy, or any other high-handed ideal, but for each other. Soldiers were not mannered and stoic, they were men freed of the constraints of society by a war they were forced to fight, and they drank, caroused, joked, and brawled with each other to pass the time between battles.

The film's director, Raoul Walsh, faced a tremendous challenge in translating the riveting and controversial dialogue from the play to a silent film format. If the blunt language used by Flagg and Quirt was the key to theatrical success, the mute version on the screen might fail in translation. Walsh recognized that simply using the same dialogue on title screens would never work. It was one thing to utter soldierly profanity on the stage, quite another to spell it out on the big screen, when those of all ages would be in attendance. Walsh kept some of the authenticity of the stage dialogue by maintaining it in the script, and viewers quickly learned to pick out the more salacious bits by lip-reading. Walsh recalled that when the two lead actors, Victor McLaglen (Captain Flagg) and Edmund Lowe (Sergeant Quirt), were "talking to one another, they'd say 'You dirty son-of-a-bitch, you lousy bastard, you prick' and then, of course, we'd put on the title: 'I don't want nothing more to do with you. You're not a pal of mine.'"[52] Fan magazines tipped off many moviegoers to this aspect of the film, and they studiously began trying to read lips in order to partake in the more scandalous aspects of the film.[53]

The film featured the war prominently on only two occasions, when Quirt and Flagg went to the front for battle. The end of the film has them marching to the front yet again, while a title card displays these words from Charmaine, "They came back once—they came back twice—but they will not come back again."[54] Viewers might have assumed that Quirt and Flagg would meet their fate during their third tour at the front, but their death is only vaguely implied, and the film's many sequels proves that they are very much alive at the close of the war. In fact, their survival is a significant reason that many critics believed the movie glorified war.

The film critic for the *National Board of Review Magazine* believed that *The Big Parade* was a better cinematic use of war than *What Price Glory?* because death came to significant characters in the film. Slim and Bull endeared themselves to viewers during the first half of the movie before both are killed in the battle sequence. Viewers' sympathy for the characters kept their attention throughout the film without the battle scenes "being mere News reel [*sic*] inserts."[55] The argument could also be made that, because it made death personal, *The Big Parade* was a more realistic war movie. *What Price Glory?* laid bare the profane speech and vulgar actions of soldiers at war, but it was less effective at displaying the costs of war. The battle scenes were momentary distractions from the comedic conflict between Quirt and Flagg. The film contained fairly accurate, if superficial, portrayals of the front, but that the true price of glory was not paid by a main character limited the impact of these scenes. A soldier known as the "mother's boy," a frail and artistic young man who fights along with Quirt and Flagg, was killed in action, but his story was a minor subplot to the film.

Regardless of the message, the production of *What Price Glory?* on the heels of *The Big Parade* showed that Hollywood believed that the war genre had a great deal of mileage left with the general public.[56] Fox movie studio executives paid $100,000 for the film rights, reportedly the highest price paid for rights at the time, and their investment paid off handsomely. The film grossed $780,000 in four weeks at New York's Roxy Theatre, breaking a record by bringing in $160,000 at the box office in the first seven days.[57] Ticket sales exceeded 20,000 per day, and often approached or exceeded 25,000, in nineteen out of the first twenty days.[58] It was a smash success for up-and-coming filmmaker Raoul Walsh, and the *New York Times* ranked it third of the ten best films of 1924.[59]

The film did so well that Fox created one of the first successful movie franchises, producing at least three additional films based on the high jinks of Quirt and Flagg. *The Cock-Eyed World* (1929), *Women of All Nations* (1931), and *Hot Pepper* (1933) followed the two marines to different locations on the globe as they caroused and fought over women of all nationalities.[60] All three were military movies, at best, but certainly not war movies. They were vulgar, slapstick comedies about marines engaged in a different kind of "action," but all performed well with audiences, particularly *The Cock-Eyed World,* which raked in over $2.7 million in rental revenue, $700,000 more than *What Price Glory?*[61] One reviewer called it a "low comedy, of the rough variety."[62]

The continued use of military imagery in the sequels to *What Price Glory?* suggests that war films might have been popular for reasons having nothing to do with actual war. Maybe it was the action-adventure aspect of war films, combined with the mystique of a soldier's life lived outside the normal constraints of society, that packed theaters. Many critics agreed with this premise. They argued that war films were unable to adequately portray war or promote pacifism because, no matter how graphic the violence or strident the antiwar message, audiences were drawn to the thrilling battle scenes, love stories, and bawdy lives of soldiers more than the underlying story of a particular war. One young moviegoer said that what he desired most at the movies was, "shootin' and kissin'."[63] Film was not likely to be the vehicle by which audiences would remember the story of Americans at war, but rather war was the vehicle by which Hollywood made blockbusters.

Seventh Heaven

The war-film boom continued in 1927 with a third silent feature, *Seventh Heaven,* a film in which war is central to the plot, but the battlefield only appears in a few brief scenes. The film was based on a well-reviewed 1922 romance fantasy play that viewed the war through the eyes of a young French couple. It was the fairy-tale story of a girl, Diane, beaten regularly by her wicked sister, rescued from her tragic life by a sewer worker, Chico. Chico reluctantly intervenes as Diane's sister viciously beats her on the street and takes her to the safety of his home on the seventh, and top, floor of an apartment with a beautiful view of the Eiffel Tower. Their cohabitation was to be temporary, but they are forced to recognize their love for one another when Chico is called to fight in the war, resulting in their hurried marriage before he leaves.[64] The play ran for three solid seasons on Broadway, with over seven hundred sold-out performances.[65]

The movie follows the same plot as the play and, and as the title suggests, is suffused with references to religion. When Chico meets Diane, he is an avowed atheist because God has never responded to his prayers to find a good job and a wife. His faith is restored when both a job and Diane come into his life, making it clear that God is indeed watching over him. Upon Chico's departure for the front, he and Diane make a pact to think about one another at eleven o'clock each day, thereby facilitating a sort of spiritual connection while they are apart. Each day both faithfully engage in the ritual, Chico from the trenches and Diane from the munitions factory where she works. At the close of the war, Diane gets word that Chico has died in battle, but she refuses to believe it. Clutching the religious medals that Chico gave her before he left, Diane insists that Chico is still alive. The closing scenes depict an injured, dirty, and tired Chico painstakingly making his way through jubilant post-armistice crowds back to Diane. God protected Chico, as well as the people of France, during the war and rewarded Chico and Diane's faith by reuniting them in the end.

An advertisement for the film depicts a ghost-like Chico returning to Diane, clad in her wedding dress, but makes no mention of the war at all, calling the film a "drama of spiritual awakening through love and courage." The war scenes are pivotal to the plot, but the film is not a statement about war, it is an exploration of romantic love, a theme that director Frank Borzage used to great effect in almost all his films.[66] According to one reviewer, the battle scenes are almost de rigueur in war films, as they provide a "spectacular punch," but, in this case, he believes the "mental appeal" of the film far outweighs the spectacle of war. By this he means the love story of Chico and Diane, not a thoughtful understanding of war.[67] Its success as a play in 1922, a time when talk of the war was largely frowned upon, also suggests that people were drawn more to the story of Chico and Diane than the story about war.

The few battle scenes extol the valor of the French more than the violence and uselessness of war. These scenes demonstrate the patriotism of the men who went from the sewers to the front lines as gallant heroes of France. One of the most discussed segments of the film portrays the caravan of taxicabs, buses, and cars that shuttled men to the pivotal Battle of the Marne, and producers were not shy about associating the movie with war. They secured an authentic French cab used during the war, "Eloise," that traveled to theaters across the country to garner publicity. The cab was accompanied by a French lieutenant from the Eighth Chasseurs.[68] The producers also capitalized on the fact that some scenes were filmed in France and the actors wore military uniforms secured from the French government. The studio seemed to take advantage of every angle, touting the film as a realistic war drama and a love story at the same time. By 1927, after the success of both *The Big Parade* and *What Price Glory?*, war films were gold at the box office, and love stories were perennial favorites as well. *Seventh Heaven* brought the war to the American public, but like many novels, presented the war from the perspective of foreigners, in this case, a French couple, which only lent credence to an American attitude that saw the war as a European phenomenon and added little to the public consciousness of the American experience at war.

Just a year or two after its release, *Seventh Heaven* and other silent films about the war were effectively made obsolete as vectors of memory, to some extent, by the advent of sound technology. Although sound was considered a wild experiment at the time, one that might have disappeared as quickly as it emerged, it quickly became the standard format for feature films. Many movies that came out in the mid-1920s were remade with the new technology, but the films discussed here were not among them. As such, their appeal to film audiences waned in the face of a much more complex theater experience. Their format stunted their potential for continued re-release in collaboration with other war films, on Armistice Day, or in conjunction with significant anniversaries. As such, their ability to influence memory beyond their original audiences was curtailed as well. Silent films about war would not be competitive with war films that took advantage of sound to bring the cacophony of an artillery bombardment to life. *All Quiet on the Western Front* would be the first successful war film to use the new technology.

All Quiet on the Western Front

By 1930, when *All Quiet on the Western Front* was released, sound films dominated the market, and director Lewis Milestone used sound to great effect in translating the horrors of war for audiences. Ironically, it was a carefully crafted story of the experience of the enemy that would emerge as the most iconic celluloid representation of the war for many British and American veterans. The film built on the tremendous success of Erich Maria Remarque's 1929 book of the same name. Within the first ten days of publication in Germany, the book sold seventy-two thousand copies, more than many other war books sold in years. The book had a strong reception in the United States, with sixty-four American newspapers carrying serializations of the novel.[69] The book captured the mood of many soldiers who were happy to see their growing dissatisfaction with war so perfectly contained in Remarque's prose. Veterans and youth were likely the strongest audiences for the book, the first group to revisit the war in a cathartic exercise, the second to find out more about a conflict about which many fathers were often silent.[70] Historian Modris Eksteins argues that the book's popularity was also fostered by the economic depression in the1930s. He suggests, "The novel became enormously successful not because it was an accurate expression of the frontline soldier's experience, but because it was a passionate evocation of current public feeling, not so much even about the war as about existence in general in 1929. It was a poignant cry of 'help' on behalf of a distraught generation."[71] Just as Paul Baumer was caught, helpless, in a war waged by others, millions were struggling to survive during an economic crisis beyond their control.

The film closely follows the storyline of the book. In both, a group of German classmates get caught up in the martial spirit and enlist as young lions ready to fight for the fatherland. Once in the trenches it quickly becomes clear that the rewards of war have been vastly oversold. When Baumer goes on leave and visits his old classroom, he shares his newfound insight into war, telling students, "It's dirty and painful to die for your country. When it comes to dying for your country, it's better not to die at all. There are millions out there dying for their country, and what good is it?" The movie portrays war as bleakly as possible, with no heroes, or significant subplots, no romances or rivalries that distract from the dirty business of war. The film used new sound technology to demonstrate the horror of perpetual barrages of artillery raining down over a dugout filled with young German soldiers. The specter of death hovers over each man every minute of the day and the mental anguish causes many to break under the strain.

The film's use of American actors as German soldiers helped soften the public's image of the enemy and made them more sympathetic. Baumer and his fellow classmates, although technically the enemy, became human, and the many deaths that happen during the course of the film were meaningful to the viewer. Until *All Quiet on the Western Front*, with the exception of Julio Desnoyers in *The Four Horsemen of the Apocalypse*, the lead characters in popular war films emerged from the war alive. The deaths of each of the main characters in *All Quiet on the Western Front*, one by one, until none were left standing, was a stark departure from previous versions of the war on the screen. The last scene, in particular, brought home the wrenching realities of war. A sniper kills Paul Baumer, the last remaining student from the original group of enlistees, as he reaches out to grasp a butterfly fluttering on weeds in front of the trench parapet (a scene that is not in the book). A cautious and fragile symbol of hope for the future was instead a portent of death, reinforcing the ideas presented throughout the film.

The film was not only a box office success, but many reviewers called it the best war film ever made, and many still believe that to be true.[72] *Harrison's Reports* called it "a picture that will live forever."[73] *Time* lauded the courage required to make such a risky film, since "from such materials the popular cinema is rarely drawn," and called it "a freak, almost a monstrosity among pictures."[74] In fact, the content weighed heavily against the film ever even being produced. It was a grim story with little redeeming entertainment value—no pretty girls and no swashbuckling heroes.[75] There were some humorous scenes sprinkled throughout, but it was certainly not a comedy.

While *All Quiet on the Western Front* was almost universally praised as a pacifist film, one leftist commentator believed that it was not substantially different in tone from the films that had come before. He grouped *All Quiet* with films like *The Big Parade*, arguing that "by their nostalgic tone, their uncritical, non-incisive pacifism, their placing blame on the lesser individual and the stay at home, their sympathy with the protagonist, their excitement, their comic interludes, make war interesting."[76] These claims may be more difficult to levy against *All Quiet*, as it attempted to avoid all the pitfalls of previous movies in glamorizing war, but there is still some validity to the critic's point. Other critics made the same point when debating the usefulness of any film as propaganda for pacifism. Regardless of the antiwar statement that a director intends to make, presenting war on film always involves entertainment, and, as such, the worst of war, including the shattered limbs, festering wounds, and the pestilence of rats and lice, was always watered down by Hollywood. To the extent that the wounds endured by the German soldiers appeared relatively bloodless and clean in *All Quiet on the Western Front*, the film does shy away from true war. The British writer John Galsworthy noted that the "reproduction of one-millionth part of the horror and misery which every day of the war brought would be enough to insure the utter failure of any of these films."[77]

Ultimately, the film won Academy Awards for Best Picture and Best Director, as well as the *Photoplay Magazine* Gold Medal.[78] The English and French joined with Americans in embracing the film, but other countries were less impressed and censored or banned it outright, including Germany, Italy, Austria, New Zealand, and Australia. Universal released the film in Berlin even though opposition forces led by the Nazi Party had indicated their strenuous objection. Protestors interrupted the movie's premier with mice, stink bombs, and sneezing powder, creating chaos and riots outside the theater. The film was banned by the German Supreme Film Censorship board just days later.[79] The strident antiwar tone of the film did not concern American officials because the whole mess could be written off as uniquely German. As one film historian astutely noted, "American moviemakers were having their cake and eating it too. They were able to condemn war without involving either the war aims or the war conduct of the United States."[80] Of course, the film's European and, worse yet, German focus makes it just one more successful film about the war that marginalized, or ignored, the American role. The film did little to instill a collective memory of the war because, while some American soldiers may have felt that their experiences were well represented by the film, those who had not experienced the war saw a disorganized, militaristic German army, an army that bore little resemblance to their perceptions of American forces, or the war they envisioned. American audiences might witness the downward spiral of morale in the German army and lament the horrors of "that European war," but they were not prepared to embrace a similar story as part of their own history.

With the exception of *Cavalcade,* a 1933 film that covered a span of thirty years, including World War I, a decade would pass between *All Quiet on the Western Front* and the next blockbuster war film. To a certain extent this gap can be attributed to a desire to block out the harshness of the world during the 1930s as the stock market crash had made life precarious for so many across the globe. Filmmakers were more apt to use the peacetime military as the backdrop for films to make people laugh, as was the case with the many sequels to *What Price Glory?* that appeared in the 1930s.[81]

The War in the Sky

Military aviation films also grew in popularity between the late 1920s and 1930s, and these films deserve special attention before we move on to the last two of the seven box office hits, produced in 1940 and 1941. Charles Lindbergh spawned an American fascination with the skies after his famous transatlantic flight in 1927. Audiences enthusiastically greeted several air war films that premiered in 1927 and 1928, including *Wings, Hell's Angels,* and *Dawn Patrol.* These films capitalized on the public craze for flying in much the same way that pulp magazines did. A second spurt of aviation war films between 1930 and 1933 took full advantage of the advent of movie sound.

The aviation genre of war film dawned in 1927 with the release of director William Wellman's *Wings. Wings* was the first, and arguably most popular, of twenty-six aviation war films Hollywood producers released between 1927 and 1938. Wellman, a veteran of the Lafayette Escadrille and the United States Army Air Division, presented the story of the air war in Europe with the addition of a romantic triangle involving 1920s "It" girl Clara Bow and two male leads.[82] The United States Army sanctioned the film and supplied a five-acre battlefield re-creation, tanks, and over five thousand soldiers as extras.[83] The film traced the lives of two American pilots from flight training school to combat against "The Flying Circus of Captain Kellerman," the fictional version of Manfred von Richthofen's Flying Circus. An unknown Gary Cooper played a pilot who dies on his first solo flight, a level of realism in the film that was championed by critics and veterans alike. The premiere of *Wings* in New York City was a runaway sellout, breaking all previous records for advance sales.[84] Moviegoers raved about the thrilling air sequences, and the film remained in theaters for over a year in New York and six months in Los Angeles.[85] It ultimately won the first Academy Award for Best Picture in 1928.

The success of *Wings* spawned many imitators, including Howard Hughes's epic *Hell's Angels,* released in 1930. The film gained a great deal of visibility because of Hughes's larger-than-life personality and its reported $4 million price tag.[86] The controversy surrounding the film and its maverick director seemed to overshadow its incredibly strident message about war. The film contained many of the same elements that helped make most war movies commercially viable (romances, tough guys, hard-drinking soldiers, and thrilling action sequences) but also had one of the most gut-wrenching scenes from any war narrative except for Humphrey Cobb's *Paths of Glory*. Cobb's novel illuminated the complete senselessness of war by highlighting the execution of three innocent soldiers as an example of military discipline. *Hell's Angels* involved the execution of one of two brother pilots caught behind enemy lines. Their German captors offer them a reprieve from a death sentence as spies if they were to divulge information about a pending British attack. One brother kills the other to stop him from accepting the deal, leaving the viewer to ponder the mental anguish caused by war, even long after the closing credits.

The Dawn Patrol was one of the few war movies that eschewed a central romance and in doing so likely failed to entice some audiences. Many critics lauded the picture, however, for sticking to a more thorough interpretation of the true war experience, without the advantage of a beautiful woman and an uplifting storyline to draw in crowds. *The Dawn Patrol* first came out in 1930 as a silent feature and was remade in 1938 using sound with David Niven and Errol Flynn. Neither the first nor the second version had a single female character, and both limited the action to just a handful of sets. The films had an unswerving focus on the flyers and their experiences serving under an unseen and unrelenting group of officers who send one crew after another out to their deaths in the sky. Many championed its realism, but the film presented many of the same contradictory images of war as previous war movies. Was the film denouncing the brutality of war, or glorifying its heroes?

It was ultimately a little bit of both. Pilots were individuals in a war made up of faceless armies, and their exploits were ripe for Hollywood because they provided hero figures. Some reviewers praised *The Dawn Patrol* along with *The Eagle and the Hawk*, another aviation war film starring a young Cary Grant, as being pacifist in orientation because both films focused primarily on the war, and both leading men sacrificed themselves to save a friend. In that way, the films highlight the senseless death brought about by war, but film historian Michael Isenberg notes that this is a perverse view of true pacifism, which "would find neither virtue in duty nor glory in honor."[87]

The aviation war-film genre had a devoted following, much like aviation pulp fiction. However, unlike pulp fiction, the messages conveyed by these films were less straightforward in articulating a common memory of war. Moreover, like other war films, they often explored the war from the perspective of foreigners. *The Dawn Patrol* was about British pilots, as was *Hell's Angels*. *Wings* was a hybrid of a love story and a war story, a commercial success largely because of its groundbreaking visual effects, portrayal of pilots, and a popular leading lady, not because it was about war. Film historians count these movies amongst the best films of their era, but none is inextricably linked to the American war experience. The genre is notable because it had great endurance through the 1930s, a time in which successful movies about the ground war were scarce.

While there were few successful war movies outside of the air war genre in the 1930s, several films emerged in 1932 and 1933 that referenced the plight of veterans. The Bonus Army inspired three of these films, *Gold Diggers of 1933* (1933), *Gabriel Over the White House* (1933), and *Heroes for Sale* (1933). The Bonus Army was a group of disgruntled veterans, over forty thousand strong, who converged on Washington DC in the summer of 1932 to demand payment of a bonus promised to them eight years earlier (the bonus was not to be paid out until 1945). During the height of the Depression the Bonus Army camped near the Capitol to persuade congressmen to make the payments ahead of schedule. The camp was ultimately dispersed at gunpoint by U.S. military troops under the command of Gen. Douglas MacArthur. The bonus was eventually paid early, but not until 1936.[88]

Gold Diggers of 1933 was a movie about chorus girls and rich men, not war, but its last scene featured a musical number to the song "Forgotten Man" about the neglected veterans of the war. Soldiers in uniform marching in parade transformed into shabbily dressed veterans marching in a breadline as one of the lead chorus girls, the actress Joan Blondell, sang dolefully about their plight.[89] The director had reserved the finale, and biggest production number, for World War I veterans, and he explained it to the chorus girls as the "Big Parade of Tears."[90]

In *Gabriel Over the White House,* the newly elected president dismisses Congress and his cabinet when they fail to agree to a plan to get the country out of the Depression. After having established, essentially, a dictatorship, President Hammond addresses the plight of thousands of poverty-stricken men marching on Washington DC by ordering the military to set up a jobs program.[91] The plot garnered the attention of the Motion Picture Producers and Distributors of America (MPPDA), which imposed a production code for the film industry that became effective in 1930.[92] The code usually targeted sexual content, but in this case the MPPDA was particularly concerned with the fascistic overtones of the film and made some changes to the script before it was approved.[93] No independent body or agency centrally enforced censorship in the 1920s, but state and local review boards had influenced content before the advent of the Hays Code. Prior to the code being implemented, the industry attempted to police itself by creating lists of particularly troublesome topics to avoid. The first list crafted by the National Association of the Motion Picture Industry proscribed sex, nudity, crime, gambling, gratuitous violence, and ridicule of public officials and governmental authority as particularly apt to draw the attention of censors.[94] Reformers included these same categories in the Production Code instituted in 1930, along with proscriptions on topics related to "National Feelings."[95] Presumably, the restrictions on abrogating national feelings and ridicule of government officials and authority might have influenced the production of some war movies. However, there is little evidence indicating that censorship played an important role in dictating the content of war films. Furthermore, many of the most significant war films were produced before 1930, when censorship became more oppressive. By the late 1930s a different sort of influence would come to bear from war hawks and isolationists seeking to influence the movie-going public.

The Fighting 69th and Sergeant York

Warner Brothers released *The Fighting 69th* in 1940 to a different world than that which had received the antiwar *All Quiet on the Western Front* enthusiastically. Hitler had already invaded Poland, prompting declarations of war by France and Great Britain. Pacifists, isolationists, war hawks, and those who wanted to come to the aid of the Allies were already attempting to influence American involvement in the war. Henry and Jack Warner at Warner Brothers were outspoken opponents of the Nazis and the Fascists, and this probably influenced their move to secure the rights to *The Fighting 69th*. The film tells the World War I story of a real-life New York regiment that first gained acclaim during the Civil War. The primarily Irish regiment included the poet Joyce Kilmer in its ranks, as well as a Catholic priest,

Father Duffy, who gained fame for his devotion to the regiment, even following his men to the trenches. "Wild Bill" Donovan, an officer of the regiment, went on to become a confidant of Franklin Roosevelt and the director of the Office of Strategic Services during World War II. In the film, the real-life stories of Duffy, Kilmer, and Donovan are supplemented by the fictional character Jerry Plunkett, an arrogant kid from Brooklyn played by James Cagney, who picks fights with men in the regiment but cowers in the face of the enemy. Plunkett gets in trouble at every turn, even with the affable Father Duffy trying to guide him. Plunkett's escapades turn tragic when he causes the deaths of several soldiers. A military court finds him guilty of cowardice and sentences him to execution, but before he faces the firing squad, an artillery bombardment of the jail allows him to escape. With the inspirational words of Father Duffy ringing in his ears, he repents his earlier actions and charges the front lines to save men from his regiment who have been pinned down by machine-gun fire. After the dramatic rescue, Plunkett succumbs to his own wounds. Like Claude Wheeler in *One of Ours*, Plunkett finds redemption on the battlefields of France.

Many critics praised *The Fighting 69th* as a realistic film about war because of the brutality it depicted, but there was actually little truth presented. Early in the creative process producers had strayed from the film's original focus on Father Duffy to Plunkett, perhaps because of Cagney's appeal to American audiences. So the film did not document the experiences of the real men of the 69th, but co-opted an inspirational character, Father Duffy, in crafting a story about one man's redemption. Instead of capitalizing on the intriguing tales of some of the larger-than-life members of the regiment, and using the opportunity to represent the experiences of the American Expeditionary Force, the film crafted an alternate reality of the war, one that focused on the failings and heroics of a fictional man. Very little of the actual experiences of the regiment were presented to audiences. They fought "somewhere in France," like other fictional regiments, although they were really at the deadly battle of the Meuse-Argonne, and there was little to distinguish their war from that of any other nation's experience.

As with other popular war films, critics differed in their analysis of what type of propaganda was put forth by *The Fighting 69th.* Some suggested that the war scenes were sufficiently graphic and horrifying as to promote pacifism and discourage thoughts of American intervention. However, the film's appeals to patriotism, heroism, and loyalty, combined with a closing scene that shows victorious and proud soldiers marching in a New York City parade, seemed to argue the opposite. The film also suggested that intervention in the war might have had a heavenly sanction. Father Duffy offered his men inspirational speeches about fulfilling their duty to God and country.

It is also clear that *The Fighting 69th*, at least on some level, played into a growing interest in Americanism and appeals to patriotism. By 1939, chorus singers appeared against the backdrop of a waving flag on the screen and serenaded audiences with "The Star-Spangled Banner" before and after feature presentations.[96] The producers also arranged for many tie-ins with the military when promoting the film. They encouraged local exhibitors to arrange for radio interviews of local World War I heroes, plastered theater lobbies with war pictures clipped from twenty-two-year-old newspapers, and staged announcements with members of the Veterans of Foreign Wars and American Legion.[97] It would take a second world war to encourage remembrance of the first.

To generate publicity for the film, Warner Brothers organized 365 simultaneous openings on the same night as Rainbow Division dinners around the country. The 69th was part of the Rainbow Division.[98] This close association between veterans groups and the military suggests that the film's patriotic and glory-filled scenes outweighed those that conveyed war as fruitless, but studio head Jack Warner proclaimed that it "carries the strongest plea to keep America out of the war."[99] Warner's anti-Nazi stance was clearly in place by 1940, but he maintained neutrality because of the need to have access to the international market.[100] The film was produced at a time of great ambivalence about the new war in Europe and was caught up in the transition from isolationism to intervention.[101] Like many Americans, Jack Warner's public stance as an isolationist would be short lived.

By 1941, when *Sergeant York* was released, there was little pretense to neutrality. Alvin York, the title character, underwent a conversion from pacifist to fighter and made a powerful statement about humanity's obligation to fight evil. Warner Brothers released the film in 1941, just before Pearl Harbor, and it was quickly caught in the crossfire between isolationist and prowar factions. Isolationists argued that Hollywood stoked the fires of war by putting out films that seemed to play to Americans' sense of patriotism and promote the idea of German duplicity. Films like the *Fighting 69th, Convoy, Flight Command*, and *I Married a Nazi*, all of which premiered in 1940, were part of a propaganda campaign propelling America toward war. Pacifists considered *Sergeant York* another propaganda film with the same goal.

Producers and literary agents had deluged the Medal of Honor winner with offers to tell his story since he stepped off the boat from France, but York had always demurred by pointing out that his uniform was not for sale. He finally agreed to participate in writing his life story in order to help his fellow Tennesseans with the many philanthropic educational endeavors he promoted throughout his life, but

Hollywood movies were far too commercial an exploit for the God-fearing and humble veteran—even if the money might help others. At least that was true until 1940, when York relented. His financial situation had always been precarious because of his generosity, but it had deteriorated further and his latest project to create a fundamentalist Bible school was floundering.[102] A persistent Hollywood studio executive, financial troubles, and appeals to patriotism were the persuasive trifecta that prompted York's reversal on seeing his name in lights.

Promoter Jesse Lasky, who had worked on *Wings*, appealed to York's sense of pride as an American, provided him a lucrative contract, and promised to get Gary Cooper to play the lead.[103] Warner Brothers also gave him a great deal of control over other casting and the script to secure his participation.[104] Relinquishing control to this extent was atypical in Hollywood, but the studio was motivated by more than profit to produce York's story. The brothers Warner were becoming more active proponents of American intervention. Their Jewish parents had fled Poland during a pogrom in 1883, and there was never any doubt where their sympathies lay. Much of Hollywood may have shared their views, but few other studios were as overt, particularly since many Americans remained staunchly isolationist.[105]

The resulting screenplay was based on York's earlier biography, and written in collaboration with Tom Skeyhill. Originally the script focused more on York's life after the war. The film was to convey that the war was a turning point in York's life that led him on the path of trying to enrich the educational opportunities of those in Tennessee. The original screenplay had a scene where York visited the Louvre with a fellow soldier from the North, which was the beginning of his intellectual enlightenment.[106] Writers went through several revisions before the focus was shifted to York's conversion from conscientious objector to fighter with a cause. York's views on the second European war evolved during production of the film as he heard reports of German atrocities. He had been convinced to bear arms against Germans in World War I because the circumstances required men to stand up for God's laws and justice, and he was coming around to the same perspective on the new war.

Interestingly, producers briefly toyed with casting Ronald Reagan as York because he was cheaper and easier to procure than Gary Cooper, but Cooper ended up with the part, largely because of York's insistence.[107] The film was not considered a sure bet, as war movies had not been big sellers as of late, with the genre peaking in the late 1920s and early 1930s. But it turned out to be an unqualified success from the moment of its premier in New York in July 1941. *Sergeant York* sold tickets more quickly than any film since *Gone With the Wind*. It ranked ninth in rental revenue of all films produced between 1941 and 1950, earning over $6 million and eclipsing the next highest grossing film about World War I, *The Four Horsemen of the Apocalypse*, by $1.5 million.[108]

Reviews were overwhelmingly positive, and few failed to mention the film's importance in light of world events. One reviewer noted that it paid "a fine tribute to patriotism, making one proud to be an American."[109] The reviewer for *Newsweek* wrote:

> In such times and in less capable hands, the story of the conscientious objector whom General Pershing was to call "the greatest civilian soldier of all time" might have been a jingoistic cross between *Billy the Kid* and *The Fighting 69th*. Instead it is an engrossing and humorous record of the American way of life in a backwoods community, as well as a timely drama of the inner struggle of a deeply religious

man who weighs his horror of killing against what he feels is the greater necessity to stop all the killing.[110]

Reviewers understood that the film was preparing the country for war, but Warner Brothers executives and York had agreed to steer clear of labeling the project a war movie, partially to avoid the taint of propaganda, and partially because York saw it as the struggle of right versus wrong rather than a typical war film. Scriptwriters strove to make the film a story of an Appalachian farmer, "'rather than to aggrandize war or even heroism' . . . Their objective, they reported, was not to 'wave any flags' in the movie, 'but when the picture is over to have made the audience wave flags.'"[111] York argued, "It would be a true picture of my life . . . my contributions to my community since the war. It wouldn't be a war picture . . . I don't like war pictures."[112]

As much as York might protest otherwise, the film could hardly be labeled anything but a war film. The plot pivoted on an American soldier's experience during the war, and it was produced in 1941 precisely because it served up a case study about war. In fact, it was the closest thing to a quintessential American war story since *The Big Parade* in 1925. In many ways York represented a typical American soldier of the Great War. He was from a rural part of the country, had never before left his hometown, and he fought because he was compelled, drafted, rather than volunteering. He struggled with the cause, although his concerns were religious rather than practical or political, and he served as an enlisted man, not an officer. York also demonstrated spectacular heroics that viewers could connect to the war. All of this suggests that *Sergeant York* might have endured as an iconic representation of the war. York came closest of any American participant in the war to leaving an indelible mark on collective memory, but he never quite became a full-fledged icon of the war, largely because he refused to play that role upon his return home. When the film launched him in front of the public once again, his fame was shifted out of context, and he became more associated with a later war in which he never fought.

Sergeant York lost much of its connection to World War I when it was co-opted to fight World War II. If one were to scan the television listings of classic movie channels today and see that *Sergeant York*, a film from 1941, was showing, an educated person might easily deduce that it was a World War II film. And, because Warner Brothers purchased the rights to the screenplay and financed the film based solely on the film's potential to influence American attitudes about the coming war, it, largely, *is* a World War II film. It is often cited in film histories of World War II, not World War I. In fact, the Japanese bombing of Pearl Harbor happened just months after the film's premier. York was well known for his military exploits by most Americans in 1941, but by tying his story to America's entry into a bigger, more deadly war, he may have inadvertently diluted his iconic representation of World War I. The biggest hero of the first world war became inextricably linked with the second.

The Legacy of World War I Films in America

It would be disingenuous to discuss the marginalization of the American war experience on film without exploring those who were marginalized most—African Americans. It is important to note that, while *Sergeant York* paints a fairly accurate picture of the experience for many American soldiers, there was no film that even attempted to represent the experience of African American soldiers, who are absent from the mainstream war-film canon. None of the films discussed in this chapter feature black soldiers, and judging by the historical record made by Hollywood, one might assume that African Americans never served or fought. Because African American troops were segregated in their own divisions during the war, unless a film specifically focused on black soldiers, they were invisible on the screen. White Hollywood would have seen little advantage in featuring black soldiers on screen, since their mere presence in real life on the streets of America was enough to cause riots in some parts of the country.[113]

While black writers chronicled the stories of black soldiers in documentary volumes and fiction, the nascent black film industry was too new to have much influence in the immediate postwar years. One struggling black-owned film company attempted to contract with the CPI to create news footage of black soldiers during the war but failed.[114] Black production companies were involved in a few other documented efforts, including *A Trooper in Troop K* (1917), about the African American cavalry fighting against the Mexicans in 1916, and *Spying the Spy* (1918), about a character named Sambo Sam's ill-fated effort to catch German spies. There is also evidence of a documentary film, *The Heroic Black Soldiers of the War*, made up of war department footage from France that was shown by the Frederick Douglass Company in New York City, but no copy of the film survives.[115]

African Americans were not missing much, however, as most of the popular war films fell short of the mark for commemoration for any soldier because they represented a distinctly foreign perspective. One cannot remember America at war by witnessing the acts of other nations' soldiers, particularly in a war where the participants went through vastly different experiences. Even those films that portrayed some semblance of the American experience fell short because they failed to make the experience iconic. None of the films created an impression of the war that was distinctly American, although there were opportunities to do so. American involvement in the war is synonymous with the battles of Meuse-Argonne and Belleau Wood, yet none of the films made these battles the primary focus. At the Meuse-Argonne, Gen. John Pershing led one million U.S. soldiers against a German position in a battle that spanned 47 days, resulted in 120,000 casualties, and killed more than 26,000. It was the largest battle in American military history and certainly the most important American contribution to Allied victory during the war.[116] With statistics like this, it is hard to understand why the battle is virtually unknown to Americans. Historian Edward Lengel argues, "Young officers who entered the army in the 1920s and 1930s knew more about the Battle of Gettysburg than the Meuse-Argonne. . . . So far as the American public is concerned, the Meuse-Argonne might as well never have occurred."[117] Not even the American military seemed to comprehend, or wished to publicize, the scope of the battle and its importance in history, since no official history of the Meuse-Argonne was ever issued. If the United States Army was not reflecting on its greatest achievement of the war, it is not surprising that no one else was either.[118]

There was also plenty of ripe film material in the fight put up by the Second Division's Marine Brigade as it clawed through the Bois de Belleau using only rifles and bayonets against the machine-gun nests arrayed in front of them. The marines took possession of a forest that other Allied forces had refused to attack. They lost an appalling number of men doing it, but they accomplished a task many thought impossible.[119] As momentous as the battles at the Meuse-Argonne and Belleau Wood were, they were largely absent from the plots of war films in the 1920s and 1930s. Perhaps it is because focusing on battles meant focusing on deaths. Any feature film exploring a specific battle would have had little opportunity to squeeze in a romance or comedic relief. The film would have had to revolve around battle itself, something that is intrinsically bloody, cruel, and violent. These are characteristics that might be alluded to in a film, splashed on the screen sparingly, but they could not dominate a commercially viable American war film. The exploits of Jim, Slim, and Bull in *The Big Parade* were at Belleau Wood, but few, if any, reviews mentioned it, and most viewers likely never realized that fact.[120] The limited infantry scenes in *Wings* were supposed to represent Saint-Mihiel, but again, this was not a well-publicized fact, and most audiences were probably ignorant of this fact. The battles for most feature films about the war were set "somewhere in France." That amorphous description of the locus for fighting seemed to have been enough for many Americans, who never identified with the war and therefore never needed to identify with its battlefields.

The representations of World War II on film relied significantly on battles of significant importance to the war and American involvement, like Normandy, the Battle of the Bulge, and Guadalcanal—terms that are instantly recognizable by many Americans, then and today. Major box-office successes, like *Battleground* (1949), about the Battle of the Bulge; *Sands of Iwo Jima* (1949), with John Wayne, *Bataan* (1943); and *From Here to Eternity* (1953), about Pearl Harbor, reinforced the importance of these engagements in collective memory. These films were joined by a host of others, like *Battle Cry* (1955), about Guadalcanal and Tarawa; *The Longest Day* (1962), about the Normandy invasion; and *Midway* (1976), that rounded out the canon.[121] Movies grew in popularity during the 1940s and 1950s as disposable income rose, meaning that even larger numbers of Americans fell under the influence of Hollywood's iconic representations of battles of significance to Americans.[122]

Unlike American World War I films, many of the films produced by British companies focused intently on those events that came to symbolize the war in their country. The war devastated European film production, and Hollywood had filled the void, eventually dominating the film industry for many years as a result of this head start. This makes English criticism that films like *The Big Parade* overshadowed the other Allies in cinematic history much more understandable. The few European companies that remained viable after the war attempted to put out quality films that represented their own unique perspective on the war, whether it was English, French, or German. Much of the body of work produced in Britain focused on the engagements that entangled the most British citizens. British producers created many features about single battles, including *The Battle of the Somme* (1916); *The Battle of Jutland* (1921); *Armageddon* (1923), about the Palestinian campaign; *Zeebrugge* (1924); *Ypres* (1925); *Mons* (1926); *The Battles of Coronel and Falkland Islands* (1927); and *The Somme* (1927).[123] French producers were less battle-specific with most of their films, but did bring *Verdun, visions d'histoire* to the screen in 1928, a film released to coincide with the tenth anniversary of the armistice. An antiwar film, it was popular with the public and was re-released in 1932 with sound.[124] These films created a stronger understanding of each nation's unique contributions to the war and the suffering experienced by native soldiers. They also provided a point of reference around which their respective citizens might remember the war, something that never happened in American films. German filmmakers, not surprisingly, did not focus on battles. German producers primarily released antiwar films in the late 1920s, before Nazi censorship made these films impossible to make or release. The most famous was *Westfront 1918* (1930), which many believed presented an even bleaker antiwar perspective than *All Quiet on the Western Front*, although the latter film is much better known.[125]

The Big Parade was the closest that the American cinema came to "owning" the reality of the war for Americans. King

Vidor presented the full story of an American boy experiencing peer pressure to join the army, leaving his family's home, bonding with fellow soldiers from different stations in life, and witnessing the horrors of the battlefield. However, the story arc was generic enough to be that of almost any soldier from any country, and it was muddled by a concurrent love story. Notwithstanding these issues, it still might have been the iconic movie of the war, but the first big film to pack theaters was doomed to obsolescence by talking films just a few short years after its release. Movie studios churned out a fair body of work about the war after *The Big Parade* and the advent of sound, but nothing stuck as an iconic representation of the American war then, and nothing has emerged since. How could so many popular and critically acclaimed movies fail to produce even one film truly representing the American experience at war?

There seem to be several reasons why this is so. First, pervasive apathy about the war, as demonstrated in the first three chapters, meant that audiences were not clamoring to know about the authentic doughboy experience. Most of the public simply wanted to forget the war. Hollywood could use the war simply as a plot device, and no one really cared. Audiences weren't concerned that they were missing out on the real thing. Many of the war films that followed *The Big Parade* appropriated the basic theme presented by Vidor but focused even more on Hollywood's obligation to entertain rather than inform. Producers used war as a raison d'être for portraying the raucous lives of Captain Flagg and Sergeant Quirt in *What Price Glory?*, for creating an obstacle to the love of Chico and Diane in *Seventh Heaven*, and for providing thrilling aerial dogfights between heroic knights in the sky in *Wings*. War was usually a backdrop, not the main attraction. As such, Americans could blithely acknowledge the war without grappling with its meaning.

On the rare occasion when the war was front and center, as it was in *All Quiet on the Western Front*, viewers could abhor war as foreigners practiced it without contemplating their own country's complicity or participation. The beauty of film is that it allows one to enter an alternate reality, and Americans were clearly accepting of an alternate reality of war that was both generic and diffuse. Throughout the 1920s and 1930s, film studios churned out a series of war films that catered to a thrill-seeking public with nonspecific battle scenes set "somewhere in France." And, as was true with some writers, film producers failed to clarify murky perceptions of American involvement in the war. War films had split personalities, exposing the death and destruction of war in carefully measured doses alongside portrayals of male bonding, romance, and comedic interludes. As such, the celluloid narrative of war lacked touchstones for remembrance and defied easy categorization into a single collective memory. Film studios watered down the war to a muddle of foreign armies, indistinct locations, and uncertain lessons, all of which did not produce an iconic film about the war, much less help shape a distinctive American vision of the country's role in the conflict.

Conclusion

The youth of America flocked to war movies as surely as they had taken to pulp-fiction magazines about daredevil pilots. Both mediums had great potential for fostering collective memory of the war among a younger generation of Americans. Children were the vast majority of film audiences, with some exhibitors claiming that as much as 85 percent of their customer base was made up of children. Teen and young adult audiences were also significant, with the age group from seventeen to twenty-three considered particularly strong.[1] But, as was true for pulp fiction, the youths who bought these books and watched these movies would become much more intimately involved in a bigger war that would come to dominate their generation's consciousness. Children ages five to seventeen who began watching these movies in the late 1920s and 1930s would be ages nineteen to thirty-one in 1941, prime age for service in the military or on the home front. So, even the glamorized version of American war would slip into obscurity when the young men who could not get enough of the war in magazines and films got plenty to remember with their own war.

Samuel Hynes spoke for the interwar generation when he talked about "the war in the head" that many of them carried with them into World War II. Their expectations were a mixture of dread and excitement. They were chastened by the death and destruction conveyed by novels and movies, but still anxious to take their turn in the maelstrom of war.[2] Ultimately, their stories of war would displace those they had read as children and proliferate into a cult of respect for the "good war," effectively blotting out the memory of an earlier war that was perhaps not so "good." Films joined written documentation of World War I in taking a back seat to a war that benefitted from clearer aims, more popular support, and, in America, many more men mobilized for action for a longer time. When it was over, Americans would not shove the war to the backs of their minds. There would be no purposeful forgetting or a prevailing mood of apathy. There also would not be a larger war to eclipse it twenty years, or even fifty years, later. World War II remains the last just war. Its supremacy in American memory hinders a potential resurgence in remembrance of World War I, which only perpetuates the attitude of apathy that dominated the 1920s and 1930s into the twenty-first century.

However, it is too simplistic to say that the enormity of World War II simply overshadowed World War I. It is certainly true that World War II resulted in more American deaths, lasted much longer, and involved many more citizens and soldiers, but that is not the only reason, or even the primary reason, that World War I registers so faintly in American public consciousness. The war was lost to collective memory because the interwar generation never established a "collected memory" of the war. Americans never reconciled their conflicting views of the war, and many simply chose to forget the war entirely. In chapter 1 of this volume I demonstrated that veterans and the public foiled efforts to craft war histories. Some Americans clearly thought that such histories would be valuable as a memorial to those who served, others either disagreed with the "heroic" narrative that was being crafted by the state or just chose to put the war out of their minds. In chapter 2 I identified almost five hundred personal narratives that framed the American part in the war for posterity. A significant number of soldiers believed that the war could teach enduring lessons that they were obligated to tell, but most Americans simply ignored them. The novels explored in chapter 3 attracted many more readers, but the bifurcated narratives they presented did little to bridge divided American opinions about the war. Willa Cather and Dorothy Canfield Fisher found an audience among those who believed the war served a purpose, while Ernest Hemingway and Humphrey Cobb found common cause with those who rejected the war, and all wars, outright. The same duality is evident in the films analyzed in chapter 4. War films were multidimensional and fleeting, but they had the awesome power of offering iconic representations of the war to millions of Americans. They could have subtly left messages about the war in the minds of an engaged audience, but they failed to focus on those experiences that were uniquely American.

Film studios presented the quintessential experiences of World War II, including Pearl Harbor, Normandy, and the Battle of the Bulge, on movie screens across the country in a way that forged a homogeneous view about why Americans fought that war. Films, as well as personal narratives and fiction, demonstrated why the enemy was evil and how teamwork won the war. The figure of the kaiser and the Battle of Meuse-Argonne have never resonated with the public in the same way. The kaiser cannot rival the shock value of Hitler, although the earlier German leader played a key role in bringing on a war that ultimately led to the death of over eight million soldiers. In turn, in terms of military history, Pearl Harbor was a minor engagement compared to the death wrought at the Battle of Meuse-Argonne. But, there was an overriding moral imperative to World War II that contributed to the ease with which American thought coalesced around similar memories of the war. Fascism and Hitler were spreading evil, and the war effectively halted that malignity.[3] There was no comparable principled stand during World War I that bound Americans to the cause. The world was not saved for democracy, and the outcomes of the war left the world teetering on the edge of an even bigger war.

The one hundredth anniversaries of World War I in Europe (2014) and the United States (2017) have seen a resurgence of interest in the war. The one hundredth anniversary of the Civil War brought the creation of a centennial commission, commemorative postage stamps, and renewed funding for battlefield commemoration in the United States. A similarly charged World War I centennial commission has been created by Congress and is working diligently to raise American awareness of the war and its consequences. However, given the dearth of cultural touchstones left by the war generation, remembrance in this country remains uncertain at best. The lack of public support in documenting the war and the determined attitude to forget it, fundamental disagreements about the war's meaning in books and films produced during the 1920s and 1930s, and the primacy of World War II in the memory of many Americans since the 1940s has affected collective memory of the war in each generation since the armistice. Memoirs and films of World War II have dominated war remembrance for over fifty years, to the detriment of remembrance of World War I. Maybe, when Americans have fully dissected the anatomy of victory and the "greatest generation," they will be able to reach farther back in history and examine the war that started it all.

APPENDIX 1

Selected Bibliography of World War I Personal Narratives

Aaronsohn, Alexander. *With the Turks in Palestine.* 1916.

Abbey, Edwin. *An American Soldier.* 1918.

Adams, Briggs Kilburn. "The American Spirit." 1918.

Albertson, Ralph. *Fighting Without a War: An Account of Military Intervention in North Russia.* 1920.

Aldrich, Mildred. *A Hilltop on the Marne.* 1915.

———. *On the Edge of the War Zone.* 1917.

———. *The Peak of the Load.* 1918.

Alexander, Robert. *Memories of the World War, 1917–1918.* 1931.

Allen, Henry. *My Rhineland Journal.* 1923.

Allen, Hervey. *Toward the Flame.* 1926.

Anderson, Isabel. *Zigzagging.* 1918.

Andrews, Paul Shipman. *Guns of the A.E.F..* 1920.

Anonymous. *Field Ambulance Sketches.* 1919.

Anonymous. *My Secret Service.* 1916.

Anonymous. *One Woman's War.* 1930.

Anonymous. *Red Triangle Girl in France.* 1918.

Anonymous. *What I Found Out in the House of a German Prince: By an English-American Governess.* 1915.

Archibald, Norman. *Heaven High, Hell Deep, 1917–1918.* 1935.

Ashe, Elizabeth H. *Intimate Letters from France, and Extracts from the Diary of Elizabeth Ashe, 1917–1919.* 1931.

Ashford, Bailey K. *A Soldier in Science: The Autobiography of Bailey K. Ashford.* 1934.

Atwood, John H. *What I Saw of the War: Notes of My Trip Through England & France.* 1919.

Austin, W. *War Zone Gadabout.* 1917.

Bagenal, H. *Fields and Battlefields.* 1918.

Baker, Horace L. "Argonne Days: Experiences of a World War Private on the Meuse-Argonne Front." 1927.

Baldwin, Marian. *Canteening Overseas.* 1920.

Barber, Thomas H. *Along the Road.* 1924.

Barclay, Harold. *A Doctor in France, 1917–1919.* 1923.

Barkley, John Lewis. *No Hard Feelings!* 1930.

Barnard, Charles Inman. *Paris War Days: Diary of an American.* 1914.

Bartley, Albert Lea. *Tales of the World War.* 1935.

Beal, Howard W. *The Letters of Major Howard W. Beal.* 1926.

Beaufort, J. M. *Behind the German Veil.* 1918.

Benson, S. C. *Back From Hell.* 1918.

Bernheim, Bertram. *Passed as Censored.* 1917.

Biddle, Charles John. *The Way of the Eagle.* 1919.

Bigelow, Glenna Lindsley. *Liege, on the line of March: An American Girls Experience when the Germans came through Belgium.* 1918.

Bingham, Hiram. *An Explorer in the Air Service.* 1920.

Bittle, Celestine Nicholas Charles. *Soldiering for Cross and Flag; Impressions of a War Chaplain.* 1929.

Blake, Catherine. *Some Letters Written to Maude Gray and Marian Wickes 1917–1918.* 1920.

Blakenhorn, Heber. *Adventures in Propaganda: Letters from an Intelligence Officer in France.* 1919.

Blodgett, Richard Ashley. *Life and Letters of Richard Ashley Blodgett.* 192-?

Blumenstein, Christian. *Whiz Bang!* 1927.

Borden, Mary. *The Forbidden Zone.* 1929.

Borden, Raymond D., and Prosper Buranelli. *Maggie of the Suicide Fleet.* 1930.

Braddan, William S. *Under Fire with the 370th Infantry.* 1919.

Bradley, Amy. *Back of the Front in France.* 1918.

Brittain, Harry. *To Verdun from the Somme.* 1917.

Britton, Emmet Nicholson. *"As it Looked to Him": Intimate Letters on the War.* 1919.

Brooks, Alden. *As I Saw It.* 1930.

Broun, Heywood. *The A.E.F.* 1918.

Brown, Hilton. *Hilton Brown, Jr., One of Three Brothers in the Artillery.* 1920.

Brown, William. *The Adventures of an American Doughboy.* 1919.

Bryan, Julien. *Ambulance 464.* 1918.

Buck, Beaumont. *Memories of Peace and War.* 1935.

Buell, Charles Townshend. *The Great World War and the Americans on the Field of Battle.* 1924.

Bullard, Robert Lee. *Personalities and Reminiscences of War.* 1925.

Bullitt, Ernesta Drinker. *An Uncensored Diary from the Central Empire.* 1917.

Burdick, Joel Wakeman. *Lorraine: 1918.* 1919.

Burton, Caspar Henry. *Letters of Caspar Henry Burton, Jr.* 1921.

Buswell, Leslie. *Ambulance No. 10: Personal Letters from the Front.* 1915.

Butters, Harry. *Harry Butters R.F.A.—"An American Citizen."* 1918.

Cade, John Brother. *Twenty-Two Months with "Uncle Sam," Being the Experiences and Observations of a Negro Student Who Volunteered.* 1929.

Callaway, A.B. *With Packs and Rifles: A Story of the World War.* 1939.

Cameron, John. *Ten Months in a German Raider.* 1918.

Campbell, Peyton Randolph. *The Diary-Letters of Sergt. Peyton Randolph Campbell.* 1919.

Canfield, Dorothy. *Home Fires in France.* 1918.

Carstairs, Carroll. *A Generation Missing.* 1930.

Carter, William Arthur. *The Tale of a Devil Dog.* 1920.

Casey, Robert Joseph. *The Cannoneers Have Hairy Ears: A Diary of the Front Lines.* 1927.

Catlin, Albertus Wright. *"With the Help of God and a Few Marines."* 1919.

Center, Charles. *Things Usually Left Unsaid.* 1927.

Chamberlin, Joseph Edgar. *The Only Thing for a Man to Do: The Story of Raymond Chamberlin.* 1921.

Chambers, Hilary Ranald, Jr. *United States Submarine Chasers in the Mediterranean, Adriatic and the Attack on Durazzo.* 1920.

Chapin, Harold. *Soldier and Dramatist.* 1916.

Chapin, Hope. *Experience of an American Refugee.* 1914.

Chapman, Charles Wesley. *Letters of Second Lieutenant Charles Wesley Chapman, Jr.* 1919.

Chapman, Victor Emmanuel. *Victor Chapman's Letters from France.* 1917.

Chapple, Joseph. *We'll Stick to the Finish: C'est la Guerre.* 1918.

Christian, Royal A. *Roy's Trip to the Battlefields of Europe.* 192-?

Churchill, Mary Smith. *You Who Can Help.* 1918.

Clark, Coleman Tileston. *Soldier Letters, Coleman Tileston Clark.* 1919.

Clarke, Carolyn. *"Evacuation 114" as Seen from Within.* 1919.

Clarke, M. E. *Paris Waits.* 1914.

Clover, Greayer. *A Stop at Suzanne's and Lower Flights.* 1919.

Cobb, Irwin Shrewsbury. *The Glory of the Coming.* 1918.

———. *Paths of Glory.* 1918.

———. *Speaking of Prussians.* 1917.

Codman, Charles R. *Contact.* 1937.

Cohen, Israel. *Ruhleben Prison Camp.* 1917.

Coolidge, Hamilton. *Letters of an American Airman.* 1919.

Coolidge, John Gardner. *A War Diary in Paris.* 1931.

Corning, Walter D. *The Yanks Crusade: A Book of Reminiscences.* 1927.

Coyle, Edward Royal. *Ambulancing on the French Front.* 1918.

Crane-Gartz, Kate. *A Woman and War.* 1928.

Cravath, Paul. *Great Britain's Part.* 1917.

Crosby, Henry Grew. *War Letters.* 1932.

Crowe, James Richard. *Pat Crowe, Aviator: Skylark Views and Letters from France, Including the Story of "Jacqueline."* 1919.

Cummings, E. E. *The Enormous Room.* 1922.

Curtin, Daniel. *The Land of Deepening Shadow.* 1917.

Curtiss, Elmer E. *Going and Coming as a Doughboy.* 1920.

Cushing, Harvey. *From a Surgeon's Journal, 1915–1918.* 1936.

Cutchins, John A. *An Amateur Diplomat in the World War.* 1938.

Davis, Richard Harding. *With the Allies.* 1915.

———. *With the French in France and Salonika.* 1916.

Dawes, Charles Gates. *A Journal of the Great War.* 1921.

Dawson, Coningsby. *Carry On: Letters in War-time.* 1917.

———. *Glory of the Trenches.* 1917.

———. *Out to Win.* 1918.

Day, Kirkland Hart. *Camion Cartoons.* 1919.

Dearing, Vinton Adams. *My Galahad of the Trenches.* 1918.

Deckard, Percy Edward. *List of Officers Who Served with the 371st Infantry and Headquarters.* 1929.

Depew, Albert. *Gunner Depew.* 1918.

Derby, Richard. *"Wade in Sanitary!": The Story of a Division Surgeon in France.* 1919.

Detzer, Karl. *True Tales of the D.C.I.* 1925.

Devan, Scoville T. *Overseas Letters from a Y Secretary.* 1919.

DeVarila, Osborne. *The First Shot for Liberty.* 1918.

DeVille, Father Jean B. *Back from Belgium.* 1918.

Dexter, Mary. *In the Soldier's Service.* 1918.

Dickman, Joseph Theodore. *The Great Crusade: A Narrative of the World War.* 1927.

Dodd, Anna Bowman. *Heroic France.* 1915.

Dorr, Rheta. *Soldier's Mother in France.* 1918.

Doty, Madeleine. *Short Rations: An American Woman in Germany.* 1917.

Downer, Earl. *Highway of Death.* 1916.

Duffy, Francis Patrick. *Father Duffy's Story.* 1919.

Dunn, Robert. *At the Furthest Front.* 1915.

———. *Five Fronts.* 1915.

DuPuy, Charles M. *A Machine Gunner's Notes, France 1918.* 1920.

Eddy, Sherwood. *With Our Soldiers in France.* 1917.

Einstein, Lewis. *Inside Constantinople.* 1918.

Ellinwood, Ralph E. *Behind the German Lines, a Narrative of the Everyday Life of an American Prisoner of War.* 1920.

Elliot, Paul Blodgett, ed. *On the Field of Honor.* 1920.

Ely, Dinsmore. *Dinsmore Ely, One Who Served.* 1919.

Emmett, Chris. *Way to the Right: Serving with the A.E.F. in France During the World War.* 1934.

Empey, Arthur Guy. *First Call.* 1918.

———. *Over the Top; by an American Soldier Who Went.* 1917.

———. *Tales from a Dugout.* 1918.

Evans, Frank E. *Daddy Pat of the Marines.* 1919.

Evarts, Jeremiah Maxwell. *Cantigny, A Corner of the War.* 1938.

Farnham, Ruth. *A Nation at Bay: What an American Woman Saw and Did in Suffering Serbia.* 1918.

Farrar, Reginald. *Void of War.* 1918.

Ferguson, John B. *Through the War with a Y Man.* 1919.

Fitch, Willis Stetson. *Wings in the Night.* 1938.

Fitzgerald, Alice. *The Edith Cavell Nurse from Massachusetts.* 1917.

Flight [pseud.]. *Flying Yankee.* 1918.

Flores, C. *No. 6: A Few Pages from the Diary of an Ambulance Driver.* 1918.

Flowthow, Marie. *Letters to My Son.* 1926.

Foote, Katherine. "88 Bis and V.I.H.: Letters from Two Hospitals by an American V.A.D." 1919.

Ford, Torrey Sylvester. *Cheer-up Letters from a Private with Pershing.* 1918.

Fortescue, Granville. *At the Front with Three Armies.* 1914.

———. *France Bears the Burden.* 1917.

———. *Frontline & Deadline; the Experiences of a War Correspondent.* 1937.

———. *Russia, the Balkans, and the Dardanelles (At the Front with Three Armies?).* 1915.

Fox, Edward. *Behind the Scenes in Warring Germany.* 1915.

Frazer, Elizabeth. *Old Glory and Verdun.* 1918.

Fredenberg, Theodore. *Soldier's March.* 1930.

Gaines, Ruth. *A Village in Picardy.* 1918.

Gallagher, David B. *The Battle of Bolts and Nuts in the Sector of Cognac Hill.* 1931.

Gallishaw, John. *Trenching at Gallipoli.* 1916.

Genet, Edmond Charles. *War Letters.* 1918.

Gerard, James Watson. *Face to Face with Kaiserism.* 1917.

———. *My Four Years in Germany.* 1917.

Gibbons, Floyd. *"And They Thought We Wouldn't Fight".* 1918.

Gibbons, Helen Davenport. *A Little Gray Home in France.* 1919.

Gibbons, Herbert. *Paris Reborn: A Study in Civic Psychology.* 1915.

Gibson, Hugh. *A Journal From Our Legation in Belgium.* 1917.

Gibson, Preston. *Battering the Boche.* 1918.

Gleason, Arthur H. *With the First World War Ambulances in Belgium.* 1918.

Gleason, Arthur H., and Helen Hays. *Golden Lads.* 1916.

Gordon, George Vincent. *Leathernecks and Doughboys.* 1927.

Gow, Kenneth. *Letters of a Soldier.* 1920.

Grant, Robert. *Their Spirit.* 1916.

Grasty, Charles. *Flashes from the Front.* 1918.

Green, Horace. *Log of a Non-Combatant.* 1915.

Greene, Warwick. *Letters of Warwick Greene, 1915–1928.* 1931.

Grider, John MacGavock, and Elliott White Springs. *War Birds: Diary of an Unknown Aviator.* 1926.

Grow, Malcolm. *Surgeon Grow: American in the Russian Fighting.* 1918.

Gulberg, Martin Gus. *A War Diary: into This Story Is Woven an Experience of Two Years' Service in the World War with the 75th Company.* 1927.

Gutterson, Granville. *Granville: Tales and Tail Spins from a Flyer's Diary.* 1919.

Hagood, Johnson. *The Services of Supply: A Memoir of the Great War.* 1927.

Hale, Walter. *By Motor to the Firing Line.* 1916.

Hall, Bert. *En L'Air. Three Years on and Above the Fronts.* 1918.

Hall, Bert, and John J. Niles. *One Man's War: The Story of the Lafayette Escadrille.* 1929.

Hall, James Norman. *Flying With Chaucer.* 1930.

———. *High Adventure.* 1917.

———. *"Kitchener's Mob."* 1916.

Halyburton, Edgar, and Ralph Gall. *Shoot and Be Damned.* 1932.

Harbord, James G. *Leaves from a War Diary.* 1925.

Harden, Elmer Stetson. *An American Poilu.* 1919.

Harrison, Henry Sydnor. *When I Come Back.* 1919.

Hartney, Harold Evans. *Up and at 'Em.* 1940.

Harvey, Bartle M. *Me and Bad Eye Slim: The Diary of a Buck Private.* 1932.

Haslet, Elmer. *Luck on the Wing: Thirteen Stories of a Sky Spy.* 1920.

Hayes, Ralph. *Secretary Baker at the Front.* 1918.

Hays, Harold Melvin. *Cheerio!* 1919.

Herring, Ray DeWitt. *Trifling with War.* 1934.

Herzog, Stanley J. *The Fightin' Yanks; A Book of Plain Facts, Written with the Intention of Perpetuating the Deeds of the Boys of Battery F.* 1922.

Hightower, Thomas W. *My Experience as a Soldier During the "World War."* 1919.

Hinckley, Faith Jane. *Forgotten Fires.* 1923.

Hoffman, Conrad. *In the Prison Camps of Germany.* 1920.

Hoffman, Robert C. *I Remember the Last War.* 1940.

Hogan, Martin Joseph. *The Shamrock Battalion of the Rainbow; A Story of the Fighting Sixty-Ninth.* 1919.

Hoggson, Noble Foster. *Just Behind the Front in France.* 1918.

Holden, Frank A. *War Memories.* 1922.

Holmes, Robert Derby. *A Yankee in the Trenches.* 1918.

Hopkins, Nevil. *Over the Threshold of War.* 1918.

Huard, Frances Wilson. *My Home in the Field of Honor.* 1916.

———. *My Home in the Field of Mercy.* 1917.

Hungerford, Edward. *With the Doughboy in France: A Few Chapters of an American Effort.* 1920.

Hunt, Edward Eyre. *War Bread.* 1916.

Hunton, Addie W., and Kathryn M. Johnson. *Two Colored Women with the American Expeditionary Forces.* 1920.

Husband, Joseph. *A Year in the Navy.* 1919.

Imbrie, Robert. *Behind the Wheel of a War Ambulance.* 1918.

Irvine, Alexander Fitzgerald. *A Yankee with the Soldiers of the King.* 1923.

Irwin, William Henry. *The Latin at War.* 1917.

———. *Men Women and War.* 1915.

———. *Reporter at Armageddon.* 1918.

Isaacs, Edouard Victor. *Prisoner of the U-90.* 1919.

Jacks, Leo Vincent. *Service Record: by an Artilleryman.* 1928.

Jacobs, Josephine Grider. *Marse John Goes to War.* 1933.

Janis, Elsie. *The Big Show: My Six Months with the American Expeditionary Forces.* 1919.

Jeffries, J. *War Diary of an American Woman to the Proclamation of the Holy War.* 1915.

Jelke, Ferdinand Frazier. *Letters from a Liaison Officer.* 1919.

Jenkins, Burris. *Facing the Hindenburg Line.* 1917.

Jenks, Chester Walton. *Our First Ten Thousand.* 1919.

Johnson, E. A. *Torpedoed in the Mediterranean.* 1918.

Johnson, Owen. *The Spirit of France.* 1916.

Jones, E. Powis. *From the Side Lines.* 1925.

Jordan, Walker Harrison. *With "Old Elph" in the Army (not a history) a Simple Treatise on the Human Side of a Colored Soldier.* 1919.

Judd, James Robert. *With the American Ambulance in France.* 1919.

Judy, Will. *A Soldier's Diary: A Day to Day Record in the World War.* 1930.

Kauffman, Reginald. *In a Moment of Time: Things Seen on the Bread-Line of Belgium.* 1915.

Kautz, John. *My Escape From Germany.* 1919.

———. *Trucking to the Trenches.* 1918.

Kellogg, Doris. *Canteening Under Two Flags: Letters of Doris Kellogg.* 1920.

Kelly, Russell. *Kelly of the Foreign Legion.* 1917.

Kendall, Harry. *A New York Actor on the Western Front: Giving an Account of Many Hitherto Unrecorded Incidents and Unusual Actions that Took Place During the Great Conflict.* 1932.

Kennedy, Laurence Sarsfield. *War Letters of Laurence Sarsfield Kennedy.* 1932.

Kilham, Eleanor B. *Letters from France, 1915–1919.* 1941.

Kimmel, Stanley. *Crucifixion.* 1922.

King, David Wooster. *L.M. 8046.* 1929.

Knapp, Shepard. *On the Edge of the Storm: The Story of a Year in France.* 1921.

Kramer, Harold Morton. *With Seeing Eyes: The Unusual Story of an Observant Thinker at the Front.* 1919.

Kurtz, Leonard Paul. *Beyond No Man's Land.* 1937.

LaMotte, Ellen. *The Backwash Of War.* 1934.

Langer, William Leonard, and Robert B. MacMullin. *With "E" of the First Gas.* 1919.

Langille, Leslie. *Men of the Rainbow.* 1933.

Lardner, Ring. *My Four Weeks in France.* 1918.

Leach, George E. *War Diary.* 1923.

Leach, Maud Shipley. *Hill 7; A Life Sketch of George Elliot Shipley.* 1935.

Leach, William James. *Poems and War Letters.* 1922.

Lee, Benjamin. *Benjamin Lee, 2d: A Record Gathered from Letters, Notebooks and Narratives of Friends.* 1920.

Le Guiner, Jeanne. *Letters from France.* 1916.

Lejeune, John Archer. *The Reminiscences of a Marine.* 1930.

Lettau, Joseph L. *In Italy with the 332nd Infantry.* 1921.

Levell, Robert O. *"War on the Ocean": A Sailor's Souvenir.* 1937.

Liggett, Hunter. *A.E.F. Ten Years Ago in France.* 1927–28.

Lindner, Clarence R. *Private Lindner's Letters: Censored and Uncensored.* 1939.

Little, Arthur W. *From Harlem to the Rhine: The Story of New York's Colored Volunteers.* 1936.

Livingston, St. Clair, and Ingeborg Steen-Hanson. *Under Three Flags.* 1916.

Long, Robert Edward Crozier. *Colours of War.* 1915.

Lucas, June Richardson. *The Children of France and the Red Cross.* 1917.

Lukens, Edward C. *A Blue Ridge Memoir.* 1922.

Macarthur, Charles. *War Bugs.* 1929.

Mack, Arthur. *Shellproof Mack.* 1918.

Mackay, Helen Gansevoort. *Journal of Small Things.* 1917.

MacLeish, Kenneth. *Kenneth: A Collection of Letters.* 1919.

MacNider, Hanford. *The A.E.F. of a Conscientious Subaltern.* 1924.

Mahon, John C. *The United States and World Peace.* 1920.

March, Peyton Conway. *The Nation at War.* 1932.

Markle, Clifford Milton. *A Yankee Prisoner in Hunland.* 1920.

Maverick, Maury. *A Maverick American.* 1937.

Mayo, Katherine. *"That Damn Y"; A Record of Overseas Service.* 1920.

Mayo, Margaret. *Trouping for the Troops.* 1919.

McBride, Herbert. *Emma Gees.* 1918.

——. *A Rifleman Went to War.* 1935.

McCarthy, George T. *The Greater Love.* 1920.

McCarthy, T. F. *A Year at Camp Gordon.* 1920.

McClintock, A. *Best O' Luck.* 1917.

McCollum, Lee. *Our Sons at War.* 1940.

McConnell, James. *Flying for France.* 1917.

McCormick, Robert R. *The Army of 1918.* 1920.

——. *With the Russian Army, Being the Experiences of a National Guardsman.* 1915.

McCoy, Patrick [pseud.]. *Kiltie McCoy.* 1918.

McDougal, Grace. *Nurse at the War.* 1917.

McElroy, John Lee. *War Diary of John Lee McElroy.* 1929.

Mela, Alvin S. *My Little Part in a Big War.* 1919.

Mellon, Thomas Jr. *Army "Y" Diary.* 1920.

Meriwether, Lee. *The War Diary of a Diplomat.* 1919.

Merrill, Wainwright. *A College Man in Khaki: Letters of an American in the British Artillery.* 1918.

Metcalf, Stanley. *Personal Memoirs: A Narrative of the Experiences of an American in France and Germany in 1917–1919.* 1927.

Millard, Shirley. *I Saw Them Die: Diary and Recollections of Shirley Millard.* 1936.

Millen, DeWitt Clinton. *Memoirs of 591 in the World War.* 1932.

Millholland, Ray. *The Splinter Feet of the Otranto Barrage.* 1936.

Mills, Quincy Sharpe. *One Who Gave His Life: War Letters of Quincy Sharpe Mills; with a Sketch of His Life and Ideals.* 1922.

Minder, Charles Frank. *This Man's War: The Day-by-Day Record of an American Private on the Western Front.* 1931.

Minturn, Joseph Allen. *The American Spirit.* 1921.

Mitchell, Clarence van Shaick. *Letters from a Liaison Officer 1918–1919.* 1920.

Mitchell, Mildred. *Letters from an American Girl in the War Zone 1917–1919*. 1920.

Morgan, Daniel E. *When the World Went Mad: A Thrilling Story of the Late War, Told in the Language of the Trenches*. 1931.

Morganthau, Henry. *Ambassador Morgenthau's Story*. 1918.

Morlae, Edward. *A Soldier of the Legion*. 1916.

Morse, Katherine Duncan. *The Uncensored Letters of a Canteen Girl*. 1920.

Mortimer, Maud. *Green Tent in Flanders*. 1917.

Mosely, George Clark. *Extracts from Letters of George Clark Moseley During the Period of the Great War*. 1923.

Muse, Benjamin. *The Memoirs of a Swine in a Land of Kultur*. 1919.

Musgrave, George Clark. *Under Four Flags for France*. 1918.

Muston, W. H. *Over There: The Story of a Sky Pilot*. 1923.

Needham, Mary. *Tomorrow to Fresh Fields*. 1936.

Noble, Carl. *Jugheads Behind the Lines*. 1938.

O'Brian, Alice Lord. *No Glory; Letters from France, 1917–1919*. 1936.

O'Brien, Howard Vincent. *Wine, Women and War: A Diary of Disillusionment*. 1926.

O'Brien, Pat. *Outwitting the Hun; My Escape from a German Prison Camp*. 1918.

Orcutt, Philip Dana. *The White Road of Mystery; The Notebook of an American Ambulancier*. 1918.

O'Shaughnessy, Edith. *My Lorraine Journal*. 1918.

Page, L. Rodman. *War Without Fighting: Being the Experiences of L. Rodman Page, Jr. on the Mexican Border and in the World War Against Germany*. 1928.

Palmer, Frederick. *My Second Year of the War*. 1917.

———. *My Third Year of the War*. 1918.

———. *My Year of the Great War*. 1915.

———. *With My Own Eyes: A Personal Story of Battle Years*. 1933.

Parsons, Edwin C. *The Great Adventure: The Story of the Lafayette Escadrille*. 1937.

Patterson, Joseph. *Notebook of a Neutral*. 1915.

Peixotto, Ernest. *The American Front*. 1919.

Pershing, John J. *My Experiences in the World War*. 1931.

Peterson, Wilbur. *I Went to War*. 1938.

Pickell, James Ralph. *Twenty-Four Days on a Troopship*. 1919.

Pierce, Ruth. *Trapped in "Black Russia"*. 1918.

Piper, Edgar Bramwell. *Somewhere Near the War; Being an Authentic and More or Less Diverting Chronicle of the Pilgrimage of Twelve American Journalists to the War Zone*. 1919.

Poling, Daniel Alfred. *Hats in Hell.* 1918.

Porter, William Townsend. *Shock at the Front.* 1918.

Pottle, Frederick Albert. *Stretchers; The Story of a Hospital Unit on the Western Front.* 1929.

Powell, Edward Alexander. *Italy at War.* 1917.

———. *Slanting Lines of Steel.* 1933.

———. *Vive La France!* 1915.

Putnam, Elizabeth Cabot. *On Duty and Off: Letters of Elizabeth Cabot Putnam: Written in France, May 1917–September 1918.* 1919.

Pratt, Joseph Hyde. *Diary of Colonel Joseph Hyde Pratt.* 1926.

Pressly, Harry. *Saving the World for Democracy.* 1933.

Prince, Norman. *A Volunteer Who Died for the Cause He Loved.* 1917.

Pulitzer, Ralph. *Over the Frontier in an Aeroplane.* 1915.

Quane, Oliver J. *West of the Meuse.* 1919.

Ranlett, Louis Felix. *Let's Go! The Story of A.S. no 2448602.* 1927.

Raymond, Anan. *Letters, April, 1917, June, 1919.* 1926.

Reece, Robert H. *Night Bombing with the Bedouins.* 1919.

Reed, David Aiken. *Letters, 1918–1919.* 1919.

Reed, John. *War in Eastern Europe.* 1916.

Reifsnyder, Henry J. *A Second Class Private in the Great World War.* 1923.

Rendinell, Joseph Edward, and George Pattullo. *One Man's War: The Diary of a Leatherneck.* 1928.

Rice, P. S. *American Crusader at Verdun.* 1918.

Richards, John Francisco. *War Diary and Letters of John Francisco Richards, II, 1917–1918.* 1925.

Rickenbacker, Eddie. *Fighting the Flying Circus.* 1919.

Ridout, George W. *The Cross and Flag: Experiences in the Great World War.* 1919.

Riegelman, Harold. *War Notes of a Casual.* 1931.

Riggs, Arthur Stanley. *With Three Armies on and Behind the Western Front.* 1918.

Rinehart, Mary Roberts. *Kings, Queens, and Pawns: An American Woman at the Front.* 1915.

Roberts, Lieutenant E. M. *A Flying Fighter.* 1918.

Robinson, William J. *My Fourteen Months at the Front.* 1916.

Rockwell, Kiffin Yates. *War Letters of Kiffin Yates Rockwell, Foreign Legionnaire and Aviator, France, 1914–1916.* Edited by Paul Rockwell. 1925.

Rodman, Hugh. *Yarns of a Kentucky Admiral.* 1928.

Rogers, Alden. *The Hard White Road: A Chronicle of the Reserve Mallet.* 1923.

Rogers, Randolph. *Pour le Droit.* 1919.

Romeo, Giuseppe. *Diary of Pvt. Giuseppe Romeo.* 1919.

Roosevelt, Kermit. *War in the Garden of Eden.* 1919.

Roosevelt, Quinten. *Quentin Roosevelt; A Sketch with Letters.* 1921.

Root, Esther Sayles, and Marjorie Crocker. *Over Periscope Pond: Letters From Two American Girls in Paris, Oct. 1916–Jan.1918.* 1918.

Rose, Harold W. *Brittany Patrol: The Story of the Suicide Fleet.* 1937.

Ross, Warner Anthony. *My Colored Battalion.* 1920.

Ross, William O. and Duke Slaughter. *With the 351st in France.* 1923.

Rounds, Ona Mahitta. *Buck Privates on Parnassus.* 1933.

Ruhl, Arthur. *Antwerp to Gallipoli: A Year of War on Many Fronts—and Behind Them.* 1916.

Russel, William Muir. *A Happy Warrior: Letters of William Muir Russel, an American Aviator in the Great War, 1917–1918.* 1919.

Schreiner, George. *From Berlin to Bagdad.* 1918.

Schultze, Walter H. *Captain Walter H. Schultze.* 1925.

Scudder, Robert Author. *My Experience in the World War.* 1921.

Scully, Charles Alison. *The Course of the Silver Greyhound.* 1936.

Sears, Herbert Mason. *Journal of a Canteen Worker: A Record of Service with the American Red Cross in Flanders.* 1919.

Seeger, Alan. *Letters and Diary.* 1917.

Seibert, A. *Trip to Germany During Wartime.* 1915.

Sergeant, Elizabeth Shepley. *Shadow-Shapes: The Journal of a Wounded Woman, October 1918–May 1919.* 1920.

Shainwald, Richard H. *Letters and Notes from France.* 1919.

Shanks, David C. *As They Passed Through the Port.* 1927.

Sheehan, Henry. *A Volunteer Poilu.* 1916.

Shepherd, William. *Confessions of a War Correspondent.* 1917.

Sherwood, Elmer. *Diary of a Rainbow Veteran.* 1929.

Shortall, Katherine. *A "Y" Girl in France.* 1919.

Sims, William Sowden. *The Victory at Sea.* 1920.

Sinclair, May. *A Journal of Impressions in Belgium.* 1915.

Sirmon, W.A. *That's War: An Authentic Diary.* 1929.

Smith, F. B. *Observations in France.* 1918.

Smith, Harry L., and James Eckman. *Memoirs of an Ambulance Company Officer.* 1940.

Smith, Joseph L. *Over There and Back in Three Uniforms.* 1918.

Snively, Harry Hamilton. *The Battle of the Non-Combatants; The Letters of Dr. Harry Hamilton Snively to His Family from Russia, Poland, France.* 1933.

Snow, William J. *Signposts of Experience: World War Memoirs.* 1941.

Speakman, Harold. *From a Soldier's Heart.* 1919.

Speakman, Marie Anna. *Memories.* 1937.

Spencer, Carita. *War Scenes I Shall Never Forget*. 1917.

Speranza, Gino Charles. *The Diary of Gino Speranza, Italy, 1915–1919*. 1941.

Spitz, Leon. *The Memoirs of a Camp Rabbi*. 1927.

Springs, Elliot White. *Above the Bright Blue Sky; more about the war birds*. 1928.

Springs, Elliott White, and John MacGavock Grinder. *War Birds: Diary of an Unknown Aviator*. 1926.

Stansbury, Henry D. *Maryland's 117th Trench Mortar Battery*. 1942.

Stearns, Gustav. *From Army Camps and Battle-Fields*. 1919.

Steege, Klyda. *We of Italy*. 1917.

Stephens, D. Owen. *With Quakers in France*. 1921.

Sterne Elaine, ed. *Over the Seas for Uncle Sam*. 1918.

Stevenson, William Yorke. *At the Front in a Flivver*. 1917.

———. *From "Poilu" to "Yank"*. 1918.

Stewart, Lawrence O. *Rainbow Bright*. 1923.

Stidger, William. *Soldier Silhouettes on Our Front*. 1918.

Stimson, Julia C. *Finding Themselves*. 1918.

Stoddard, F. R. *War Time France*. 1918.

Stone, Ernest. *Battery B Thru the Fires of France*. 1919.

Straub, Elmer Frank. *A Sergeant's Diary in the World War*. 1923.

Strickland, Riley. *Adventures of the A.E.F. Soldier*. 1920.

Stringfellow, John S. *Hell! No! This and That: A Narrative of the Great War*. 1936.

Sullivan, Reginald Noel. *Somewhere in France*. 1917.

Sullivan, Vincent F. *With the Yanks in France: A Story of America in France*. 1921.

Summerbell, Carlyle. *A Preacher Goes to War*. 1930.

Swan, Carroll Judson. *My Company*. 1918.

Sweetser, Arthur. *Roadside Glimpses of the Great War*. 1916.

Taber, Sydney Richmond. *Arthur Richmond Taber: A Memorial Record Compiled by His Father*. 1920.

Tarbot, Jerry. *Jerry Tarbot, the Living Unknown Soldier*. 1928.

Therese, Josephine. *With Old Glory in Berlin: The Story of an American Girl's Life and Trials in Germany and her Escape from the Huns*. 1918.

Thompson, Terry Brewster. *Taker Her Down, a Submarine Portrait*. 1937.

———. *Those War Women: By One of Them*. 1929.

Tippet, Edwin James. *Who Won the War?: Letters and Notes of an M.P. in Dixie, England, France and Flanders*. 1920.

Toland, E. D. *Aftermath of Battle*. 1916.

Towne, Charles Hanson. *Shaking Hands with England*. 1919.

Trounce, Harry Davis. *Fighting the Boche Underground*. 1918.

Trueblood, Edward Alva. *Observations of an American Soldier During His Service with the A.E.F. in France, in the Flash Ranging Service.* 1919.

Truitt, C. *Wartime Letters from Italy.* 1915.

Tunney, Thomas J. and Paul Merrick Hollister. *Throttled! The Detection of the German and Anarchist Bomb Plotters.* 1919.

Turczynowicz, Laura de Gozdawa. *When the Prussians Came to Poland.* 1916.

Turnure, George Evans. *Flight Log and War Letters.* 1936.

Tyler, Elizabeth Stearns. *Letters of Elizabeth Stearns Tyler.* 1920.

Tyler, John C. *Selections from the Letters and Diary of John Cowperthwaite Tyler.* 1938.

Upson, William Hazlett. *Me and Henry and the Artillery.* 1928.

Van Dyke, Henry. *Fighting for Peace.* 1917.

Van Shaick, John, Jr. *Love That Never Failed: Memories of the World War.* 1933.

Van Vorst, Marie. *War Letters of an American Woman.* 1916.

Veil, Charles. *Adventure's a Wench: The Autobiography of Charles Veil as Told to Howard Marsh.* 1934.

Vickers, Leslie. *Training for the Trenches.* 1917.

Volk, Katherine. *Buddies in Budapest.* 1936.

Voska, Emanuel Victor and Will Irwin. *Spy and Counterspy.* 1940.

Walcott, Stuart. *Above the French Lines: Letters of an American Aviator.* 1918.

Waldo, Fullerton L. *America at the Front.* 1918.

Wallach, Mike. *"Farmer, Have You a Daughter Fair?" A Traveling Salesman Meets the Mamselles from Armentieres.* 1929.

Ward, Herbert. *Mr. Poilu.* 1917.

Warren, Maude Lavinia. *White Flame of France.* 1918.

Washburn, Slater. *One of the Yankee Division.* 1919.

Washburn, Stanley. *The Russian Advance.* 1917.

———. *The Russian Campaign, April to August 1915.* 1915.

Watson, Samuel Newell. *Those Paris Years: With the World at the Crossroads.* 1936.

Wellman, William. *Go Get 'Em!* 1918.

Werner, Morris Robert. *"Orderly!"* 1930.

West, William Benjamin. *The Fight for the Argonne, Personal Experiences of a "Y" Man.* 1919.

Westbrook, Stillman Foote. *Those Eighteen Months.* 1934.

Wharton, Edith. *Fighting France; From Dunkirque to Belfort.* 1915.

Wheeler, Curtis. *Letters from an American Soldier to His Father.* 1918.

Whitaker, Herman. *Hunting the German Shark: The American Navy in the Underseas War.* 1918.

Whitehair, Charles. *Out There.* 1918.

———. *Pictures Burned Into My Memory.* 1918.

Whitehouse, Vira B. *A Year as a Government Agent.* 1920.

Wilder, Fred Calvin. *War Experiences of F. C. Wilder.* 1926.

Wile, Frederic William. *Assault.* 1916.

Wilgus, William. *Transporting the A.E.F. in Western Europe.* 1931.

Williams, Albert Rhys. *In the Claws of the German Eagle.* 1917.

Williams, Ashby. *Experiences of the Great War; Artois, St. Mihiel, Meuse-Argonne.* 1919.

Williams, Wythe. *Passed by the Censor: the experiences of an American newspaper man in France.* 1916.

Winant, Cornelius. *A Soldier's Manuscript.* 1929.

Winn, Hiram W. *Fighting the Hun on the U.S.S. Huntington.* 1919.

Winslow, Carroll Dana. *With the French Flying Corps.* 1916.

Wise, Frederick M., and Meigs O. Frost. *A Marine Tells it to You.* 1929.

Wister, Owen. *The Pentecost of Calamity.* 1915.

Withington, Alfreda Bosworth. *Mine Eyes Have Seen; A Woman Doctor's Saga.* 1941.

Wolfe, S. Herbert. *In Service.* 1922.

Wood, Eric Fisher. *The Note-Book of an Attaché: Seven Months in a War Zone.* 1915.

———. *The Note-Book of an Intelligence Officer.* 1917.

Wood, Lambert Alexander. *His Job: Letters Written by a 22-Year-Old Lieutenant in the World War to His Parents and Others in Oregon.* 1932.

Woodward, Houston. *A Year For France: War Letters of Houston Woodward.* 1919.

Wright, Jack Morris. *A Poet of the Air.* 1918.

Wunderlich, Raymond. *From Trench and Dugout.* 1919.

Yardley, Herbert O. *The American Black Chamber.* 1931.

York, Alvin. *Sergeant York: His Own Life Story and War Diary.* 1928.

Young, Rush Stephenson. *Over the Top with the 80th.* 1933.

Zander, Harry William. *Thirteen Years in Hell.* 1933.

APPENDIX 2

Selected Bibliography of World War I Novels

Ames, Franklin T. *Between the Lines on the American Front: A Boy's Story of the Great European War.* 1919.

Anderson, Robert G. *Cross of Fire.* 1919.

Andrews, Mary R. S. *Her Country [A Story of the Liberty Loans].* 1918.

——. *His Soul Goes Marching On.* 1922.

Angellotti, Marion Polk. *The Firefly of France.* 1918.

Aspen, Don. *Mike of Company D.* 1939.

Atkinson, Eleanor. *"Poilu," A Dog of Roublaix.* 1919.

Bailey, Irene Temple. *Tin Soldier.* 1918.

Balmer, Edwin. *Ruth of the U.S.A.* 1919.

Barretto, Larry. *Horses in the Sky.* 1930.

Bellah, James Warner. *Gods of Yesterday.* 1928.

Bennet, Robert A. *The Blond Beast.* 1918.

Bishop, Giles. *Captain Comstock, U.S.M.C.* 1923.

——. *Lieutenant Comstock, U. S. Marine.* 1922.

——. *The Marines Have Landed.* 1921.

Bonner, Charles. *Legacy.* 1940.

Boyd, Thomas. *Points of Honor.* 1925.

——. *Through the Wheat.* 1923.

Brooks, Alden. *Fighting Men.* 1917.

Brown, Alice. *The Black Drop.* 1919.

Burtis, Thomson. *Russ Farrell, Airman.* 1924.

Cable, Boyd. *Front Lines.* 1918.

Campbell, William E. M. (William March). *Company K.* 1933.

Canfield, Dorothy. *The Deepening Stream.* 1930.

Cather, Willa. *One of Ours.* 1922.

Chambers, Robert W. *Barbarians.* 1917.

——. *The Dark Star.* 1917.

——. *The Laughing Girl.* 1918.

Cobb, Humphrey. *Paths of Glory.* 1935.

Commander [pseud.]. *Clear the Decks! A Tale of the American Navy Today.* 1918.

Curtis, Kent. *The Tired Captains.* 1928.

Darling, Esther B.., *Navarre of the North.* 1930.

Daly, Victor. *Not Only War.* 1932.

Dawson, Conigsby. *Kingdom Around the Corner.* 1921.

Divine, Charles. *Cognac Hill.* 1927.

Dodge, Henry Irving. *The Yellow Dog.* 1918.

Dos Passos, John R. Jr. *1919.* 1932.

———. *One Man's Initiation.* 1920.

———. *Three Soldiers.* 1921.

Driggs, L. L. *Adventures of Arnold Adair, American Ace.* 1918.

Driggs, Laurence. *On Secret Air Service.* 1930.

Dunbar, Ruth. *Swallow.* 1919.

Dunton, James G. *A Maid & A Million Men.* 1928.

Dyer, Walter. *Ben, The Battle Horse.* 1919.

Empey, Arthur G. *A Helluva War.* 1927.

Erskine, Laurie Y. *Comrades of the Clouds.* 1930.

———. *Fine Fellows.* 1929.

Faulkner, William. *Soldier's Pay.* 1926.

Foote, M. H. *The Ground-Swell.* 1919.

Fredenburgh, Theodore. *Soldiers March.* 1930.

French, Allen. *At Plattsburgh.* 1917.

Gibbs, George Fort. *The Splendid Outcast.* 1920.

Grider, John McGavock. *War Birds.* 1927.

Guthrie, Ramon. *Parachute.* 1928.

Haines, D. H. *The Dragon-Flies.* 1919.

Hall, James Norman, and Charles B. Nordhoff. *Kitchener's Mob.* 1916.

Hamilton, Robert W. *Belinda of the Red Cross.* 1917.

Harris, Credo F. *Where the Souls of Men are Calling.* 1918.

Hemingway, Ernest. *A Farewell to Arms.* 1929.

Hunt, Frazier. *Blown in by the Draft.* 1918.

Jenkins, Burris A. *It Happened Over There.* 1919.

Johnson, Owen M. *Wasted Generation.* 1921.

Kauffman, Reginald W. *Victorious.* 1919.

Keable, Robert. *Simon Called Peter.* 1922.

Kelly, Thomas H. *What Outfit, Buddy?* 1920.

Kennedy, William A. *The Invader's Son.* 1920.

Kyne, Peter B. *They Also Serve.* 1927.

Lardner, Ring. *Treat 'Em Rough.* 1918.

Lebeck, Oscar, and Gaylord DuBois. *Stratosphere Jim and His Flying Fortress.* 1941.

Lee, Mary. *It's a Great War.* 1929.

Lewis, Herbert C. *Spring Offensive.* 1940.

Lohrke, Eugene. *Overshadowed.* 1929.

Lutes, Della T. *My Boy in Khaki.* 1918.

MacGill, Patrick. *Dough Boys.* 1918.

Mack, Charles E. *Two Black Crows in the A.E.F.* 1928.

Malone, Paul B. *Barbed Wire Entanglements.* 1940.

McClure, Robert E. *Some Found Adventure.* 1926.

McKay, Claude. *Home to Harlem.* 1928.

McKay, Helen G. *Chill Hours.* 1920.

Montague, Margaret P. *England to America.* 1920.

———. *Of Water and the Spirit.* 1916.

Nason, Leonard. *Among the Trumpets.* 1930.

———. *Chevrons.* 1926.

———. *Corporal Once.* 1930.

———. *The Fighting Livingstones.* 1931.

———. *The Man in the White Slicker.* 1929.

———. *Sergeant Eadie.* 1928.

———. *Three Lights from a Match.* 1927.

———. *Top Kick.* 1928.

Newsom, J. D. *Garde à Vous!* 1928.

Nordhoff, Charles B., and James Norman Hall. *Falcons of France: A Tale of Youth in the Air.* 1929.

Norton, Roy. *Drowned Gold.* 1919.

Olmstead, Florence. *On Furlough.* 1918.

Paul, Elliot. *The Amazon.* 1930.

Perkins, L. F. *The French Twins.* 1918.

Poole, Ernest, *Blind.* 1920.

Quirk, L. W. *Jimmy Goes to War.* 1931.

Rice, A. H. *Quin.* 1921.

Rinehart, Mrs. M. R. *The Amazing Interlude.* 1918.

Scanlon, William T. *God Have Mercy on Us: A Story of 1918.* 1929.

Schauffler, R. H. *Fiddler's Luck.* 1920.

Schindel, Bayard. *The Golden Pilgrimage.* 1929.

Shepard, William G. *The Scar that Tripled.* 1918.

Sherwood, Margaret. *The Worn Doorstep.* 1916.

Springs, Elliot White. *Contact: A Romance of the Air.* 1930.

———. *Leave Me With a Smile.* 1928.

————. *Nocturne Militaire*. 1927.

————. *The Rise and Fall of Carol Banks*. 1931.

Stallings, Laurence. *Plumes*. 1924.

Steele, Dan. *Snow Trenches*. 1932.

Stevens, James. *Mattock*. 1927.

Stewart, C. D. *Valley Waters*. 1922.

Tarkington, Booth. *Ramsey Milholland*. 1919.

Tomlinson, E. T. *Scouting With General Pershing*. 1918.

Tomlinson, H. M. *All Our Yesterdays*. 1930.

Upson, William. *Me and Henry and the Artillery*. 1928.

Van Dyke, Henry. *The Broken Soldier and the Maid of France*. 1919.

Wharton, Edith. *Marne*. 1919.

————. *A Son at the Front*. 1923.

Wharton, James B. *Squad*. 1928.

White, Walter, *Fire in the Flint*. 1924.

Wise, Jennings C. *The Great Crusade*. 1930.

Witwer, Harry C. *From Baseball to Boches*. 1918.

NOTES

Introduction

1. See Lengel, *To Conquer Hell,* for an excellent review of the offensive.
2. See Terkel, *"The Good War."*
3. See Mock and Larson, *Words that Won the War;* Axelrod, *Selling the Great War;* Harries, *Last Days of Innocence;* and Capozzola, *Uncle Sam Wants You.* Each explores the proliferation of propaganda during the war.
4. Winter, *Remembering War,* 4.
5. Hynes, "Personal Narratives and Commemoration," 207.
6. Fussell, *The Great War and Modern Memory,* 153–57.
7. Hynes, *Soldiers' Tale,* 95–97.
8. Kennedy, *The First World War and American Society,* 218. Membership statistics from Jones, *History of the American Legion,* 344–45. The high point of membership in the 1920s was in 1920, when there were approximately 840,000 members. The low point was in 1925, when there were approximately 610,000.
9. Budreau, *Bodies of War,* 241.
10. Cappon, "Collection of World War I Materials in the States," 743.
11. Forman, *Our Movie Made Children,* 52.
12. Sullivan, *Our Times, 1900–1925,* 115.

1. State War Histories

1. Holbrook, "Collection of State War Service Records," 72.
2. Mereness, *American Historical Activities during the War,* 161, 165.
3. Cappon, "Collection of World War I Materials in the States," 743–44. The Illinois State Historical Society published a four-volume history of the Thirty-Third Division in 1921 and an additional two volumes on wartime organizations and war documents and addresses in 1923; the Minnesota Historical Society published a two-volume narrative history, abandoning plans for an eight-volume work that would have included

three volumes of brief service records of individuals; the State Historical Society of Iowa published a seven-volume series, *Iowa Chronicles in the World War,* which consisted primarily of home front activities; and the Indiana Historical Commission produced the *Gold Star Honor Roll* in 1921, including 3,354 biographical sketches of those who died, with photographs, followed in 1932 by the *Book of Merit,* which included profiles of those wounded or given awards. Cappon speculates that a strong showing by Midwest states was consistent with the high quality of historical societies typically found in that area. The Massachusetts Commission on Massachusetts' Part in the War published the *Gold Star Record* in 1929; the Maryland War Records Commission published two volumes in 1933, which included some service information and an honor roll; the Historical Commission of the Territory of Hawaii produced a history that was part narrative and part honor roll. Commercially produced histories or rosters were published in some states/localities as well, for instance in Kansas, Louisiana, Massachusetts, Vermont, and Wisconsin.

4. Singewald, "Progress in the Collection of War History Records by State War History Organizations," 137; McKinley, "Plans for State and Local Publications on War History," 148.

5. McKinley, "Plans for State and Local Publications on War History," 148.

6. Daniel J. Sweeney to Edward R. Foreman, August 29, 1921, ERFC.

7. Faust, *This Republic of Suffering,* 213.

8. "Notes and Queries," 215.

9. Allen, "Indiana's War History," 1.

10. See Cappon, *A Plan for the Collection and Preservation of World War II Records*; and Binkley, "Two World Wars and American Historical Scholarship."

11. Statistics Branch, General Staff, War Department, March 8, 1920, Historical Research Working Files, 1795–1945 (A3167), NYSA. New York also lost more men than any other state, more than fourteen thousand soldiers died.

12. The adjutant general of the army was provided an appropriation to share data with the states, but the data were slow in coming and often inaccurate. A test case discussed by the NASWHO in December 1920 found that Delaware collected data on 235 dead soldiers while the adjutant general recorded only 123. NASWHO Meeting Minutes, December 28, 1920, Working Files for a Publication on New York in World War I, 1917–1925 (A3166), NYSA.

13. "Dr. James Sullivan Dies of a Stroke," *New York Times*, October 9, 1931, 20.

14. "Dr. James Sullivan Dies of a Stroke," 20. The article refers to the Bureau of Public Information in Washington, it is assumed that it is referencing the CPI. Sullivan also gave speeches on behalf of the Liberty Loan and worked with the State Defense Council to implement "Wake Up America Week." Sullivan gave a series of National Security League addresses in Kentucky, Tennessee, Iowa, and Nebraska. In his role as an educational commissioner for the AEF, Sullivan was given oversight of developing a plan for the education of soldiers abroad. World War I Veterans' Service Data and Photographs, 1917–1938 (A4012), NYSA.

15. Statistics Branch, General Staff, War Department, March 8, 1920, Historical Research Working Files, 1795–1945 (A3167), NYSA.

16. James Sullivan to Karl Singewald, December 1, 1920, Working Files for a Publication on New York in World War I, 1917–1925 (A3167), NYSA. The five boroughs of New York City were not included in the bill authorizing the appointment of local historians, they were added through an amendment in 1921. Of the five, only Brooklyn submitted any information to the state.

17. State Historian Annual Report, July 1920 to June 30, 1921, Historical Research Working Files, 1795–1945 (A3167), NYSA. However, for this to be true, all 1,027 appointed local historians would have submitted reports, plus over one hundred more. These numbers are suspect on several counts. First, there are only approximately six hundred reports extant in the New York State Archives, and there is little evidence that 1,027 local historians were in office in 1925, let alone 1921. Second, Sullivan contradicts his own figures several times in different sources. For example, in 1922 he noted that over one thousand historians had been appointed, and only a "scant handful" had submitted reports by 1920. In his annual report for 1925 he reports that 60 percent of the reports have been received, 15 percent less than he had in hand in 1921.

18. Additional questions, including where a soldier trained, what ships he sailed on, and written statements about a soldier's experiences during the war were also evident in some questionnaires.

19. Charles M. Reed to James Sullivan, March 10, 1921, Historical Research Working Files (A3167), NYSA.

20. James Sullivan to Delight Keller, August 19, 1922, Historical Research Working Files (A3167), NYSA.

21. James Sullivan to Delight Keller, August 19, 1922; L. R. Lewis to James Sullivan, February 13, 1922, Historical Research Working Files (A3167), NYSA.

22. Charles M. Dow, president, Chautauqua County Historical Society, as quoted in the *Jamestown Morning Post*, September 15, 1919, Working Files for a Publication on New York in World War I, 1917–1925 (A3166), NYSA.

23. James Sullivan to Edgar J. Klock, December 21, 1921, World War I Veterans' Service Data (A0412), NYSA.

24. Edgar J. Klock to James Sullivan, December 20, 1921, World War I Veterans' Service Data (A0412), NYSA.

25. George S. Bixby, "City Historian Asks for Military Records," *Plattsburgh Sentinel*, November 10, 1922, 3.

26. "Material for the War History," *Plattsburgh Sentinel*, December 26, 1922, 5.

27. Evelyn M. Barrett to James Sullivan, October 20, 1922, World War I Veterans' Service Data (A0412), NYSA.

28. William A. Orr, State Defense Council, to County Defense Committees, December 3, 1918, Historical Research Working Files (A3167), NYSA.

29. Oneida County Honor Roll, Oneida County Defense Committee, Utica NY, World War I Veterans' Service Data (A0412), NYSA.

30. Review of "Yates County in the World War 1917–1918," 105.

31. E. D. Harrison to Edward B. Foreman, August 1, 1921, Box 2, ERFC.

32. Sweeney, *History of Buffalo & Erie County 1917–1918*.

33. Frank B. Steele, Secretary for the Sons of the American Revolution (Buffalo Chapter) to Edward Foreman, July 27, 1921, Box 2, ERFC.

34. Edward Foreman to Dr. James Sullivan, October 12, 1922, ERFC.

35. Karl Singewald to Edward Foreman, November 3, 1922, ERFC.

36. Monroe County reported 609 war dead and the New York State adjutant general reported 447, another example of the poor quality of the adjutant general's records. Some of the discrepancy may be that Monroe County also reported deaths of home front workers, but it is unlikely they totaled over 160.

37. Edward R. Foreman to Dr. James Sullivan, December 22, 1922, Box 2, ERFC.

38. "Historical Society in One of Its Most Important Works," *Rochester Post Express*, March 15, 1920.

39. Edward R. Foreman to Dr. James Sullivan, July 13, 2921, Box 2, ERFC. Organizations included the Daughters of the American Revolu-

tion, Sons of the American Revolution, Grand Army of the Republic, Soldiers' Memorial Committee, Gold Star Mothers, Mothers of Draftees, Mothers of Volunteers, Federation of Churches, and Societies of the Foreign Born.

40. No other local organizations were overt in their claim to have used veterans to collect data.

41. Leon C. Hatch to Edward R. Foreman, May 8, 1922, Box 6, ERFC.

42. "Much Data Already Gathered for War History of Former Service Men of Rochester," *Record*, March 1922.

43. Foreman, *World War Service Record of Rochester & Monroe County, New York*; Keene, *Doughboys*, 2.

44. Foreman, *World War Service Record of Rochester & Monroe County, New York*.

45. Gibson and Jung, *Historical Census Statistics on Population Totals by Race*. James Sullivan to J. Leslie Kincaid, February 21, 1921. Working Files for a Publication on New York in World War I, 1917–1925 (A3166), NYSA.

46. See Williams's comprehensive *Torchbearers of Democracy* and Barbeau and Henri, *Unknown Soldiers*.

47. Scott, *Scott's Official History of the American Negro in the World War*, 197–207; "Historical Sketch," New York State Military Museum and Veterans Research Center, http://dmna.state.ny.us/historic/reghist /wwi/infantry/369thInf/369thInfHistSketch.htm, accessed December 15, 2010.

48. "Black WWI Vet Gets Posthumous Heroism Medal," *Los Angeles Times*, March 20, 2002, http://articles.latimes.com/2002/mar/20 /news/mn-33725.

49. Johnson is recognized for his heroic exploits in *Albany's Part in the World War*.

50. "About the World War I History Commission Questionnaires Collection," Library of Virginia, http://www.lva.virginia.gov/public /guides/opac/wwiqabout.htm, accessed October 13, 2010.

51. Davis, *Publications of the Virginia War History Commission, Source Volume VII, Virginia Communities in War Time*, 3.

52. C. R. Keiley, Secretary of the War History Commission, to County Committee Chairmen, September 20, 1919, VWHC, Series XI, Office Files, 1917–1927, Boxes 151–55.

53. War History Commission Annual Report, VWHC, Series XI, Office Files, 1917–1927, Box 152, Folder 5.

54. Progress Report, VWHC, Series XI, Office Files, 1917–1927, Box 160, Folder 4.

55. Arthur James to C. R. Keiley, August 24, 1920, VWHC, Series XI, Office Files, 1917–1927, Box 156, Folder 1.

56. Walter F. Beverly to Col. C. R. Keiley, VWHC, Series XI, Office Files, 1917–1927, Box 152, Folder 7.

57. G. M. Harrison to Arthur Kyle Davis, February 14, 1922, VWHC, Series XI, Office Files, 1917–1927, Box 165, Folder 1.

58. Ruth K. Cunningham to Arthur Kyle Davis, VWHC, Series XI, Office Files, 1917–1927, Box 153, Folder 3.

59. Mrs. Turner Thomas to Secretary of the Virginia War History Commission, May 5, 1920, LOV.

60. "Police Supply 2,500 Men with War Record Blanks," *Richmond Times Dispatch*, Tuesday, March 8, 1921. The police were sent to the homes of white veterans, while students of Virginia Union University canvassed black veterans.

61. "About the World War I History Commission Questionnaires Collection," Library of Virginia, http://www.lva.virginia.gov/public/guides/opac/wwiqabout.htm, accessed November 11, 2010; Field Report from 1922 or 1923, VWHC, Series XI, Office Files, 1917–1927, Box 160, Folder 4.

62. Looney, "'I Really Never Thought War Was So Cruel,'" 128–30.

63. Lillian Webb Naylor to Julia Sully, March 16, 1920, VWHC, Series XI, Office Files, 1917–1927, Box 160, Folder 4.

64. Report of Ora Stokes, August 31, 1920, VWHC, Series XI, Office Files, 1917–1927, Box 158, Folder 2.

65. "Returning Troops Decry Dry Nation," (Albany) *Knickerbocker Press*, April 20, 1919, 3.

66. Report of Ora Stokes, August 31, 1920.

67. Barbeau and Henri, *Unknown Soldiers*. Barbeau and Henri also explore the "Red Summer" of 1919 and the role of returning black servicemen in the race riots the year after the war ended.

68. See Smith, *Managing White Supremacy*.

69. Sweeney, *History of the American Negro in the Great World War*. Inducted from Virginia were 141,714 white soldiers and 34,796 black soldiers. Gibson and Jung, *Historical Census Statistics on Population Totals by Race*.

70. Julia Sully to Arthur Kyle Davis, February 23, 1920, VWHC, Series XI, Office Files, 1917–1927, Box 158, Folder 5.

71. Julia Sully to W. S. Morton, Chairman of Charlotte County War History Commission, VWHC, Series XI, Office Files, 1917–1927, Box 158, Folder 4.

72. Lillian Webb Naylor to Miss Sully, March 16, 1920, VWHC, Series XI, Office Files, 1917–1927, Box 158, Folder 2.

73. The Chairman to T. C. Erwin, October 4, 1920, VWHC, Series XI, Office Files, 1917–1927, Box 158, Folder 4.

74. Report of Ora Brown Stokes, Field Agent, VWHC, Series XI, Office Files, 1917–1927, Box 158, Folder 2. Also see Scott, *Scott's Official History of the American Negro in the World War*, 237, 267–69, 310. While all three survivors were born in Virginia, none enlisted from Virginia, and therefore they may not have been solicited to complete a war history questionnaire.

75. Williams, *George S. Schuyler*, 22.

76. See Barbeau and Henri, *Unknown Soldiers*.

77. McWhirter, *Red Summer*, 105. See also Speer and Townsend, *Survival and Struggle*; and Tuttle, *Race Riot*.

78. Sweeney, *History of the American Negro in the Great World War*.

79. "Says Negroes Are Loyal: Head of Hampton Institute Scouts Stories of Disaffection," *New York Times*, April 6, 1917.

80. War History Commission Military Service Record of Edward Leonard Dabney, World War I War History Commission Questionnaires, Library of Virginia, http://lva1.hosted.exlibrisgroup.com/F/?func=file &file_name=find-b-clas13&local_base=clas13, accessed November 3, 2010.

81. Gov. Westmorland Davis, "A Proclamation by the Governor of Virginia," VWHC, Series XI, Office Files, 1917–1927, Boxes 151–55.

82. Looney, "I Really Never Thought War Was So Cruel," 127.

83. Looney, "I Never Really Thought War Was So Cruel," 132. In 1920 approximately 25 percent of African Americans were illiterate, while 4 percent of whites were, so blacks faced a much greater barrier to filling out questionnaires.

84. Looney, "I Never Really Thought War Was So Cruel," 132.

85. Gutiérrez, *Doughboys on the Great War*, 15.

86. "War Notes," 86.

87. H. L. Opie to the Virginia War History Commission, VWHC, Series XI, Office Files, 1917–1927, Box 158, Folder 6, Newspapers 1920–1922.

88. War History Commission Military Service Record of Hierome L. Opie, World War I War History Commission Questionnaires, LOV, http://lva1.hosted.exlibrisgroup.com/F/?func=file&file_name=find -b clas13&local_base=clas13, accessed December 15, 2010.

89. Arthur Kyle Davis to John Garland Pollard, January 17, 1923, VWHC, Series XI, Office Files, 1917–1927, Box 153, Folder 8.

90. The seven histories are for Hanover, Fluvanna, Dickenson, Cumberland, and Scott counties, and the cities of Clifton Forge and Norfolk. Census figures for these counties indicate that there is no indication that size of the county or the ratio of black to white citizens played a role in which submitted reports. See Historical Census Browser, University of Virginia, Geospatial and Statistical Data Center, http://mapserver.lib.virginia.edu/collections/stats/histcensus/index.html, accessed April 16, 2013.

91. Ruth K. Cunningham to Arthur Kyle Davis, February 25, 1921, VWHC, Series XI, Office Files, 1917–1927, Box 153, Folder 3.

92. Lyle, *My Dearest Angel*, 195–275.

93. Progress Report, VWHC, Series XI, Office Files, 1917–1927, Box 160, Folder 4.

94. See Winter, *Remembering War*, 4–5, 279–82. Winter calls remembrance "an act of symbolic exchange between those who remain and those who suffered or died. They went through much; they lost or gave much; we give the little we can—starting with recognition and acknowledgement and then moving on, at times, to material expressions of both." He also argues that many acts of remembrance are facilitated by historians, and these collective acts of remembrance, like war histories, foster and sustain collective memory.

95. Kansas State Historical Society, "World War I." Harry Truman served with the Thirty-Fifth Division as part of the Missouri National Guard.

96. "To Prepare Histories of Two Famous Divisions," Manuscript Collection 49, KSHS, Box 1.

97. English, *History of the 89th Division*. The history includes a roster of officers and a listing of soldiers who were wounded, but no general roster of the men who served.

98. William Connelly to John Beaton, May 23, 1919, Manuscript Collection 49, KSHS, Box 1.

99. William Connelly to Mrs. Hugh Bay, June 1, 1921, Manuscript Collection 49, KSHS, Box 1.

100. William Connelly to W. A. Bevis, July 9, 1919, Manuscript Collection 49, KSHS, Box 1. There is very limited extant information about the Historical Society's effort to collect data, as there are almost no administrative records detailing the process.

101. Nellie Charles Terrill, "The Military Sisterhood of the World War, 1917–1919," Manuscripts, Military Sisterhood 1917–1924, KSHS, Box 1.

102. Nellie C. Terrill to Kansas Women of the Military Sisterhood, October 25, 1918, Manuscript Collection 49, KSHS, Box 1.

103. "Gold Star Mothers Meet," *Topeka Capital,* April 9, 1922.

104. Connelly to Bay, June 1, 1921.

105. Draft layout plan for book, no known author, Manuscript Collection 49: 27.01, KSHS. The document assumes twenty-five hundred war dead from Kansas.

106. Annual Convention Meeting Minutes, 1924 and 1927, American Legion Auxiliary, Kansas Department, KSHS.

107. Records issued by the Kansas State Adjutant General's Office indicate that there were 817 men who enlisted from Marion County.

108. "Marion County Service Men," *Marion Record* (Marion County KS), August 7, 1919, 1.

109. *Honor Roll, Shawnee County, Kansas.*

110. Adjutant General, *Kansans Who Served in the World War.* N.p.: n.d.. Four volumes produced by the adjutant general that list names of soldiers and home counties, KSHS.

111. Advertisement for Crawford County History, *Pittsburg Daily Headlight* (Pittsburg KS), November 19, 1919, 4.

112. *Honor Roll, Crawford County, Kansas, 1919.* Kansas City: Union Bank Note Company, 1919.

113. "Batteries Greeted by Cheering Thousands of the Home Folks," *Pittsburg Daily Headlight,* May 8, 1919, 1.

114. Advertisement, *Pittsburg Daily Headlight,* April 19, 1919, 8.

115. Advertisement, *Pittsburg Daily Headlight,* April 4, 1919, 3.

116. Advertisement, *Pittsburg Daily Headlight,* April 19, 1919, 8.

117. Lightfoot, *Our Heroes in Our Defense.*

118. "Horton Celebrated Its 33rd Anniversary, Sept. 19 and 20," *Horton Headlight-Commercial* (Horton KS), September 25, 1919, 10.

119. *Horton Headlight-Commercial,* July 3, 1919 (reprinted from the *Atchison Globe*).

120. Browne and McManigal, *Our Part in the Great War,* 21.

121. See Britten, *American Indians in World War I.*

122. Wilson, *Russell County in the War.*

123. "Russell County Honor Roll Contains a List of Men Who Didn't Go," *Russell Record,* March 13, 1921, 2.

124. Dean and Alexander, *World War Roll of Honor 1917–1920, Marion County, Kansas.*

125. Miner, *Kansas,* 129.

126. Dean and Alexander, *World War Roll of Honor 1917–1920,* 184–85.

127. Capozzola, *Uncle Sam Wants You*, 69. Capozzola explores the increasing power of the state against Americans, especially those whose loyalty was questioned.

128. Miner, *Kansas*, 237.

129. J. E. Webber to Edward R. Foreman, July 13, 1923, ERFC.

130. Lansing B. Bloom to Edward R. Foreman, January 13, 1922, ERFC.

131. Leon C. Hatch to Edward R. Foreman, May 8, 1922, ERFC.

132. Yockelson, "They Answered the Call: Military Service in the United States Army during World War I."

2. War Memoirs

1. I compiled a select bibliography of these narratives (see appendix 1) using two comprehensive bibliographies produced in 1969 and 2004 by Genthe, *American War Narratives, 1917–1918*, and Lengel, *World War I Memories*. Additional research using numerous other less-comprehensive lists, including the American Book Publishing Record, the *Subject Catalog of the World War I Collection* for the New York Public Library (1961), and books discovered during research, provided additional titles not included in either of the first two bibliographies. For the purposes of this study, narratives were included if they were written by an American citizen who had the opportunity to experience the war from a military, diplomatic, volunteer, medical, or civilian perspective and published their story between 1914 and 1941. Generally, only books that have the war as their primary subject matter are included. Most books were published for sale to the general public, but a small number were privately printed. This list is not considered to be comprehensive but represents a close approximation of the total number of memoirs published during the interwar years.

2. See Zeigler's *World War II Books in English 1945–1965*.

3. Glende, "Victor Berger's Dangerous Ideas."

4. Aldrich, *Hilltop on the Marne*, and Huard, *My Home on the Field of Honor*.

5. Hackett, *Seventy Years of Best Sellers 1895–1965*, 115.

6. Aldrich wrote *On the Edge of the War Zone* (1915) and *The Peak of the Load* (1915), which continued her original story, and Huard wrote *My Home in the Field of Mercy* (1917), about using her home as a hospital for the wounded, and *With Those Who Wait* (1918), about the hard circumstances facing those who wait at home.

7. Ogden, "The Book Trade in War Time," 98. Irvin Cobb wrote the best seller *Paths of Glory* in 1914 while traveling with both the Bel-

gian and German armies. His book suffered because he wrote about the precision and effectiveness of the German army.

8. La Motte, *Backwash of War*, 58. The book was reissued in 1934.

9. "The Backwash of War: Realities of the Hospital Presented by an American Nurse," *Springfield Daily Republican*, October 2, 1916, 6.

10. Colby, "The War Books," 446.

11. The *Bookman* and the *Publishers' Weekly* were two of the most popular, although many other publications offered similar analyses.

12. Hackett, *Fifty Years of Best Sellers 1895–1945*, vii.

13. Mott, *Golden Multitudes*, 204–6.

14. Mott, *Golden Multitudes*, 1–3.

15. Hackett, *Seventy Years of Best Sellers*, 4–5.

16. Mott, *Golden Multitudes*, 240–42.

17. Interestingly, *See Here, Private Hargrove* by Marion Hargrove became a best seller during World War II. Hargrove takes much the same approach as Streeter by taking a humorous look at a soldier's experiences in the army.

18. Swanson, "Edward Streeter." Streeter is much better remembered for his 1949 book, *Father of the Bride*, not his wartime writing. His fictional account of a father not ready to marry off his only daughter was enshrined in public memory when Spencer Tracy and Elizabeth Taylor brought the tale to life on the silver screen in 1950.

19. Hart, *The Popular Book*, 225. Streeter's second and third books in the series were *That's Me All Over, Mable* and *Same Old Bill, eh Mable!* He also later added *As You Were, Bill!*

20. Ogden, "The Book Trade in War Time," 94–95.

21. "Wilson Heard Empey Talk," *New York Times*, August 12, 1918, 1.

22. "Captaincy Given to Author and Lecturer on July 16th, Cancelled Three Days Later," *New York Times*, July 26, 1918, http://query.nytimes.com/mem/archive-free/pdf?res=9f04e1d6103bee3abc4e51dfb1668383609ede.

23. Hackett, *Seventy Years of Best Sellers*, 25, 77, 117. Another best seller, *Rhymes of a Red Cross Man*, sold incredibly well relative to previous sales of poetry books. It was accompanied on the best-seller list by other works of poetry, including the *Poems of Alan Seeger, Over Here* by Edgar Guest, *In Flanders Fields* by John McCrae, and the *Treasury of War Poetry* by G. H. Clarke.

24. Wiegand, *"An Active Instrument for Propaganda,"* 35.

25. "'Don'ts from the Author of 'Over the Top,'" *New York Times*, October 14, 1917, 68.

26. Gordon, *Lafayette Escadrille Pilot Biographies,* 217–24.

27. Gordon, *Lafayette Escadrille Pilot Biographies,* 217–19.

28. Grech, "O'Brien, Patrick Alva MC." Grech has researched the 66th Squadron for over twenty years and has completed biographies on many of its members. He reports that family members and historians raised funds in 2007 to place an appropriate marker on O'Brien's gravesite.

29. Smith, "War Books by American Diplomatists," 94–96.

30. Smith, "War Books by American Diplomatists," 98.

31. Smith, "War Books by American Diplomatists," 96–98.

32. Genthe, "Personal War Narratives in America, 1914–1918," 228–30.

33. Nitchie et al., *Pens for Ploughshares,* 38.

34. Genthe, *American War Narratives,* 1–5.

35. Genthe, *American War Narratives,* 22.

36. The *Winds of Chance* advertisement, *Publishers' Weekly,* October 5, 1918, 1093.

37. "'War Books after the War," 1586.

38. "What's This? Yank Dubbed Highbrow?," *Stars and Stripes,* June 6, 1919, 1.

39. Tomlinson, "War Books," 450.

40. J. I. Wyer Jr. to President of the University, May 14, 1919, *University of the State of New York Bulletin,* October 1, 1919. The New York State Library published a "Best Books" list that recommended books that were appropriate for small libraries with limited appropriations for book purchases. Officials at the library boasted that "testimony to its wide use may be found in the fact that 5,000 additional copies were printed by the American Library Association and the library commissions of many other states," thus testifying to its potential reach beyond New York.

41. Lynd and Lynd, *Middletown,* 230–31.

42. Bennett, "What We Read and Why We Read It," 123–24. Bennett also estimated that there are approximately five million illiterate adults in 1925.

43. Review, Fighting the Flying Circus, 578.

44. Lewis, *Eddie Rickenbacker,* 219–34. Hervey Allen's book contract gave him a royalty of 15 percent on every book sold over 1,500. If Rickenbacker had a similar contract, this would mean it sold over 100,000 copies.

45. Simmons, "Catlin of the 6th Regiment," 3.

46. "Quentin Roosevelt Has Soldier Burial," *New York Times,* July 22, 1918, 1.

47. Trout, *On the Battlefield of Memory*, 222–25.

48. "Kermit Roosevelt's Story of Mesopotamia in the War," *New York Times*, November 9, 1919, BR5. In 1919, the American author Lowell Thomas began giving lectures in New York City about T. E. Lawrence's exploits in the Middle East.

49. Information on printings is taken from the *National Union Catalog*.

50. Nevins, *Letters and Journal of Brand Whitlock*, 249.

51. See Anderson, *Brand Whitlock*, for a biography of Whitlock's life.

52. Crunden, *A Hero in Spite of Himself*, 363, 475.

53. Nevins, *Letters and Journal of Brand Whitlock*, 240.

54. Nevins, *Letters and Journal of Brand Whitlock*, 507.

55. Spartacus Educational, "Profile of *Everybody's Magazine*." The magazine's political stance may have cost them readers after the war. Readership dropped precipitously after the war, and the magazine closed in 1929.

56. Nevins, *Letters and Journal of Brand Whitlock*, 302–3, 334.

57. Wells, "Ballade of War Books," 643.

58. Hynes, *The Soldier's Tale*, 4.

59. "War Books," 261.

60. Frick, "Katherine Mayo Biography."

61. Book review of *That Damn Y!*, *North American Review*, August 1920, 283, from Katherine Mayo's scrapbook, Katherine Mayo Papers, Series 3.

62. Book review of *That Damn Y!*, *Richmond Leader*, June 16, 1920, from Katherine Mayo's scrapbook, Katherine Mayo Papers, Series 3.

63. Frederic F. Van de Water, "Books," *New-York Tribune*, June 21, 1920, from Katherine Mayo Papers, Series 3.

64. Frick, "Katherine Mayo Biography," 1.

65. Gordon, *Lafayette Escadrille Pilot Biographies*, 69–71.

66. Gordon, *Lafayette Escadrille Pilot Biographies*, 74.

67. Gordon, *Lafayette Escadrille Pilot Biographies*, 71.

68. "Real D'Artagnans Who Seek Peril Afar," *New York Times Magazine*, April 27, 1930, 18.

69. "Bert Hall Gets 2½ Years," *New York Times*, November 11, 1933, 9.

70. "Weston Hall, 62, Flier of Fortune," *New York Times*, December 8, 1948, 31.

71. Penrose, *James G. Harbord*, 335.

72. Penrose, *James G. Harbord*, 280.

73. Book review, *Boston Transcript*, October 17, 1925, 2.

74. Woollcott, "Introducing Captain Thomason of the Marines," 70.

75. Brickell, "This New Vogue for War Books," 530.

76. Greicus, *Prose Writers of World War I*, 15.

77. Greicus, *Prose Writers of World War I*, 33.

78. Advertisements in *Publishers' Weekly*, July 20, 1929, 240; and December 28, 1929, 1882.

79. Smythe, *Pershing, General of the Armies*, 288–89.

80. Smith, *Until the Last Trumpet Sounds*, 188.

81. Hackett, *Seventy Years of Best Sellers*, 145. The book did not make the best-seller lists for 1932, although Clarence Darrow's autobiography did, but it did appear on the *Bookman*'s list of books most requested at public libraries.

82. Larry Barretto, "Does War Pay," *New-York Herald Tribune*, April 26, 1926, 7.

83. See Hynes, *The Soldiers' Tale*, 96–97.

84. Hackett, *Seventy Years of Best Sellers*, 29, 148.

85. Knee, *Hervey Allen 1889–1949*, 161.

86. Knee, *Hervey Allen*, 438.

87. Dickinson, *Best Books of the Decade, 1926–1935*, viiii, 20.

88. Perry, *Sergeant York*, 91.

89. Perry, *Sergeant York*, 17–20.

90. Perry, *Sergeant York*, 121.

91. Perry, *Sergeant York*, 200.

92. Lynd and Lynd, *Middletown*, 230–31.

93. Duffus, *Books*, 1–3. The survey found that 44 percent of the total population had no access to a public library, a figure that jumps to 83 percent for rural populations. Additionally, of the 3,065 U.S. counties, 1,135 had no public libraries (including four cities with populations 25,000–100,000).

94. Bennett, "What We Read and Why We Read It," 119.

95. See Cook and Monro, *Standard Catalog for Public Libraries*.

96. *Books for the High School Library*, 6, 7, 181.

97. Brown, *Standard Catalog for High School Libraries*, vii, 184, and "Directions for Use."

98. Schmidt, *500 Books for the Senior High School Library*.

99. Cook and Monro, *Standard Catalog for Public Libraries*, 1382–83. Additional books that were suggested, but not annotated, were *I Saw Them Die* by Shirley Millard and *American Black Chamber* by H. O. Yardley; both were out of print in 1939.

100. See Drury, *What Books Shall I Read?*

101. Costello, *A List of Books for A College Student's Reading*.

102. National Council of Teachers of English, *Good Reading*, 43–44.

103. National Council of Teachers of English, *Good Reading*, 56.

104. Waples and Tyler, *What People Want to Read About*, 10–15. The survey solicited opinions from a wide range of respondents, including high school and college students, skilled craftsmen, postal clerks, farmers, prisoners, waiters, shop girls, housewives, telephone operators, factory girls, and teachers. The survey did not address fiction and excluded humorous and historical writing.

105. Waples and Tyler, *What People Want to Read About*, 284–85.

106. Waples and Tyler, *What People Want to Read About*, 83.

107. Waples and Tyler, *What People Want to Read About*, 103.

108. Waples and Tyler, *What People Want to Read About*, 45.

109. Moreland, "What Young People Want to Read About," 469–93.

110. Dawson's war stories were best sellers during the war. Gertrude Atherton was a controversial novelist who was also the protégé of the bitter Civil War writer Ambrose Bierce.

111. Dawson, "The Unharvested Literature of the War," 1. Although Dawson was American, he bases much of his commentary on the situation in Great Britain, but indicates that he feels his criticisms are equally applicable to America.

112. W. J. Locke wrote several best-selling novels before the war, many of which were dramatized in Broadway plays and film.

113. Locke, "The Novelist's Dilemma," 176.

114. "Must Novelists Forget the War?," 35.

115. "The Plight of Novelists," *New-York Tribune*, August 3, 1920, 8. For more information about the Red Scare just after World War I, see Ceplair, *Anti-Communism in Twentieth Century America*; or Powers, *Not Without Honor*.

116. Ceplair, *Anti-Communism in Twentieth Century America*, 38.

117. Coningsby, "Unharvested Literature of the War," 1.

118. *Publishers' Weekly*, October 9, 1920, 1084.

119. Graves, "Poets in War and Peace."

120. Fussell, *The Great War and Modern Memory*, 153–57.

121. Hynes, *Soldiers' Tale*, 95–97.

122. "Marks of a Classic," 222–23.

123. Obituary for Cyril Falls, *Times* (London), April 24, 1971. Falls was the Military Correspondent to the *Times* for fourteen years and the Chichele Professor of the History of War at Oxford University from 1946–53. He had a "vast knowledge of French, as well as of English literature," and his credibility in this field is well established.

124. Falls, *War Books.*

125. Hemingway, *Men at War.* While Hemingway might have liked Thomason's writing, he only used one selection about World War I ("The Marines at Soissons"). Thomason's other selections are about the Civil War. The contributions from Stallings ("Vale of Tears") and Hall and Nordhoff ("Air Battle") are both about World War I.

126. Flowers, *A Century of Best Sellers, 1830–1930,* 3.

127. Egremont, *Siegfried Sassoon,* 361, 429, 436.

128. See Trout, introduction to *Goodbye to All That and Other Great War Writings,* xi, xxi; and Seymour, *Robert Graves,* 192.

129. Fussell, *The Great War and Modern Memory,* 256; and Fayn, *Writing Disenchantment,* 232–33.

130. Sherriff, *No Leading Lady: An Autobiography,* 192.

131. Gene Weingarten, "Pearls before Breakfast," *Washington Post,* April 8, 2007, http://www.washingtonpost.com/wpdyn/content/article /2007/04/04/ar2007040401721.html. Weingarten won a 2008 Pulitzer Prize for his articles about this experiment. While not scientifically valid, the experiment demonstrates that taste is purely subjective and can be defined by the ideas of those around us or the environment in which we live.

3. War Stories

1. The chapter subtitle is taken from "With Malice Toward None," *War Stories,* November 1926, 2, PFC.

2. "Must Novelists Forget the War," *Literary Digest,* August 21, 1920, 35.

3. Kammen, *Mystic Chords of Memory,* 488, 497. Another scholar on war and memory, G. Kurt Piehler, also notes American ambivalence in the postwar era. He cites the popularity of Erich Maria Remarque and Ernest Hemingway on the one hand with the copious commemoration efforts of government agencies, communities, and the American Legion on the other.

4. Fitzgerald, *This Side of Paradise.*

5. Edward Gutiérrez makes a similar argument in *Doughboys on the Great War.*

6. See Hackett, *Seventy Years of Best Sellers.* Another is Mott's *Golden Multitudes,* which rates a book a best seller if it sold an amount equivalent to 1 percent of the population in the decade in which it was published.

7. Hackett, *Seventy Years of Best Sellers,* 19.

8. Fenton, "American Ambulance Drivers in France and Italy: 1914–1918," 326. For further reading on the "lost generation," see Wohl, *The*

Generation of 1914. Wohl tries to separate the history of the war generation from the myth that has evolved. Interestingly, Wohl ignores the American perspective entirely, focusing only on the European experience.

9. Baker, *Ernest Hemingway*, 30.

10. Baker, *Ernest Hemingway*, 44–52.

11. Hemingway was awarded the Croce di Guerra (Italian war cross for military valor) and Medaglia d'Argento al Valore (Italian medal for gallantry).

12. Noble, review of *Hemingway in Love and War: The Lost Diary of Agnes von Kurowsky*, 138.

13. Ernest Hemingway, "How to Be Popular in Peace Though a Slacker in War," *Toronto Star Weekly*, March 13, 1920, 11.

14. Fitzgerald, This Side of Paradise.

15. Bruccoli and Trogdon, *The Only Thing That Counts*, 126.

16. Hemingway, *The Sun Also Rises*; Hutner, *What America Read*.

17. Mott, *Golden Multitudes*, 241.

18. Mulvey, "A Defense of *A Farewell to Arms*," 243.

19. Herrick, "What Is Dirt?," 258–62.

20. Woodress, *Willa Cather*, 334.

21. Woodress, *Willa Cather*, 228.

22. Robinson, *Willa*, 222.

23. Cather, *One of Ours*, 370.

24. Mencken, review of One of Ours, 140.

25. Woodress, *Willa Cather*, 333.

26. Woodress, "A Note on *One of Ours*," 1, 4.

27. "Comment on Two Decisions," *New York Times*, May 15, 1923, 18.

28. Trout, *Memorial Fictions*, see chapter 1, "Americans Lost."

29. Trout, *Memorial Fictions*, 11.

30. Hohenberg, *Pulitzer Prizes*, 19, 87. In 1929 the wording was changed to "the whole atmosphere of American life," instead of "wholesome."

31. Stuckey, *Pulitzer Prize Novels*, 41.

32. Stuckey, *Pulitzer Prize Novels*, 44–45.

33. Hohenberg, *Pulitzer Prizes*, 91.

34. Woodress, *Willa Cather*, 85–93.

35. Washington, *Dorothy Canfield Fisher*, 20–21.

36. Phelps, review of *The Deepening Stream*, 199.

37. Washington, *Dorothy Canfield Fisher*, 173.

38. Yates, *The Lady from Vermont*, 174.

39. SeBoyar, *Pocket Library of the World's Essential Knowledge*, 193–204.

40. Review of *Ramsey Milholland*, *New Republic*, 158.

41. Woodress, *Booth Tarkington*, 200–201.

42. Woodress, *Booth Tarkington*, 201.

43. "Latest Works of Fiction," *New York Times*, August 17, 1919, 78.

44. "Humphrey Cobb, 44, War Story Author," *New York Times*, April 26, 1944, 19.

45. "War, First Degree," 83.

46. "Book Notes," *New York Times*, June 5, 1935, 17.

47. "Mutiny of Troops Reviewed in Paris," *New York Times*, June 3, 1934, 26.

48. Robert Van Gelder, "A Talk with the Author of '*Paths of Glory*,'" *New York Times*, September 22, 1940, BR2.

49. Eyster, "Warren Eyster on Humphrey Cobb's Paths of Glory," 138, 135.

50. Simon, introduction to *Paths of Glory*, by Humphrey Cobb.

51. Eyster, "Warren Eyster on Humphrey Cobb's Paths of Glory," 138, 135. Publishing statistics from the *National Union Catalog*.

52. Trout, *American Prose Writers of World War I*, 299–300.

53. Grider, *War Birds*, 201.

54. Grider, *War Birds*, 330.

55. Davis, *War Bird*, 106–7. Springs was originally offered $5,000 for the story, but he negotiated for extra payment for text in excess of thirty thousand words and ultimately earned $9,388.70.

56. Vaughan, *Letters from a War Bird*, 284, 308.

57. Hart, *The Popular Book*, 243.

58. Whitehouse, *Heroes of the Sunlit Sky*, 5–6.

59. Vaughan, *Letters from a War Bird*, 345.

60. The family business, Springs Cotton Mills, produced the Spring-maid brand of sheets and pillowcases. Elliot Springs would also be remembered for a famously risqué advertising campaign.

61. Hart, *The Popular Book*, 237.

62. Hemingway's poor showing at the Boston Public Library was because much of his writing was banned in that city.

63. Hutner, *What America Read*, 47. Hutner's claim that the "intelligentsia" hijacked memory of the war is representative of many other scholars who come to the same conclusion, including Walsh, *American War Literature 1914 to Vietnam*, and Isenberg, "The Great War Viewed from the Twenties: The Big Parade."

64. Publishing information is taken from the *National Union Catalog*. Sales figures from Hackett, *70 Years of Best Sellers*.

65. Hutner, *What America Read*, 2.

66. Hutner, *What America Read*, 4.

67. Hutner, *What America Read*, 64. Newspapers and magazines depend on advertising revenue and publishing houses make up part of that revenue. Hutner notes that, for example, the *New York Times* maintains a high proportion of positive reviews versus negative reviews, presumably because of the financial incentive to do so.

68. Hutner, *What America Read*, 26.

69. Hutner, *What America Read*, 45.

70. Modern Library, "One Hundred Best Novels."

71. See Oliver, *Ernest Hemingway's A Farewell to Arms*.

72. There were also many other well-known authors who could be considered here, for example, E. E. Cummings (*The Enormous Room*, 1922), William Faulkner (*Soldiers' Pay*, 1926), and Laurence Stallings (*Plumes*, 1924), all of whom wrote well-respected novels about disillusionment and World War I.

73. Mencken, "Portrait of an American Citizen," 141.

74. Coningsby Dawson, "Insulting the Army," *New York Times*, October 2, 1921, 43.

75. Ludington, *John Dos Passos*, 213.

76. Ludington, *John Dos Passos*, 203.

77. Ludington, *John Dos Passos*, 213.

78. Dos Passos's political views were well known to publishers. An editor at the *Bookman* called Dos Passos and others "insoluble alien influences" who were proselytizing their "creeds." Boyar, *Purity in Print*, 110. Little evidence has been uncovered, however, that indicates that the Red Scare had a significant effect on war books in general.

79. Matsen, *The Great War and the American Novel*, 54.

80. Pizer, *John Dos Passos's U.S.A.*, 274.

81. Bruce, *Thomas Boyd*, 46.

82. Fitzgerald and Boyd became friends when both lived in St. Paul, Minnesota, after the war.

83. Trout, *American Prose Writers of World War I*, 67, 76.

84. Trout, *American Prose Writers of World War I*, 67.

85. Matsen, *The Great War and the American Novel*, 91.

86. Bruce, *Thomas Boyd*, 141.

87. See Simmonds, *Two Worlds of William March*.

88. Simmonds, *Two Worlds of William March*, 75.

89. Waldmeir, "Novelists of Two Wars," 304.

90. See Greene, *Blacks in Eden*, and James, *A Freedom Bought with Blood*.

91. Davis, "Not Only War Is Hell," 479.

92. Waldron, *Walter White and the Harlem Renaissance*, 42.

93. Waldron, *Walter White and the Harlem Renaissance*, 74–76.

94. Andrews, Foster, and Harris, *African American Literature*, 6.

95. Andrews, Foster, and Harris, *African American Literature*, 71–72.

96. Bassett, *Harlem in Review*, 18.

97. Tillery, *Claude McKay*, 84–85.

98. Bassett, *Harlem in Review*, 92–93.

99. Poetry Foundation, "Claude McKay, 1889–1948."

100. Piehler, *Remembering War the American Way*, 111, 113.

101. "For the Best War Novel, $25,000," *American Legion Monthly*, April 1928, 20–21.

102. Trout, *On the Battlefield of American Memory*, 101–5.

103. Trout, *On the Battlefield of American Memory*, 104–5. Finding aid for Mary Lee's papers at the Radcliffe Institute for Advanced Study.

104. MacLeish, "Lines for an Internment," 159–60.

105. MacLeish, "A Communication, the Dead of the Next War," 215.

106. Cowley, response to review of *The First World War* by Archibald MacLeish, 160–161.

107. Pottle, "Creed Not Annulled," 359–62. Pottle wrote *Stretchers, the Story of a Hospital Unit on the Western Front* in 1929.

108. Wilder, "At the Nethermost Piers of History," 345, 354–57.

109. Waldmeir, "Novelists of Two Wars," 304–5. See also Eisinger, "The American War Novel."

110. Eisinger, "American War Novel," 272.

111. Lundberg, "American Literature of War," 384.

112. The other six were *The Wall* (John Hersey), *Melville Goodwin USA* (John Phillips Marquand), *No Time for Sergeants* (Mac Hyman), *Don't Go Near the Water* (William Brinkley), *Mila 18* (Leon Uris), and *This Above All* (Eric Knight). See Hackett, *Seventy Years of Best Sellers*.

113. *From Here to Eternity* was at the top of the list of six, with sales of 3,646,004.

114. Remarque's success with *All Quiet on the Western Front* in America is puzzling considering Humphrey Cobb's equally stark antiwar novel, *Paths of Glory*, sold poorly.

115. The Modern Library published *A Farewell to Arms* and *The Deepening Stream,* and Mercury Books published *Company K* in cheaper editions.

116. "Popular Fiction as It Is Today," 32; and *N.W. Ayer and Son's American Newspaper Annual and Directory*.

117. Goulart, *Cheap Thrills*, 13.

118. "With Malice toward None," *War Stories*, November 1926, 2, PFC.

119. "Bed-Time War Stories," *New Republic*, 178. "Vin-blink" was a poor representation of *vin blanc*, or white wine.

120. Letter to the editor of *War Stories* from Capt. Harry W. Hiltz, *War Stories*, April 1927, 253–54, PFC.

121. "The Firing Step," *Battle Stories*, September 1927, 169, PFC.

122. Whitehouse, *Heroes of the Sunlit Sky*, 6.

123. Corn, *Winged Gospel*, 10–13.

124. Morrow, *The Great War in the Air*, 365.

125. "Melvin Lostutter Gets Personal," letter to the editor from Melvin Lostutter, *Under Fire Magazine*, May 1929, 496, PFC.

126. "The Humor in *Under Fire*," letter to the editor from Thomas O'Roorke, *Under Fire*, April 1929, 373, PFC.

127. "The Humor in *Under Fire*," 373.

128. Royce B. Howes, "Men: Pink tea ideas didn't count in that red horror at the front," *War Stories*, February 16, 1928, PFC.

129. "Magazines of General Circulation," *N.W. Ayer & Son's Directory of Magazines and Periodicals*, 1250–52.

130. These numbers are conservative. A writer for the magazine estimated that successful pulps averaged about two hundred thousand copies per issue.

131. Barclay, "Magazines for Morons," 42.

132. Rasche, *Reading Interests of Young Workers*, 65.

133. Aaron A. Wyn, "Pulp Magazines (Letter to the Editor)," *New York Times*, September 4, 1935, 18.

134. Hynes, *The Soldiers' Tale*, 110.

135. Robinson, "The Wood-Pulp Racket," 651.

4. War Films

1. Quoted in Berger, "Ev'ry Time We Say Goodbye."

2. Lynd and Lynd, *Middletown*, 263–64; and Koszarski, *Evening's Entertainment*, 26.

3. Forman, *Our Movie Made Children*, 10–11.

4. Forman, *Our Movie Made Children*, 46.

5. Hampton, *History of the American Film Industry*, 201.

6. "Dogs of War Let Loose on Screen," 2320.

7. Isenberg, "The Great War Viewed from the Twenties," 29.

8. These films are easily accessible via online archives or DVD.

9. Blasco Ibáñez, *Four Horsemen of the Apocalypse*.

10. Hackett, *Seventy Years of Best Sellers*, 120.

11. "Book Is Sensation of Publishing World," 2236.

12. Isenberg, *War on Film*, 71–72.

13. Soderbergh, "Aux Armes!," 513.

14. For an overview of wartime movies, see DeBauche, *Reel Patriotism*.

15. Ross, *Working Class Hollywood*, 124.

16. See Campbell, *Reel America and World War I*. There were only a few films before 1917 that were antiwar; one of the most successful was *War Brides*, in which a British soldier's pregnant wife protests the war and its voracious appetite for the young men of England.

17. "Dogs of War Let Loose on Screen," 2320.

18. Spears, "World War I on the Screen: Part 2," 347.

19. "Filming Story Was Gigantic Task," *Motion Picture News*, March 26, 1921. Twelve thousand extras would have been quite the feat, and some have questioned this figure.

20. Sargent, "Got the Pick of New York Windows for the 'Four Horsemen' Production."

21. Finler, The Hollywood Story, 276.

22. "Our Boys and Girls," *Time*, June 11, 1923, 15.

23. Quoted in Soderbergh, "Aux Armes!," 515.

24. Ramsaye, *A Million and One Nights*, 802.

25. Valentino died in 1926 at age thirty-one from a perforated ulcer and prompted the first "extra" newspaper edition for an actor's death. See *Dark Lover* by Emily W. Leider.

26. Review of "The Four Horsemen," March 5, 1921, 1859.

27. Review of "The Four Horsemen," February 26, 1921, 1235.

28. "Realistic Bombardment in Metro Special," 2223. Five thousand veterans were reportedly used to shoot the main battle scene, the second Battle of the Marne.

29. "On the Screen in City Theaters," *Sun* (New York), March 7, 1921, 12.

30. Koszarski, *An Evening's Entertainment*, 29.

31. There were few war pictures produced from 1919 to 1925, and almost all were failures at the box office. See Isenberg, "The Great War Viewed from the Twenties."

32. "Dogs of War Let Loose on Screen," 2320.

33. Vidor, *A Tree Is a Tree*, 111.

34. Schickel, *Men Who Made the Movies*, 139.

35. "Dogs of War Let Loose on Screen," 2320.

36. Spears, "World War I on the Screen," 351.

37. Vidor, *A Tree Is a Tree*, 111–12.

38. Koszarski, *Evening's Entertainment*, 311.

39. Lawrence Stallings also lost a leg during the war, so this aspect of the story brought a bit of his life experience to the screen.

40. Isenberg, "The Great War Viewed from the Twenties," 29.

41. Isenberg, "The Great War Viewed from the Twenties," 116.

42. Wheelock, "The Years," 18–19.

43. Charles Higham, "He Directed 'em All—from Doug Fairbanks to Bogey," *New York Times*, April 14, 1974, 103.

44. A World War Veteran, "Flashes from the Past," *New York Times*, May 30, 1926, x2.

45. "Film Reviews, The Big Parade," 40.

46. Vidor, *A Tree Is a Tree*, 124–26.

47. "Over There," *New York Times*, June 13, 1926, xx2; "Flashes from the Past," x2.

48. "French Like 'Big Parade,'" *New York Times*, November 10, 1926, 6.

49. "Grim Film of War," *New York Times*, November 20, 1927, x5.

50. "Dogs of War Let Loose on Screen," 2320. The films were both drama and comedy, including *We're in the Navy, Wings, Private Izzy Murphy, The Big Gun, Remember, The Patent Leather Kid, Corporal Kate* (about the role of women in the war), and *Men of the Dawn*.

51. Jacobs, "Men without Women," 310.

52. Schickel, *The Men Who Made the Movies*, 33.

53. "Strange Screen Confidences," 24.

54. "'What Price Glory' a Brilliant Triumph for Producer, Author, Cast and Director," *Motion Picture News*, November 27, 1926, 2016.

55. Review of *What Price Glory*, 15.

56. Walsh, *Each Man in His Time*, 186.

57. Walsh, *Each Man in His Time*, 193.

58. "$408,152 Glory Record at New York Roxy," 842.

59. Moss, *Raoul Walsh*, 93.

60. IMDB Movie Database.

61. Schader, "The Cock-Eyed World," 603–4.

62. "The Cock-Eyed World," *Harrison Reports*, August 10, 1929, 127.

63. Forman, *Our Movie Made Children*, 52.

64. John Corbin, "The Play," *New York Times*, October 31, 1922, 20.

65. Dumont, *Frank Borzage, the Life and Films of a Hollywood Romantic*, 111.

66. Borzage also directed two other war-romance movies, the screen version of *A Farewell to Arms* and *The Mortal Storm*.

67. Review of *Seventh Heaven*, 289.

68. "'7th Heaven' Taxi Feature of Fox Ballyhoo Through the East," 734. The cab was purchased by Fox Studios from the French War Office

as one of the actual cabs used to rush troops to the River Orcq during the fight to save Paris.

69. Kelly, *Filming All Quiet on the Western Front*, 112.

70. Eksteins, "All Quiet on the Western Front and the Fate of a War," 361.

71. Eksteins, "All Quiet on the Western Front and the Fate of a War," 362.

72. Eksteins, "All Quiet on the Western Front and the Fate of a War," 50–51.

73. Review of *All Quiet on the Western Front*, 75.

74. "Cinema: The New Pictures, May 5, 1930."

75. Kelly, *Cinema and the Great War*, 44.

76. Harry Allen Potamkin, "The Eyes of the Movie."

77. "Untruthful War Films," 27.

78. Kelly, *Filming All Quiet on the Western Front*, 112.

79. Kelly, *Cinema and the Great War*, 50–51.

80. Isenberg, *War on Film*, 139. Isenberg noted that only two films released in America suggested that the war was in any way controversial for Americans, *Beyond Victory* (1931), which suggested that American soldiers saw no purpose in the war, and *Private Jones* (1933), which featured a draft dodger and caricatures of the dollar-a-year man, YMCA staff, and the venereal disease lecturer.

81. Suid, *Guts & Glory*, 41.

82. Behlmer, "World War I Aviation Films," 413–14.

83. Paris, "Wings," 12.

84. "Big Advance Sale of Tickets for 'Wings,'" 104.

85. Suid, *Guts & Glory*, 39.

86. "Films–'Hell's Angels," 254.

87. Isenberg, *War on Film*, 125–27.

88. Dickson and Allen, *Bonus Army*, 254.

89. Dickson and Allen, *Bonus Army*, 284.

90. *Gold Diggers of 1933*, dir. Busby Berkeley and Marvin LeRoy.

91. While the Bonus March is significant to the evolving memory of the war, it is generally insignificant to this study through chapter 3 because there was not much of interest published in 1932, or for that matter, after 1932. The only significant book published after the Bonus March was Humphrey Cobb's *Paths of Glory*, which came out three years after the march, and as such was likely not affected.

92. The Production Code was administered by the Motion Pictures Producers and Distributors of America (MPPDA) beginning in 1930. It

was called the Hays Code because the director was Will H. Hays, a former postmaster general. The 1930 code would be altered and enforced more vigorously beginning in 1934, when the Catholic-based National League of Decency was formed. See Doherty, "A Code Is Born, 55–60.

93. Dickson and Allen, *Bonus Army*, 284.

94. Dickson and Allen, *Bonus Army*, 48.

95. Dickson and Allen, *Bonus Army*, 55.

96. Jacobs, *Rise of the American Film*, 531.

97. "Giant Board Shows War Shots for '69th' Harrisburg Date," 78.

98. "Fighting 69th," 26.

99. Leab, "*The Fighting 69th*," 114.

100. Leab, "*The Fighting 69th*," 113, 117.

101. Leab, "*The Fighting 69th*," 117.

102. Birdwell, *Celluloid Soldiers*, 104.

103. See Perry, *Sergeant York*.

104. York was said to have been opposed to the "wrong type" of girl playing his wife, Gracie, in the film. He was opposed to anyone who smoked or had an overtly sexual persona, which led to the casting of fifteen-year-old Joan Leslie over a more bankable Jane Russell.

105. Birdwell, *Celluloid Soldiers*, 1–2, 103–4.

106. Birdwell, *Celluloid Soldiers*, 118.

107. Cooper was initially concerned about portraying a living person on screen, but he ultimately earned his first Best Actor Academy Award for his work.

108. Finler, "Box-Office Hits 1914–1986," 276.

109. "'Sergeant York' with Gary Cooper," 111.

110. Quoted in Birdwell, "'The Devil's Tool': Alvin York and *Sergeant York*,"136.

111. Perry, *Sergeant York*, 246–47.

112. "Cinema, Sergeant York Surrenders."

113. See McWhirter, *Red Summer*.

114. Cripps, *Slow Fade to Black*, 78–81.

115. Winter, "The Training of Colored Troops," 18.

116. See Lengel, *To Conquer Hell*.

117. Lengel, *To Conquer Hell*, 4–5.

118. Lengel, *To Conquer Hell*, 4–5.

119. Stallings, *The Doughboys*, 97–113.

120. One account places the action at Belleau Wood, but Jim and his colleagues wear the insignia of the Forty-Second "Rainbow" Division, which was not at Belleau Wood.

121. See Suid, *Guts & Glory.*

122. McLaughlin and Parry, *We'll Always Have the Movies.*

123. Kelly, *Cinema and the Great War,* 61.

124. Kelly, *Cinema and the Great War,* 107.

125. Kelly, *Cinema and the Great War,* 91.

Conclusion

1. Koszarski, *An Evening's Entertainment,* 26–27.

2. See Hynes, *The Soldiers' Tale.*

3. McLaughlin and Parry, *We'll Always Have the Movies,* 299. For other works on memory and World War II, see Beidler, *The Good War's Greatest Hits;* and Wood, *Worshipping the Myths of World War II.*

Archives and Manuscript Materials

ERFC. Edward R. Foreman Correspondence, Office of the City Historian, Rochester NY.

Historical Research Working Files, NYSA.

Katherine Mayo Papers, Manuscripts and Archives, Yale University Library, New Haven CT.

KSHS. Kansas State Historical Society Manuscript Collection, Topeka KS.

LOV. State Records Collection. Library of Virginia, Richmond VA.

NYSA. New York State Archives, Albany NY.

PFC. Pulp Fiction Collection, Serial and Government Publications Division, Library of Congress, Washington DC.

VWHC. Virginia War History Commission, 1915–1931, LOV.

Working Files for a Publication on New York in World War I, NYSA.

World War I History Commission Questionnaires, LOV.

World War I Veterans' Service Data, NYSA.

Published Works

Albany's Part in the World War. Albany NY: General Publishing, 1919.

Aldrich, Mildred. *Hilltop on the Marne.* Boston: Riverside Press, 1916.

Allen, Max P. "Indiana's War History." The War Records Collector 2, no. 5 (July 1945): 1–2.

Anderson, David D. *Brand Whitlock.* New York: Twain Publishers, 1968.

Andrews, William L., Frances Smith Foster, and Trudier Harris, eds. *The Concise Oxford Companion to African American Literature.* New York: Oxford University Press, 2001.

Ashley, Michael. *The Age of the Storytellers: British Popular Fiction Magazines, 1880–1950.* London and New Castle: British Library and Oak Knoll Press, 2006.

Axelrod, Alan. *Selling the Great War: The Making of American Propaganda.* New York: Palgrave Macmillan, 2009.

Ayers, Edward L. *The Promise of a New South: Life After Reconstruction.* New York: Oxford University Press, 1992.

Baird, Robert. *"Hell's Angels above the Western Front."* In *Hollywood's World War I: Motion Picture Images,* edited by Peter C. Rollins and John E. O'Connor, 79–100. Bowling Green OH: Bowling Green State University Popular Press, 1997.

Baker, Carlos. *Ernest Hemingway, A Life Story.* New York: Charles Scribner's Sons, 1969.

Barbeau, Arthur E., and Florette Henri. *The Unknown Soldiers: Black American Troops in World War I.* Philadelphia: Temple University Press, 1974.

Barclay, Alvin. "Magazines for Morons." New Republic, August 28, 1929, 42.

Bassett, John E. *Harlem in Review: Critical Reactions to Black American Writers, 1917–1939.* Selinsgrove PA: Susquehanna University Press, 1992.

"Bed-Time War Stories." *New Republic* (January 5, 1927): 178.

Behlmer, Rudy. "World War I Aviation Films." *Films in Review,* August/September 1967, 413–14.

Beidler, Philip D. *The Good War's Greatest Hits.* Athens: University of Georgia Press, 1998.

Bennett, Jesse Lee. "What We Read and Why We Read It." *Bookman,* September 25, 1925.

Berger, John. "Ev'ry Time We Say Goodbye." *Sight and Sound* (London) June 1991.

Bergonzi, Bernard. *Heroes' Twilight: A Study of the Literature of the Great War.* New York: Coward-McCann, 1965.

"Big Advance Sale of Tickets for 'Wings." *Moving Picture World,* September 1927, 104.

Binkley, William C. "Two World Wars and American Historical Scholarship." *Mississippi Valley Historical Review* 33, no. 1 (June 1946): 3–26.

Birdwell, Michael. *Celluloid Soldiers, The Warner Bros. Campaign Against Nazism.* New York: New York University Press, 1999.

———. "'The Devil's Tool': Alvin York and *Sergeant York.*" In *Hollywood's World War I: Motion Picture Images,* edited by Peter C. Rollins and John E. O'Connor, 121–42. Bowling Green OH: Bowling Green State University Popular Press, 1997.

Blair, William Allen. *Cities of the Dead: Contesting the Memory of the Civil War in the South, 1865–1914.* Chapel Hill: University of North Carolina Press, 2004.

Blakely, George T. *Historians on the Homefront.* Lexington: University Press of Kentucky, 1970.

Blasco Ibáñez, Vincent. *The Four Horsemen of the Apocalypse.* New York: E. P. Dutton, 1918.

Blight, David. *Race and Reunion: The Civil War in American Memory.* Cambridge MA: Belknap Press of Harvard University Press, 2001.

Blystone, John G., dir. *Hot Pepper.* Fox Film Corporation, 1933.

Bodnar, John. *The Good War in American Memory.* Baltimore: Johns Hopkins University Press, 2010.

"Book Is Sensation of Publishing World." *Motion Picture News,* March 26, 1921, 236.

Books for the High School Library. Chicago: American Library Association, 1924.

Borzage, Frank, dir. *Seventh Heaven.* Fox Film Corporation, 1927. Digital file.

Boyar, Paul S. *Purity in Print: Book Censorship in America from the Gilded Age to the Computer Age.* Madison: University of Wisconsin Press, 2002.

Brickell, Herschel. "This New Vogue for War Books." *Publishers' Weekly,* August 10, 1929, 530.

Britten, Thomas. *American Indians in World War I.* Albuquerque: University of New Mexico Press, 1997.

Brown, Zaidee, ed. *Standard Catalog for High School Libraries.* New York: H. W. Wilson, 1929.

Browne, Charles Herbert, and J. W. McManigal. *Our Part in the Great War and Historical Record: The War Work of the Horton Community and a Record of the Activities of Our Soldiers, Sailors and Marines 1917–1918–1919.* Horton KS: Headlight Commercial, 1919.

Bruccoli, Matthew J., and Robert W. Trogdon, eds. *The Only Thing That Counts: The Ernest Hemingway/Maxwell Perkins Correspondence, 1925–1947.* New York: Scribner, 1996.

Bruce, Brian. *Thomas Boyd: Lost Author of the 'Lost Generation.'* Akron OH: University of Akron Press, 2006.

Budreau, Lisa. *Bodies of War: World War I and the Politics of Commemoration in America 1919–1933.* New York: New York University Press, 2011.

Campbell, Craig W. *Reel America and World War I: A Comprehensive Filmography and History of Motion Pictures in the United States, 1914–1920.* Jefferson NC: McFarland & Company, 1985.

Capozzola, Christopher. *Uncle Sam Wants You: World War I and the Making of the Modern American Citizen.* New York: Oxford University Press, 2008.

Cappon, Lester J. "The Collection of World War I Materials in the States." *American Historical Review* 48 (July 1943): 733–45.

——. *A Plan for the Collection and Preservation of World War II Records.* New York: Social Science Research Council, October 1942. http://babel.hathitrust.org/cgi/pt?id=ucl.b4078888;view=1up;seq=16. Accessed April 10, 2016.

Capps, Jack. "The Literature of the AEF, A Doughboy Legacy." In *Unknown Soldiers: The American Expeditionary Forces in Memory and Remembrance,* edited by Mark A. Snell, 195–237. Kent OH: Kent State University Press, 2008.

Cather, Willa. *One of Ours.* New York: Vintage Classics, 1991.

Ceplair, Larry. *Anti-Communism in Twentieth Century America: A Critical History.* Santa Barbara CA: Praeger, 2011.

"Cinema, Sergeant York Surrenders." *Time,* April 1, 1940.

"Cinema: The New Pictures, May 5, 1930." *Time,* May 5, 1930.

Cobb, Humphrey. *Paths of Glory.* New York: Penguin Classics, 2010.

"The Cock-Eyed World." *Harrison Reports,* August 10, 1929, 127.

Colby, Elbridge. "The War Books." *Nation,* April 11, 1918, 446.

Cook, Dorothy E., and Isabel Stevenson Monro. *Standard Catalog for Public Libraries.* New York: H. W. Wilson Company, 1940.

Cooperman, Stanley. *World War I and the American Novel.* Baltimore: Johns Hopkins University Press, 1967.

Corn, Joseph J. *Winged Gospel: America's Romance with Aviation, 1900–1950.* New York: Oxford University Press, 1983.

Costello, Harry Todd, ed. *A List of Books for a College Student's Reading.* 2nd ed. Hartford CT: Trinity College, 1928.

Cowley, Malcolm. Response to review of *The First World War* by Archibald MacLeish. *New Republic,* September 20, 1933, 160–61.

Cripps, Thomas. *Slow Fade to Black: The Negro in American Film 1900–1942.* New York: Oxford University Press, 1977.

Crunden, Robert. *A Hero in Spite of Himself.* New York: Alfred A. Knopf, 1969.

Daly, Victor. *Not Only War: A Story of Two Great Conflicts.* College Park MD: McGrath Publishing Company, 1932.

Damousi, Joy. *The Labor of Loss: Mourning, Memory and Wartime Bereavement in Australia.* New York: Cambridge University Press, 1999.

Davis, Arthur Kyle. *Publications of the Virginia War History Commission.* Source volumes 1–7. Richmond VA: State Capitol, 1927.

Davis, Burke. *War Bird: The Life and Times of Elliott White Springs.* Chapel Hill: University of North Carolina Press, 1987.

Davis, David A. "Not Only War Is Hell: World War I and African American Lynching Narratives." *African American Review* 42, nos. 3–4 (Fall–Winter 2008): 477–91.

Davis, Dernoral. "Toward a Socio-Historical and Demographic Portrait of Twentieth Century African-Americans." In *Black Exodus: The Great Migration from the American South*, edited by Alferdteen Harrison, 1–19. Jackson: University Press of Mississippi, 1991.

Dawson, Coningsby. "The Unharvested Literature of the War." *New York Times Book Review*, December 7, 1919, 1.

Dean, E. R., and J. H. Alexander. *World War Roll of Honor 1917–1920, Marion County, Kansas.* Marion KS, 1920.

DeBauche, Leslie Midkiff. *Reel Patriotism: The Movies and World War I.* Madison: University of Wisconsin Press, 1997.

Dial. Unsigned review of *Fighting the Flying Circus.* May 31, 1919, 578.

Dickinson, Asa Don. *The Best Books of the Decade, 1926–1935.* New York: H. W. Wilson, 1937.

Dickson, Paul, and Thomas B. Allen. *The Bonus Army: An American Epic.* New York: Walker and Company, 2004.

"Dogs of War Let Loose on Screen." *Motion Picture News,* December 1926, 2320.

Doherty, Thomas. "A Code Is Born." *Reason,* January 2008, 55–60.

Drury, Francis K. *What Books Shall I Read?* Boston: Houghton Mifflin, 1933.

Duffus, R. L. *Books: Their Place in a Democracy.* Boston: Riverside Press, 1930.

Dumont, Hervé. *Frank Borzage, the Life and Films of a Hollywood Romantic.* Jefferson NC: McFarland & Company, 2006.

Eisinger, Chester E. "The American War Novel: An Affirming Flame." *Pacific Spectator,* Summer 1955, 272–87.

Egremont, Max. *Siegfried Sassoon: A Life.* New York: Farrar, Straus and Giroux, 2005.

Eksteins, Modris. "All Quiet on the Western Front and the Fate of a War." *Journal of Contemporary History* 15, no. 2 (April 1980): 345–66.

Empey, Arthur. *A Helluva War.* New York: D. Appleton and Company, 1927.

English, George, Jr. *History of the 89th Division.* War Society of the 89th Division, 1920.

Eyster, Warren. "Warren Eyster on Humphrey Cobb's Paths of Glory." In *Rediscoveries: Informal Essays in Which Well-Known Novelists Rediscover Neglected Works of Fiction by One of Their Favorite Authors,* edited by David Madden, 135–46. New York: Crown Publishers, 1971.

Falls, Cyril. *War Books: A Critical Guide.* London: Peter Davies, 1930.

Faust, Drew Gilpin. *This Republic of Suffering: Death and the American Civil War.* New York: Alfred A. Knopf, 2008.

Fayn, Andrew. *Writing Disenchantment: British First World War Prose, 1914–1930.* Manchester UK: Manchester University Press, 2014.

Fenton, Charles A. "American Ambulance Drivers in France and Italy: 1914–1918." *American Quarterly* 3, no. 4 (Winter 1951): 326–43.

Fentress, James, and Chris Wickham. *Social Memory.* Oxford: Blackwell Publishers, 1992.

"Fighting 69th." *Motion Picture Herald,* January 27, 1940, 26.

"Filming Story Was Gigantic Task." *Motion Picture News,* March 26, 1921.

"Film Reviews, The Big Parade." *Variety,* December 1925, 40.

"Films–'Hell's Angels.'" *Nation,* September 3, 1930, 254.

Finan, Christopher M. *Alfred E. Smith, The Happy Warrior.* New York: Hill and Wang, 2002.

Finding aid for Mary Lee's papers at the Radcliffe Institute for Advanced Study. Cambridge MA: Harvard University. http://oasis.lib.harvard.edu/oasis/deliver/~sch00699. Accessed July 27, 2012.

Finler, Joel W. *The Hollywood Story.* London: Octopus, 1988.

Fitzgerald, F. Scott. *This Side of Paradise.* New York: Scribner, 1920.

Flentje, Edward H., and Joseph A. Aistrup. *Kansas Politics and Government: The Clash of Political Cultures.* Lincoln: University of Nebraska, 2010.

Flowers, Desmond. *A Century of Best Sellers, 1830-1930.* London: National Book Council, 1934.

Foreman, Edward R., ed. *World War Service Record of Rochester and Monroe County, New York.* Rochester NY: 1928, 1930, and 1934.

Forman, Henry James. *Our Movie Made Children.* New York: Macmillan, 1934.

"$408,152 Glory Record at New York Roxy." *Motion Picture News,* September 16, 1927, 842.

Frick, Katherine. "Katherine Mayo Biography." Pennsylvania Center for the Book, Penn State University Libraries. http://pabook.libraries.psu.edu/palitmap/bios/Mayo__Katherine.html. Accessed October 31, 2011.

Fussell, Paul. *The Great War and Modern Memory.* New York: Oxford University Press, 1975.

Genthe, Charles V. *American War Narratives, 1917–1918: A Study and Bibliography.* New York: D. Lewis, 1969.

———. "Personal War Narratives in America, 1914–1918." PhD diss., Washington State University, 1967.

"Giant Board Shows War Shots for '69th' Harrisburg Date." *Motion Picture Herald*, February 3, 1940, 78.

Gibson, Campbell, and Kay Jung. "Historical Census Statistics on Population Totals by Race, 1790 to 1990." Population Division Working Paper No. 56 U.S. Census Bureau, Washington DC, 2002. www.census.gov.

Glende, Philip. "Victor Berger's Dangerous Ideas: Censoring the Mail to Preserve National Security During World War I." *Essays in Economic and Business History* 26 (2008): 5–20.

Goebel, Stephen. *The Great War and Medieval Memory: War, Remembrance and Medievalism in Britain and Germany, 1914–1940*. New York: Cambridge University Press, 2007.

Gordon, Dennis. *Lafayette Escadrille Pilot Biographies*. Missoula MT: Doughboy Historical Society, 1991.

Goulart, Ron. *Cheap Thrills: An Informal History of the Pulp Magazines*. New Rochelle, NY: Arlington House, 1972.

Goulding, Edmund, dir. *The Dawn Patrol*. Warner Brothers, 1938. Digital file.

Graves, Robert. "Poets in War and Peace." *Saturday Review of Literature*, November 1, 1924.

Grech, John. "O'Brien, Patrick Alva MC." *"Clickerty Click": 66squadron, RFC & RAF, 1916 to 1919.* http://www.66squadron.co.uk/biogs/obrien.htm. Accessed October 27, 2011.

Greene, J. Lee. *Blacks in Eden: The African American Novel's First Century*. Charlottesville: University Press of Virginia, 1996.

Greicus, M. S. *Prose Writers of World War I*. St. Albans UK: Staples Printers, 1973.

Grider, John McGavock, and Elliott White Springs. *War Birds: Diary of an Unknown Aviator*. New York: George H. Doran Company, 1926. Reprint, College Station: Texas A&M University Press, 1988.

Guerlac, Othon. Review of *Témoins* by Jean Norton Cru. *French Review* (May 1930): 450–52.

Gutiérrez, Edward R. *Doughboys on the Great War: How American Soldiers Viewed Their Military Experience*. Lawrence: University Press of Kansas, 2014.

Hackett, Alice Payne. *Fifty Years of Best Sellers 1895–1945*. New York: R.R. Bowker, 1945.

———. *Seventy Years of Best Sellers 1895–1965*. New York: R.R. Bowker, 1967.

Hampton, Benjamin B. *History of the American Film Industry*. New York: Covici-Friede, 1931.

Harries, Meirion, and Susie Harries. *The Last Days of Innocence: American at War 1917–1918.* New York: Random House, 1997.

Harrison's Reports. Unsigned review of *All Quiet on the Western Front.* May 10, 1930, 75.

Hart, James D. *The Popular Book: A History of America's Literary Taste.* New York: Oxford University Press, 1950.

Hatcher, Harlan. *Creating the Modern American Novel.* New York: Farrar & Rinehart, 1935.

Hawks, Howard, dir. *The Dawn Patrol.* First National Pictures and the Vitaphone Corporation, 1930. Digital file.

Hawks, Howard, dir. *Sergeant York.* Warner Brothers, 1941. DVD.

Hemingway, Ernest, ed. *Men at War: The Best War Stories of All Time.* New York: Crown Publishers, 1942.

————. *The Sun Also Rises.* New York: Scribner's, 1926.

Herrick, Robert. "What Is Dirt?" *Bookman,* November 1929, 258–62.

Hoffman, Frederick J. *The Twenties: American Writing in the Postwar Decade.* New York: Viking Press, 1949.

Hohenberg, John. *The Pulitzer Prizes, A History of the Awards in Books, Drama, Music, and Journalism, Based on the Private Files over Six Decades.* New York: Columbia University Press, 1974.

Holbrook, Franklin F. *"The Collection of War Service Records."* American *Historical Review* 25, no. 1 (October 1919): 72–78.

Honor Roll, Crawford County, Kansas, 1919. Kansas City: Union Bank Note Company, 1919.

Honor Roll, Shawnee County, Kansas. N.p. [1919].

Hughes Howard, dir. *Hell's Angels.* Caddo Company, 1930. DVD.

Hutner, Gordon. *What America Read: Taste, Class, and the Novel, 1920–1960.* Chapel Hill: University of North Carolina Press, 2009.

Hynes, Samuel. "Personal Narratives and Commemoration." In *War and Remembrance in the Twentieth Century,* edited by Jay Winter and Emmanuel Sivan, 205–20. Cambridge: Cambridge University Press, 1999.

————. *The Soldiers' Tale.* New York: Penguin Books, 1997.

IMDB Movie Database. www.imdb.com.

Ingram, Rex, dir. *The Four Horsemen of the Apocalypse.* Metro Pictures Corporation, 1921. Digital file.

Isenberg, Michael T. "The Great War Viewed from the Twenties: The Big Parade." In *American History/American Film: Interpreting the Hollywood Image,* edited by John E. O'Connor and Martin A. Jackson, 17–37. New York: Frederick Unger Publishing, 1979.

————. *War on Film: The American Cinema and World War I, 1914–1941.* London: Associated University Presses, 1981.

Jacobs, Lea. "Men without Women: The Avatars of *What Price Glory.*" *Film History: An International Journal* 17, no. 2/3 (2005): 307–33.

Jacobs, Lewis. *The Rise of the American Film.* New York: Harcourt, Brace and Company, 1939.

James, Jennifer C. *A Freedom Bought with Blood: African American War Literature from the Civil War to World War II.* Chapel Hill: University of North Carolina Press, 2007.

Jones, Richard Seelye. *A History of the American Legion.* N.p.: Bobbs-Merrill Co., 1946.

Kammen, Michael. *Mystic Chords of Memory: The Transformation of Tradition in American Culture.* New York: Alfred A. Knopf, 1991.

Kansas Adjutant General. *Kansans Who Served in the World War.* N.p.: n.d.

Kansas State Historical Society. "World War I." http://www.kshs.org/kansapedia/world-war-i/12247. Accessed November 17, 2010.

Keene, Jennifer. *Doughboys, the Great War and the Remaking of America.* Baltimore: Johns Hopkins University Press, 2003.

Keighley, William, dir. *The Fighting 69th.* Warner Brothers, 1940. DVD.

Kelly, Andrew. *Cinema and the Great War.* London: Routledge, 1997.

————. *Filming* All Quiet on the Western Front: *'Brutal Cutting, Stupid Censors, Bigoted Politicos.'* London: I.B. Tauris Publishers, 1998.

Kennedy, David M. *The First World War and American Society.* New York: Oxford University Press, 1982.

Kitch, Carolyn. *Pages from the Past: History and Memory in American Magazines.* Chapel Hill: University of North Carolina Press, 2005.

Knee, Stuart E. *Hervey Allen 1889–1949: A Literary Historian in America.* Vol. 1 of *Studies in the Historical Novel.* Lewiston NY: Edwin Mellen Press, 1988.

Koszarski, Richard. *An Evening's Entertainment: The Age of the Silent Feature Picture, 1915–1928.* New York: Scribner's Sons, 1990.

La Cava, Gregory, dir. *Gabriel Over the White House.* Metro-Goldwyn-Mayer, 1933. Digital file.

La Motte, Ellen. *The Backwash of War.* New York: Putnam's, 1916.

La Naour, Jean-Yves. *The Living Unknown Soldier: A Story of Grief in the Great War.* New York: Metropolitan Books, 2004.

Leab, Daniel J. "*The Fighting 69th*: An Ambiguous Portrait of Isolationism and Interventionism." In *Hollywood's World War I: Motion Picture Images,* edited by Peter C. Rollins and John E. O'Connor, 101–20. Bowling Green OH: Bowling Green State University Popular Press, 1997.

Lee, Charles. *The Hidden Public: The Story of the Book-of-the-Month Club.* Garden City NY: Doubleday, 1958.

Leider, Emily W. *Dark Lover.* New York: Farrar, Straus and Giroux, 2003.

Lengel, Edward G. *To Conquer Hell: The Meuse-Argonne 1918.* New York: Henry Holt and Company, 2008.

———. *World War I Memories: An Annotated Bibliography of Personal Accounts Published in English Since 1919.* Lanham MD: Scarecrow Press, 2004.

LeRoy, Mervyn, dir. *Gold Diggers of 1933.* Warner Brothers, 1933. Digital file.

———. *I Am a Fugitive from a Chain Gang.* Warner Brothers, 1932.

Lewis, W. David. *Eddie Rickenbacker: An American Hero in the Twentieth Century.* Baltimore: Johns Hopkins University Press, 2005.

Lightfoot, W. H. *Our Heroes in Our Defense, Labette County, Kansas.* Kansas: Commercial Publishing, 1921.

Locke, William J. "The Novelist's Dilemma." *Atlantic Monthly,* July 1920, 176–77.

Looney, J. Jefferson. "'I Really Never Thought War Was So Cruel,' The Veterans' Questionnaires of the Virginia War History Commission." *Virginia Cavalcade* 50, no. 3 (Summer 2001): 128–30.

Lundberg, David. "The American Literature of War: The Civil War, World War I and World War II." *American Quarterly* 36, no. 3 (1984): 373–88.

Ludington, Townsend. *John Dos Passos: A Twentieth Century Odyssey.* New York: E. P. Dutton, 1980.

Lyle, Katie Letcher. *My Dearest Angel: A Virginia Family Chronicle, 1895–1947.* Athens: Ohio University Press, 2002.

Lynd, Robert S., and Helen Merrell Lynd. *Middletown: A Study in Modern American Culture.* San Diego: Harcourt Brace and Company, 1929.

MacLeish, Archibald. "A Communication, the Dead of the Next War." *New Republic,* October 4, 1933, 215.

———. "Lines for an Internment." Review of *The First World War* by Laurence Stallings. *New Republic,* September 20, 1933, 159–60.

Madden, David, ed. *Rediscoveries: Informal Essays in Which Well-Known Novelists Rediscover Neglected Works of Fiction by One of Their Favorite Authors.* New York: Crown Publishers, 1971.

"Marks of a Classic." *Bookman,* April 1926, 222–23.

Matsen, William E. *The Great War and the American Novel: Versions of Reality and the Writer's Craft in Selected Fiction of the First World War.* New York: Peter Lang Publishing, 1993.

McKinley, Albert E. "Plans for State and Local Publications on War History." Proceedings of the Sixth Annual Conference of Historical Societies, Washington DC, December 28, 1920.

McLaughlin, Robert L., and Sally E. Parry. *We'll Always Have the Movies: American Cinema During World War II.* Lexington: University Press of Kentucky, 2006.

McWhirter, Cameron. *Red Summer: The Summer of 1919 and the Awakening of Black America.* New York: Henry Holt and Company, 2011.

Medal of Honor Society. "Medal of Honor Citation for Alvin C. York." http://www.cmohs.org/recipient-detail/2613/york-alvin-c.php. Accessed August 3, 2014.

Mencken, H. L. "Portrait of an American Citizen." *Smart Set* 69, no. 3 (November 1922): 141.

——. Review of One of Ours. *Smart Set* 69, no.1 (September 1922): 140.

Mereness, Newton D., ed. *American Historical Activities during the War.* Washington DC: Government Printing Office, 1923.

Miner, Craig. *Kansas: The History of the Sunflower: 1854–2000.* Lawrence: University Press of Kansas, 2002.

Mock, James Robert, and Cedric Larson. *Words That Won the War, the Story of the Committee of Public Information.* Princeton NJ: Princeton University Press, 1939.

Modern Library. "One Hundred Best Novels." http://www.modernlibrary.com/top-100/100-best-novels/. Accessed July 5, 2012.

Moorhouse, Geoffrey. *Hell's Foundations: A Town, Its Myths, and Gallipoli.* London: Hodder and Stoughton, 1992.

Moreland, George B., Jr. "What Young People Want to Read About." *Library Quarterly* 10 (October 1940): 469–93.

Morrow, John H., Jr. *The Great War in the Air: Military Aviation from 1909 to 1921.* Shrewsbury UK: Airlife Publishing, 1993.

Moscow, Warren. *Politics in the Empire State.* New York: Alfred A. Knopf, 1948.

Moss, Marilyn Ann. *Raoul Walsh, The True Adventures of Hollywood's Legendary Director.* Lexington: University Press of Kentucky, 2011.

Motion Picture News. Unsigned review of "The Four Horsemen." February 26, 1921, 1235.

——. Unsigned review of "The Four Horsemen." March 5, 1921, 1859.

Motion Picture World. Unsigned review of *Seventh Heaven.* May 28, 1927, 289.

Mott, Frank Luther. *Golden Multitudes: The Story of Bestsellers in the United States.* New York: R.R. Bowker, 1966.

Mulvey, Jim. "A Defense of *A Farewell to Arms.*" In *Censored Books, Critical Viewpoints,* edited by Nicholas Karolides, Lee Burress, and John M. Kean. Metuchen NJ: Scarecrow Press, 1993.

"Must Novelists Forget the War?" *Literary Digest*, August 21, 1920, 35.

National Board of Review Magazine. Unsigned review of *What Price Glory*. December 1926, 15.

National Council of Teachers of English Committee on College Reading, College English Association. *Good Reading: A Guide for College Students and Adult Readers*. Chicago: National Council of Teachers of English, 1934.

National Union Catalog, Pre-1956 Imprints. London: Mansell, 1968–81.

Neff, John R. *Honoring the Civil War Dead: Commemoration and the Problem of Reconciliation*. Lawrence: University Press of Kansas, 2005.

Nevins, Allen, ed. *The Letters and Journal of Brand Whitlock*. New York: D. Appleton-Century Company, 1936.

New Republic. Unsigned review of *Ramsey Milholland* by Booth Tarkington. September 3, 1919, 158.

Nielson, David Gordon. *Black Ethos: Northern Urban Negro Life and Thought, 1890–1930*. Westport CT: Greenwood Press, 1977.

Nitchie, Elizabeth, Jane Faulkner Goodloe, Marion E. Hawes, and Grace Morley, eds. *Pens for Ploughshares: A Bibliography of Creative Literature That Encourages World Peace*. Boston: F. W. Faxon Company, 1930.

Noble, Donald R. Review of *Hemingway in Love and War: The Lost Diary of Agnes von Kurowsky*, by Agnes von Kurowsky, Ernest Hemingway, Henry Serrano Villard, and James Nagel. *South Atlantic Review* 56, no. 1 (January 1991): 136–39.

"Notes and Queries." *Quarterly Journal of the New York State Historical Society* 1, no. 4 (July 1920): 194–218.

Novick, Peter. *That Noble Dream: The Objectivity Question and the American Historical Profession*. Cambridge: Cambridge University Press, 1988.

N. W. Ayer & Son. *American Newspaper Annual and Directory*. Philadelphia: N. W. Ayer & Son, 1928.

———. *N. W. Ayer & Son's Directory of Newspapers and Periodicals*. Philadelphia: N.W. Ayer & Son, 1931.

Ogden, Archibald G. "The Book Trade in War Time." *Publishers' Weekly*, July 8, 1939, 94–98.

Oliver, Charles, ed. *Ernest Hemingway's A Farewell to Arms: A Documentary Volume*, Vol. 308. Detroit MI: Thomson Gale, 2005.

Ortiz, Stephen. *Beyond the Bonus March and GI Bill: How Veteran Politics Shaped the New Deal Era*. New York: New York University Press, 2010.

Paris, Michael. "Wings." In *The Movies as History: Visions of the Twentieth Century*, edited by David W. Ellwood. London: Sutton Publishing, 2000.

Penrose, Charles. *James G. Harbord (1866–1947), Lieutenant General: USA, Chairman of the Board: RCA.* New York: Newcomen Society, 1956.

Perry, John. *Sergeant York: His Life, Legend and Legacy.* Nashville TN: Broadman & Holman Publishers, 1997.

Phelps, William Lyon. Review of *The Deepening Stream. Saturday Review of Literature,* October 11, 1930, 199.

Piehler, G. Kurt. *Remembering War the American Way.* Washington DC: Smithsonian Institution Press, 1995.

Pizer, Donald, ed. *John Dos Passos's U.S.A.: A Documentary Volume.* Vol. 274 of *The Dictionary of Literary Biography.* Detroit MI: Thomson Gale, 2003.

Poetry Foundation. "Claude McKay, 1889–1948." www.poetryfoundation .org/bio/claude-mckay. Accessed July 25, 2012.

Polenberg, Richard. *Fighting Faiths: The Abrams Case, the Supreme Court, and Free Speech.* New York: Viking, 1987.

"Popular Fiction as It Is Today." *Writer's Digest,* October 1930. In *Pulp Fictioneers,* edited by John Locke. Silver Spring MD: Adventure House, 2004.

Potamkin, Harry Allen. "The Eyes of the Movie." *International Pamphlets* no. 38 (1934).

Pottle, Frederick A. "Creed Not Annulled." In *Promise of Greatness: The War of 1914–1918,* edited by George A. Panichas. New York: John Day Company, 1968.

Powers, Richard Gid. *Not without Honor: The History of American Anticommunism.* New York: The Free Press, 1995.

Pulley, Raymond H. *Old Virginia Restored: An Interpretation of the Progressive Impulse 1870–1930.* Charlottesville: University Press of Virginia, 1968.

"Yates County in the World War, 1917–1918." *Quarterly Journal of the New York State Historical Association* 11, no. 2 (April 1921): 105.

Radway, Janice A. *A Feeling for Books: The Book-of-the-Month Club, Literary Taste, and Middle-Class Desire.* Chapel Hill: University of North Carolina Press, 1997.

Ramsaye, Terry. *A Million and One Nights.* New York: Simon & Schuster, 1926.

Rasche, William Frank. *The Reading Interests of Young Workers.* Chicago: University of Chicago Libraries, 1937.

"Realistic Bombardment in Metro Special." *Motion Picture News,* March 26, 1921, 2223.

Remarque, Erich Maria. *All Quiet on the Western Front.* New York: Grosset & Dunlap, 1929.

Robinson, Henry Morton. "The Wood-Pulp Racket." *Bookman,* August 1928, 651.

Robinson, Phyllis C. *Willa, The Life of Willa Cather.* Garden City NY: Doubleday & Co., 1983.

Ross, Steve J. *Working Class Hollywood: Silent Film and the Shaping of Class in America.* Princeton NJ: Princeton University Press, 1998.

Sargent, Epes Winthrop. "Got the Pick of New York Windows for the 'Four Horsemen' Production." *Moving Picture World,* April 30, 1921.

Schickel, Richard. *The Men Who Made the Movies.* New York: Atheneum, 1975.

Schader, Freddie. "The Cock-Eyed World." *Motion Picture News,* August 10, 1929, 603–4.

Schmidt, Meta. *500 Books for the Senior High School Library.* Chicago: American Library Association, 1930.

Scott, Emmett J. *Scott's Official History of the American Negro in the World War.* New York: Arno Press, 1919.

SeBoyar, Gerald E. *Pocket Library of the World's Essential Knowledge.* Vol. 7, *Outline of Literature.* New York: Funk & Wagnalls Company, 1929.

"'Sergeant York' with Gary Cooper." *Harrison Reports,* July 12, 1941, 111.

"'7th Heaven' Taxi Feature of Fox Ballyhoo Through the East." *Moving Picture World,* April 1927, 734.

Seymour, Miranda. *Robert Graves: A Life on the Edge.* New York: Henry Holt and Company, 1995.

Simon, David. Introduction to *Paths of Glory,* by Humphrey Cobb. New York: Penguin Classics, 2010.

Simmons, Edwin H. "Catlin of the 6th Regiment." *Fortitudine* 22, no. 4 (Spring 1993): 3–12.

Simmonds, Roy S. *The Two Worlds of William March.* Tuscaloosa: University of Alabama Press, 1984.

Singewald, Karl. "Progress in the Collection of War History Records by State War History Organizations." Proceedings of the Sixth Annual Conference of Historical Societies, Washington DC, December 28, 1920.

Sherriff, R. C. *No Leading Lady: An Autobiography.* London: Victor Gollancz, 1968.

Sklar, Robert. *Movie-Made America: A Cultural History of the Movies.* New York: Random House, 1975. Reprint, New York: Vintage Books, 1994.

Smith, Erin A. *Hard-Boiled: Working Class Readers and Pulp Magazines.* Philadelphia: Temple University Press, 2000.

Smith, Gene. *Until the Last Trumpet Sounds: The Life of General of the Armies John J. Pershing.* New York: John Wiley, 1999.

Smith, J. Douglas. *Managing White Supremacy: Race, Politics and Citizenship in Jim Crow Virginia.* Chapel Hill: University of North Carolina Press, 2002.

Smith, Leonard V. *The Embattled Self: French Soldiers' Testimony of the Great War.* Ithaca NY: Cornell University Press, 2007.

Smith, Munroe. "War Books by American Diplomatists." *Political Science Quarterly* 35, no. 1 (March 1920): 94–125.

Smythe, Donald. *Pershing, General of the Armies.* Bloomington: Indiana University Press, 1986.

Soderbergh, Peter. "Aux Armes!: The Rise of the Hollywood War Film, 1916–1930." *South Atlantic Quarterly* 65 (1966): 509–22.

Spartacus Educational. "Profile of *Everybody's Magazine.*" http://www.spartacus.schoolnet.co.uk/usaeverybodys.htm. Accessed November 21, 2011.

Spears, Jack. "World War I on the Screen: Part 2." *Films in Review,* June–July 1966, 347.

Speer, Allan H., and Ruth J. Townsend. *Survival and Struggle: Racial Minorities in American History.* Needham Heights MA: Ginn Press, 1989.

Stallings, Lawrence. *The Doughboys.* New York: Harper and Row, 1963.

"Strange Screen Confidences." *Literary Digest,* March 5, 1927, 24.

Streeter, Edward. *Dere Mable, Love Letters of a Rookie.* New York: Frederick A. Stokes, 1918.

Stuckey, W. J. *The Pulitzer Prize Novels, A Critical Backward Look.* Norman: University of Oklahoma Press, 1981.

Suid, Lawrence. *Guts & Glory: the Making of the American Military Image in Film.* Lexington: University Press of Kentucky, 2002.

Sullivan, Mark. *Our Times, 1900–1925.* Vol. 6. New York: Charles Scribner's Sons, 1935.

Swanson, Roy Arthur. "Edward Streeter." In *American Humorists, 1800–1950,* edited by Stanley Trachtenberg. Detroit MI: Gale Research, 1982.

Sweeney, Daniel, ed. *History of Buffalo and Erie County 1917–1918.* N.p.: Committee of One Hundred, 1919.

Sweeney, W. Allison. *History of the American Negro in the Great World War, 1919.* N.p.: G.G. Sapp, 1919. Reprint, n.p.: Negro Universities Press, 1969.

Terkel, Studs. *"The Good War": An Oral History of World War II*. New York: Pantheon Books, 1984.

Thomson, Alistair. *Anzac Memories: Living with the Legend*. Melbourne: Oxford University Press, 1984.

Tillery, Tyrone. *Claude McKay: A Black Poet's Struggle for Identity*. Amherst: The University of Massachusetts Press, 1992.

Tomlinson, H. M. "War Books." *Yale Review* (March 1930).

Torgovnick, Marianna. *The War Complex: World War II in Our Time*. Chicago: University of Chicago Press, 2005.

Trout, Steven. *American Prose Writers of World War I: A Documentary Volume*. Detroit MI: Thomson Gale, 2005.

———. *On the Battlefield of Memory: The First World War and American Remembrance, 1919–1941*. Tuscaloosa: University of Alabama Press, 2010.

———. *Goodbye to All That and Other Great War Writings*. Manchester UK: Carcanet Press, 2007.

———. *Memorial Fictions: Willa Cather and the First World War*. Lincoln: University of Nebraska Press, 2002.

Tuttle, William M. *Race Riot: Chicago in the Red Summer of 1919*. New York: Atheneum, 1970.

"Untruthful War Films." *Literary Digest,* March 17, 1928, 27.

Vance, Jonathan. *Death So Noble: Memory, Meaning and the First World War*. Vancouver: UBC Press, 1997.

Vandiver, Frank E. *Black Jack: The Life and Times of John J. Pershing*. Vol. 2. College Station: Texas A&M University Press, 1977.

Vaughan, David K., ed. *Letters from a War Bird: The World War I Correspondence of Elliott White Springs*. Columbia: University of South Carolina Press, 2012.

Vidor, King, dir. *The Big Parade*. Metro-Goldwyn-Mayer, 1925. VHS.

———. *A Tree Is a Tree*. New York: Garland Publishing, 1977.

Waldmeir, Joseph. "Novelists of Two Wars." *Nation,* November 1, 1958, 304.

Waldron, Edward E. *Walter White and the Harlem Renaissance*. Port Washington NY: National University Publications, Kennikat Press, 1978.

Walker, Stuart, dir. *The Eagle and the Hawk*. Paramount, 1933. Digital file.

Walsh, Jeffrey. *American War Literature 1914 to Vietnam*. London: Macmillan Press, 1982.

Walsh, Raoul, dir. *The Cock-Eyed World*. Fox Film Corporation, 1929.

———. *Each Man In His Time: The Life Story of a Director*. New York: Farrar, Straus and Giroux, 1974.

———, dir. *What Price Glory.* Fox Film Corporation, 1926. Digital file.

———, dir. *Women of All Nations.* Fox Film Corporation, 1931.

Waples, Douglas, and Ralph W. Tyler. *What People Want to Read About.* Chicago: University of Chicago Press and the American Library Association, 1931.

"War Books." *Bookman,* November 11, 1926, 261.

"War Books after the War." *Publishers' Weekly,* November 9, 1918, 1586.

"War, First Degree." *Time,* June 3, 1935, 83.

"War Notes." *Virginia Magazine of History and Biography* 27 (1919): 71–98.

Washington, Ida H. *Dorothy Canfield Fisher: A Biography.* Shelburne VT: New England Press, 1982.

Wellman, William A., dir. *Heroes for Sale.* Warner Brothers, 1933.

———, dir. *Wings.* Paramount Famous Lasky Corporation, 1927.

Wells, Carolyn. "Ballade of War Books." *Bookman,* January 1919, 643.

Wheelock, John Hall. "The Years." *Outlook,* January 6, 1926, 18–19.

Whitehouse, Arch. *Heroes of the Sunlit Sky.* Garden City NY: Doubleday & Company, 1967.

Wiegand, Wayne A. *"An Active Instrument for Propaganda":* The American Public Library During World War I. New York: Greenwood Press, 1989.

Wilder, Amos. "At the Nethermost Piers of History: World War I, a View from the Ranks." In *Promise of Greatness: The War of 1914–1918,* edited by George A. Panichas. New York: John Day Company, 1968.

Williams, Chad L. *Torchbearers of Democracy: African American Soldiers in the World War I Era.* Chapel Hill: University of North Carolina, 2010.

Williams, Lilian Serece. *Strangers in the Land of Paradise: The Creation of an African American Community, Buffalo, New York 1900–1940.* Bloomington: Indiana University Press, 1999.

Williams, Oscar R. *George S. Schuyler: Portrait of a Black Conservative.* Knoxville: University of Tennessee Press, 2007.

Willock, Roger. *Lone Star Marine.* Princeton NJ: Privately Published, 1961.

Wilson, John. *Russell County in the War.* Russell KS: 1921.

Winter, Jay. *Remembering War: The Great War between Memory and History in the 20th Century.* New Haven CT: Yale University Press, 2006.

———. *Sites of Memory, Sites of Mourning: The Great War in European Cultural History.* New York: Cambridge University Press, 1999.

Winter, Jay, Karen Tilmans, and Frank Van Vree, eds. *Performing the Past: Memory, History and Identity in Modern Europe.* Amsterdam: Amsterdam University Press, 2010.

Winter, Thomas. "The Training of Colored Troops: A Cinematic Effort to Promote National Cohesion." In *Hollywood's World War I: Motion Picture Images,* edited by Peter C. Rollins and John E. O'Connor, 13–26. Bowling Green OH: Bowling Green State University Popular Press, 1997.

Wittern-Keller, Laura. *Freedom of the Screen: Legal Challenges to State Film Censorship, 1915–1981.* Lexington: University Press of Kentucky, 2008.

Wohl, Robert. *The Generation of 1914.* Cambridge MA: Harvard University Press, 1979.

Wood, Edward W., Jr. *Worshipping the Myths of World War II: Reflections on America's Dedication to the War.* Washington DC: Potomac Books, 2006.

Woodress, James. *Booth Tarkington: Gentleman from Indiana.* New York: Greenwood Press, 1969.

———. *Willa Cather: A Literary Life.* Lincoln: University of Nebraska Press, 1987.

———. "A Note on *One of Ours.*" *Willa Cather Pioneer Memorial Newsletter* 37, no. 1 (Spring 1993): 1, 4.

Woodward, C. Van. *Origins of the New South, 1877–1913.* Baton Rouge: Louisiana State University Press, 1951.

Woollcott, Alexander. "Introducing Captain Thomason of the Marines." *Vanity Fair,* June 1925, 70.

World War Roll of Honor, 1917–1920. Marion County Kansas [1920].

Yates, Elizabeth. *The Lady from Vermont: Dorothy Canfield Fisher's Life and World.* Brattleboro VT: Stephen Greene Press, 1971.

Yockelson, Mitchell. "They Answered the Call: Military Service in the United States Army during World War I, 1917–1919." *Prologue Magazine* 30, no. 3 (Fall 1998). http://www.archives.gov/publications/prologue/1998/fall/military-service-in-world-war-one.html. Accessed December 14, 2010.

Ziegler, Janet. *World War II Books in English, 1945–1968.* Stanford CA: Hoover Institution Press, 1971.

INDEX

Books are listed by author last name; films are listed by title.

35th Infantry Division, 30–31, 222n95

89th Infantry Division, 30–31

369th Regiment (Harlem Hellfighters), 16

African American authors, 124–28

African American soldiers, xiv, 14, 220n67, 220n69

African American war histories, 15–17, 22–27, 220n60, 221n74, 221n83

African American war movies, 184–85

Aldrich, Mildred: *Hilltop on the Marne*, 46, 79; *On the Edge of the War Zone*, 224n6; *Peak of the Load*, 224n6

Allen, Hervey, 74–75, 89–90, 226n44; *Anthony Adverse*, 74–75; *Toward the Flame*, 74–75, 89–90, 226n44

American Legion, xix, 14, 19, 23, 32, 83, 128, 179

American Legion Monthly, 128–29

American Library Association, 58, 68, 75, 78, 226n40

Atherton, Gertrude, 82, 229n110

Barabusse, Henry, *Under Fire*, 80

Belleau Wood, xxi, xxiii, 60, 70, 71, 123, 150, 185, 186, 187, 239n120

The Big Parade (Vidor), 149, 150, 156–61, 163, 170, 187, 188–89

Bonus Army, 175–76, 238n91

Bookman, 48, 68, 101, 119, 225n11, 228n81, 233n78

Book of the Month Club, 113

bookstores, 48, 59, 78

Borzage, Frank, 166, 237n66

Boudreau, Lisa: *Bodies of War*, xix

Boyd, Thomas, 80, 120, 122; *Through the Wheat*, 122–23; *In Time of Peace*, 123

Buckles, Frank, 1

Bullard, Robert Lee: *Personalities and Reminiscences of the War*, 86

Buswell, Leslie: *Ambulance No. 10*, 46

Cather, Willa, 108; *One of Ours*, 95, 96, 102–7, 118

Catlin, Albert, 60; *With the Help of God and a Few Good Marines*, 59, 60

Cavalcade (Lloyd), 172

censorship, 45, 176–77

Civil War, xvii, 1, 3–4, 8, 109, 110, 146, 194, 229n110

Cobb, Humphrey, 111; *Paths of Glory*, 97, 111–14

Cobb, Irvin, 46, 224n7; *The Glory of the Coming*, 51, 55

collective memory: definition of, xvi–xvii

Committee on Public Information (CPI), 6–7, 152–53, 217n14

Connelly, William, 31–32

conscientious objectors, 36

Cowley, Malcolm, 98, 103, 129

Curtin, Daniel: *The Land of Deepening Shadows*, 51, 55
Cushing, Harvey: *From a Surgeon's Journal 1915–1918*, 79

Daly, Victor: *Not Only War*, 127–28
Davis, Arthur Kyle, 17–19, 28–29
Davis, Richard Harding: *With the Allies*, 46
Dawn Patrol (Goulding), 173–74
Dawn Patrol (Hawks), 173–74
Dawson, Coningsby, 82, 90, 121; *Carry On*, 51
Dos Passos, John, 120–22, 130; *Three Soldiers*, 104, 120–21

The Eagle and the Hawk (Walker), 175
Eksteins, Modris, 169
Empey, Arthur, 50, 52, 82, 139, 141; *A Helluva War*, 56; *Over the Top*, 48, 50, 51; *Tales from a Dugout*, 50

Falls, Cyril, 86–87, 229n123
Faulkner, William, 85; *Soldiers' Pay*, 233n72
The Fighting 69th (Keighley), 95, 150, 177–80
Fisher, Dorothy Canfield: *The Deepening Stream*, 96, 107–9
Fitzgerald, F. Scott, 85, 94, 122, 233n82
Foreman, Edward, 13–14
The Four Horsemen of the Apocalypse (Ingram), 150, 151–56, 170, 182
Fussell, Paul, xviii, 85

Gabriel Over the White House (La Cava), 175, 176
Gerard, James, 51, 53–54; *My Four Years in Germany*, 51, 54
Gibson, Hugh, 53–54, 61–62; *Journal from Our Legation*, 51, 54
Gilbert, John, 156, 157–58, 160
Glasgow, Ellen: *The Builders*, 109
Gold Diggers of 1933 (LeRoy), 175–76
Gold Star Mothers, 30, 32

Grey, Zane, 50
Grider, John McGavock, 86
Gutiérrez, Edward, 27

Hall, Bert, 68–70, 87, *One Man's War*, 66, 68–70
Hall, James Norman, 52–53, 87; *High Adventure*, 51, 52; *Kitchener's Mob*, 46
Hampton Institute, 25
Harbord, James, 65, 70–71
Hell's Angels (Hughes), 173–74
Hemingway, Ernest, 98–102, 104, 117, 232n62; *A Farewell to Arms*, 94–102, 116–18, 119–20, 171; *Men at War*, 87, 230n125
Heroes for Sale (Wellman), 175
honor medal, 15
Huard, Frances Wilson: *My Home on the Field of Honor*, 46; *With Those Who Wait*, 224n6
Hutner, Gordon: *What America Read*, 118, 119, 232n63, 233n67
Hynes, Samuel, xvi–xvii, xviii, 65, 85, 191; *The Soldiers' Tale*, 144

Ibáñez, Vincente Blasco: *The Four Horsemen of the Apocalypse*, 101, 151, 152
Isenberg, Michael, 159, 175, 238n80

Johnson, Henry, 16–17

Kammen, Michael: *Mystic Chords of Memory*, 94
Kansas Historical Society, 30–32, 37
Keene, Jennifer, 22
Kellogg, Vernon: *Headquarters' Nights*, 79

La Motte, Ellen: *The Backwash of War*, 46–47
Lafayette Escadrille, 51–52, 68–70, 87, 173
Lee, Mary: "*It's a Great War!*," 128–29
Lengel, Edward, 186
Lewis, Sinclair, 107, 116–17
libraries, 57, 58–59, 78–81, 117, 226n40, 228n93

Liggett, Hunter: *A.E.F. Ten Years Ago in France,* 87
Lindbergh, Charles, 115
Locke, William, 84–85
lost generation, xv, 38, 56, 89, 94, 95, 98, 100, 120, 124, 230n8
Lynd, Robert and Helen: *Middletown,* 77, 147–48

MacLeish, Archibald, 129–30
March, William, 123; *Company K,* 123–24
Masefield, John: *Gallipoli,* 80
Mayo, Katherine: *That Damn Y,* 65, 66–68, 77
McKay, Claude: *Home to Harlem,* 126–27
Mencken, H. L., 103, 121, 125
Meuse-Argonne Offensive, xiii, xxi, 24, 36, 73, 75, 150, 179, 185–86, 193, 195, 208–9, 250
Modern Library Series, 109 117, 119
Morgenthau, Henry, 53–54; *Ambassador Morgenthau,* 51
Motion Picture Producers and Distributors of America (MPPDA), 176

National Military Sisterhood, 30–31

O'Brien, Howard: *Wine, Women and War,* 44, 86
O'Brien, Pat, 53; *Outwitting the Hun,* 51, 53

pacifists: Mennonites, 37
Paine, R. D.: *Fighting Fleets,* 79
paperback books, 118, 132, 144
Peat, Harold, 55–56; *The Inexcusable Lie,* 56
Pershing, John J., 13, 72, 74, 75, 77, 186; *My Experiences in the World War,* 66, 72, 73–74
Piehler, Kurt: *Remembering War the American Way,* 230n3
publishers: inhibiting memoirists, 82–84; and liberalism, 83–84, 128–29

Publishers' Weekly, 48, 58, 84, 96, 225n11
Pulitzer Prize, 74, 105, 106–7, 231n30
pulp fiction, xxii, 95–96, 115, 132–45; circulation, 143–44; and collective memory, 144–45; content of, 141
pulp fiction serials: *Battle Stories* (Fawcett), 136–37, 138; *Love and War Stories* (Good Story Magazine), 136, 138; *Navy Stories* (Dell), 136, 138; *Over the Top* (Street & Smith), 138; *Under Fire* (Magazine Publishers), 136, 138, 141; *War Aces* (Dell), 136, 138; *War Birds* (Dell), 136, 139, 143; *War Novels* (Dell), 136, 138, 143; *War Stories* (Dell), 133–36, 138, 139, 141, 142, 143; *War Stories* (in Great Britain), 142

questionnaires, 5–6, 13, 27, 32, 42; return rate for, 25–26, 37

reading habits, 58–59, 75, 80–81, 93–94, 95, 229n104
Red Triangle Club, 13–14
Remarque, Erich Maria: *All Quiet on the Western Front,* 72–73, 80, 88, 101, 113, 116–17, 132, 156, 168–69, 230n3, 234n114Rickenbacker, Eddie, xxi, 44, 59–60, 89–90; *Fighting the Flying Circus,* 59–60, 89–90, 226n44
Roosevelt, Kermit, 59, 60–61; *War in the Garden of Eden,* 59, 61
Roosevelt, Quentin, 61
Roosevelt, Theodore, 61, 63, 66

Saint-Mihiel, battle of, xxiii, 112, 123, 187
Sassoon, Siegfried: *Memoirs of a Fox Hunting Man,* 88–89
Scanlon, William: *God Have Mercy on Us,* 128–29
Schuyler, George, 25
SeBoyar, Gerald, 109–10
Seeger, Alan, 85; *Poems of Alan Seeger,* 225n23

Sergeant York (Hawks), 150, 180–84,
239n104
serials, 63, 73, 77–78, 102, 115, 133,
136, 141, 168
Seventh Heaven (Borzage), 150, 165–68
Sherriff, R. C.: *Journey's End*, 88–89
Springs, Elliot White, 114, 116,
232n60; *Leave Me with a Smile*,
116; *War Birds*, 86, 87, 97, 114–16,
232n55
Stallings, Laurence, 71–72, 87, 129–
30, 159, 230n125, 237n39; *What
Price Glory?*, 156–57; *Plumes*, 233n72
Standard Catalog for Public Libraries,
58, 79–80
Streeter, Edward, 48–50, 225n18–19;
Dere Mable, 48–50
Sullivan, James, 6–8, 35

Tarkington, Booth, 119; *Ramsey Mil-
holland*, 97, 109–11
Thomason, John, 87, 230n125; *Fix
Bayonets!*, 65, 71–72, 77, 80, 87
Trout, Steven, xii, xix, 106; *On the
Battlefield of Memory*, xix
Trumbo, Dalton, 124, 131

Valentino, Rudolph, 154, 156, 236n25
veterans, war histories of, 38–41
Vidor, King, 157–61, 189
Virginia War History Commission
(VWHC), 17, 19, 24
Virginia War History source books,
29–30

war books: popularity in Great Britain, 87–89; popularity in the
United States, 48, 50, 57–58, 72–73,
76–77, 82, 85, 122, 133, 168

war films, 165, 184–90; British, 188;
French, 188; German, 188
war histories, 1–42; Crawford County
KS, 33–35; Cumberland County
VA, 21, 222n90; Erie County NY, 12;
Horton KS 35–36; Labette County
KS, 35; Marion County KS, 33, 36–
37; Monroe County N.Y., 9, 12–15;
Norfolk VA, 25, 28, 222n90; Oneida
County N.Y. 9–11, 41; Richmond
VA, 19, 21, 330n60; Rockbridge
County VA, 28–29; Russell County
KS, 35–36; Shawnee County KS, 33;
Shenandoah County VA, 21; Yates
County N.Y., 9, 11
Warner Brothers, 177, 179–80, 181, 184
Wells, Carolyn: "Ballade of War
Books," 64–65
Wharton, Edith, 107, 109
What Price Glory? (play), 72, 133, 156
What Price Glory? (Walsh), 133, 150,
161–65
White, Walter: *Fire in the Flint*, 125–26
Whitehouse, Arch, 142
Whitlock, Brand, 59, 61–63; *Belgium*,
59, 61–63
Wings (Wellman), 173, 175, 187
Winter, Jay, xvi, xvii, xviii
Woodress, James, 102, 104–6
World War I: centennial celebra-
tions, 194; war memorials, xix, 26,
106
World War II: war films, 187; war his-
tories, 4–5

YMCA, 6, 66–68
York, Alvin, 74, 75–77, 180–84,
239n104

STUDIES IN WAR, SOCIETY, AND THE MILITARY

*Military Migration and State Formation: The British Military Community
in Seventeenth-Century Sweden*
Mary Elizabeth Ailes

The State at War in South Asia
Pradeep P. Barua

An American Soldier in World War I
George Browne
Edited by David L. Snead

*Beneficial Bombing: The Progressive Foundations of American
Air Power, 1917–1945*
Mark Clodfelter

Fu-go: The Curious History of the Japanese Balloon Bombs
Ross Coen

*Imagining the Unimaginable: World War, Modern Art,
and the Politics of Public Culture in Russia, 1914–1917*
Aaron J. Cohen

*The Rise of the National Guard: The Evolution of
the American Militia, 1865–1920*
Jerry Cooper

*The Thirty Years' War and German Memory
in the Nineteenth Century*
Kevin Cramer

*Political Indoctrination in the U.S. Army from
World War II to the Vietnam War*
Christopher S. DeRosa

In the Service of the Emperor: Essays on the Imperial Japanese Army
Edward J. Drea

American Journalists in the Great War: Rewriting the Rules of Reporting
Chris Dubbs

America's U-Boats: Terror Trophies of World War I
Chris Dubbs

The Age of the Ship of the Line: The British and French Navies, 1650–1815
Jonathan R. Dull

American Naval History, 1607–1865: Overcoming the Colonial Legacy
Jonathan R. Dull

Soldiers of the Nation: Military Service and Modern Puerto Rico, 1868–1952
Harry Franqui-Rivera

*You Can't Fight Tanks with Bayonets: Psychological Warfare against
the Japanese Army in the Southwest Pacific*
Allison B. Gilmore

*A Strange and Formidable Weapon: British Responses to
World War I Poison Gas*
Marion Girard

Civilians in the Path of War
Edited by Mark Grimsley and Clifford J. Rogers

*A Scientific Way of War: Antebellum Military Science, West Point,
and the Origins of American Military Thought*
Ian C. Hope

Picture This: World War I Posters and Visual Culture
Edited and with an introduction by Pearl James

Death Zones and Darling Spies: Seven Years of Vietnam War Reporting
Beverly Deepe Keever

For Home and Country: World War I Propaganda on the Home Front
Celia Malone Kingsbury

I Die with My Country: Perspectives on the Paraguayan War, 1864–1870
Edited by Hendrik Kraay and Thomas L. Whigham

North American Indians in the Great War
Susan Applegate Krouse
Photographs and original documentation by Joseph K. Dixon

Remembering World War I in America
Kimberly J. Lamay Licursi

*Citizens More than Soldiers: The Kentucky Militia and
Society in the Early Republic*
Harry S. Laver

*Soldiers as Citizens: Former German Officers in the
Federal Republic of Germany, 1945–1955*
Jay Lockenour

*Deterrence through Strength: British Naval Power and
Foreign Policy under Pax Britannica*
Rebecca Berens Matzke

Army and Empire: British Soldiers on the American Frontier, 1758–1775
Michael N. McConnell

Of Duty Well and Faithfully Done: A History of the Regular Army in the Civil War
Clayton R. Newell and Charles R. Shrader
With a foreword by Edward M. Coffman

The Militarization of Culture in the Dominican Republic, from the Captains General to General Trujillo
Valentina Peguero

Arabs at War: Military Effectiveness, 1948–1991
Kenneth M. Pollack

The Politics of Air Power: From Confrontation to Cooperation in Army Aviation Civil-Military Relations
Rondall R. Rice

Andean Tragedy: Fighting the War of the Pacific, 1879–1884
William F. Sater

The Grand Illusion: The Prussianization of the Chilean Army
William F. Sater and Holger H. Herwig

Sex Crimes under the Wehrmacht
David Raub Snyder

In the School of War
Roger J. Spiller
Foreword by John W. Shy

The Paraguayan War, Volume 1: Causes and Early Conduct
Thomas L. Whigham

The Challenge of Change: Military Institutions and New Realities, 1918–1941
Edited by Harold R. Winton and David R. Mets

To order or obtain more information on these or other University of Nebraska Press titles, visit nebraskapress.unl.edu.

CPSIA information can be obtained
at www.ICGtesting.com
Printed in the USA
LVOW10*2009230118

563702LV00006B/71/P